STUDENT LIVES IN CRISIS
Deepening inequality in times of austerity

Lorenza Antonucci

First published in Great Britain in 2016 by

Policy Press
University of Bristol
1-9 Old Park Hill
Bristol
BS2 8BB
UK
t: +44 (0)117 954 5940
pp-info@bristol.ac.uk
www.policypress.co.uk

North America office:
Policy Press
c/o The University of Chicago Press
1427 East 60th Street
Chicago, IL 60637, USA
t: +1 773 702 7700
f: +1 773-702-9756
sales@press.uchicago.edu
www.press.uchicago.edu

British Library Cataloguing in Publication Data
A catalogue record for this book is available from the British Library

Library of Congress Cataloging-in-Publication Data
A catalog record for this book has been requested

ISBN 978-1-4473-1824-8 paperback
ISBN 978-1-4473-1823-1 hardcover
ISBN 978-1-4473-1828-6 ePub
ISBN 978-1-4473-1827-9 Mobi

Cover design by Hayes Design
Front cover image kindly supplied by Giulia Bertuzzo

This book is dedicated to
the memory of my father, Renato Antonucci.

Contents

List of tables and figures

Tables

Figures

List of acronyms

BIS	Department for Business, Innovation and Skills
CSN	Centrala studiestödsnämnden/The National Board of Student Aid
EU	European Union
EU-27	European Union of 27 member states
HE	higher education
ILO	International Labour Organisation
ISCED	International Standard Classification of Education
ISCO	International Standard Classification of Occupations
KWS	Keynesian welfare state
NEET	(young people) not in education, employment or training
OECD	Organisation for Economic Co-operation and Development
PCA	principal component analysis
SWS	Schumpeterian welfare state
TLM	transitional labour market (model)
UCAS	Universities and Colleges Admissions Service
UK	United Kingdom
UNESCO	United Nations Educational, Scientific and Cultural Organisation
US	United States
YEI	Youth Employment Initiative

Note on author

Lorenza Antonucci (PhD Bristol, MSc Research LSE, MSc/BSc Bocconi) is a Senior Research Lecturer in Social Policy and Sociology at Teesside University, UK. In 2009 Lorenza was awarded with the first *Policy & Politics* award from Policy Press to conduct research on young people in university in England, Italy and Sweden. In 2015 she was awarded with the Fellowship of the Royal Society of Edinburgh to be Visiting Fellow at the European Trade Union Institute (ETUI)/ European Social Observatory (OSE) in Brussels, and to conduct research on the new politics of inequality in Europe. Lorenza is Research Associate at OSE (European Social Observatory) and a member of the project 'The Next Social Europe' of FEPS (Foundation for European Progressive Studies).

Lorenza's overarching research interest concerns the change in the distribution of welfare sources across European welfare states and its impact on inequality. She has focused on 'young adults' as a social group particularly affected by welfare reforms. She co-chaired the ESPAnet panel on 'Young people and social policy' (2012) and co-edited *Young people and social policy in Europe* (2014) for Palgrave's Work and Welfare in Europe series. Lorenza has served on the executive of the Social Policy Association, and currently sits on the editorial board of the academic magazine *Discover Society*. She writes on LGBT and inequality for the magazine *Slate*. Follow her on Twitter at @SocialLore

Preface: A post-Brexit preface

The Acknowledgements for this book were written before the results of the UK EU referendum and, almost prophetically, referred in its end to the 'analytical insularism' felt during the referendum debate – the feeling of isolation felt by European researchers who tried to contribute to a debate that revolved almost entirely around the British perspective and the British interest. European perspectives, as those put forward by this book, are now more important than ever.

This book reflects my own experience as a European researcher based in the north of England, but with a permanent affiliation with Brussels and an interest in EU affairs. This peculiar position allowed me to link the British trend of growing inequality with the evolution of EU policies. After all, this book is the product of the (maybe over-idealistic) ambition I've been pursuing since my early 20s: linking the British social policy tradition with European affairs.

The reader will find that this book is, inevitably, both unapologetically European and strongly EU-critical. Mass expanded higher education (HE) was supposed to sustain the European dream of enhancing social justice – the same one that recent EU austerity reforms have betrayed. Public sociologists have interpreted the Brexit vote as a manifestation of the malaise of the British working class, with an assumption that the conditions of the British working classes are somehow exceptional compared to that of the rest of Europe.

My study compared the experiences of young working-class students across Europe and found (see Parts 2 and 3) striking similarities between the experiences of young people from lower socio-economic backgrounds from Middlesbrough (in the north of England, at the core of the Brexit vote, and victim of UK self-imposed austerity reforms) and those from Naples (the south of Italy, and one of the places that has been mostly affected by EU austerity). Disadvantaged young people from these two places share a surprisingly similar story, namely, a materially disadvantaged experience of HE, with young people lacking basic needs (such as having to skip meals in order to buy books), insufficiency of state support, a feeling of local isolation (with lack of transport), over-reliance on families that do not have enough resources, and the subsequent cycle of debt (with banks or local communities) that this over-reliance generates. Issues of mental wellbeing are also widespread among young people living in these two geographically afar (but policy-alike) regions.

Another European trend that can be clearly identified in England is that disadvantage in HE is not only experienced by young people from lower socio-economic background, but also from those of intermediate backgrounds (young people from the so-called 'squeezed middle'). So, overall, inequality is not a story of the 'British working classes' – and not even only of the 'working classes'. It is hard to capture the Europeanism behind these dynamics unless one starts comparing British experiences to those of other European countries – and to conduct truly comparative and European studies like the one in this book.

My book also discusses how the EU pushed for privatisation of HE costs with the consequence of exacerbating inequalities among young people. Paradoxically, as Part 1 discusses, EU HE reforms have been profoundly influenced by the UK take on HE reforms of the last 20 years, consisting of shifting HE costs from the state to young people and their families, reducing grants, increasing personal debt and pursuing an individualistic view of meritocracy. The UK has had an uploading effect on EU austerity, which is very evident looking at the evolution of HE reforms presented in this book. The UK has also 'downloaded' something from European integration. If the individual experiences of young people in England are so similar to those in Italy, this is because in both regions state cutbacks and over-reliance on family (familism) are a match made in heaven.

With its distinctive Liberal features, the UK has framed HE as an exclusively individual matter. The last HE and Research Bill (2016-17) perpetuates this idea and marks a divergence from the rest of Europe which approximates the English student funding model to that of the US. The case of Sweden, also discussed and compared in this book, shows that it doesn't necessarily have to be that way, and inequalities among young people can be reduced by increasing public responsibility on HE costs.

By walking away from the EU, the real danger for the UK is to neglect discussing real policy alternatives – because no alternatives can be observed from an entirely inward-looking perspective. I hope the reader will enjoy the analytical trip that this book takes in comparing inequalities among young people from different countries, and in imagining policy alternatives to the current state of national and EU policies for young people.

Middlesbrough and Brussels, August 2016

Acknowledgements

My first thank you goes to the organisation that made this research possible, Policy Press. This is a book about student welfare, and Policy Press has been the 'welfare provider' of my doctoral journey financed through the *Policy & Politics* award (considering I was an EU migrant with limited access to other funding, Policy Press' decision has been life-changing for me). I must also thank Policy Press for having patiently waited for the final typescript of the book during the most hectic year of my life. As well as thanking the organisation, I would particularly like to thank its director, Alison Shaw, who has constantly supported me over the last few years. I hope this book will honour the trust placed in me.

My research involved a great deal of travelling and was practically and symbolically sustained by many people. With a small budget for a three-country study, this research would have not taken place without low-cost airlines. I want to thank the network of friends around Europe who I have seen only sporadically in the last few years, but who have always been present and supportive. I mention here a few people who have actively helped me with my research – my friend, Melanie Pissarius, deserves a great thank you for having shared important contacts in Malmö, and I am indebted to Anna Angelin for having put me in contact with her colleagues in Lund. My friendship with Nengak Daniel is one of the greatest outcomes of my fieldwork in Sweden, and I would like to thank him for having been so helpful during my time there. I am grateful to two special friends for having hosted me during my fieldwork in Milan: Gaia and Sybil (who are, with Christian, the 'rocks' in my life). I would like to thank all the lecturers and student unions (in particular, Rete Link) that facilitated the recruitment of participants, and, of course, the participants themselves – the interviews, and the related trips, were the best moments of this research.

I thank the many colleagues in academia who have inspired me and who commented on earlier versions of my work. They are, unfortunately, too many to be listed, but a special mention goes to the 'first readers' of the final typescript who read and commented on this work in a relatively short time: Jessie Abrahams, Georgios Antonopoulos, Ibrar Bhatt, Tom Chevalier, Nengak Daniel and Diego Escobar. The fantastic Kim Allen and Georgios Papanicolaou sent me the most comprehensive and constructive comments I could hope for.

Giulia Bertuzzo must be thanked for having done an amazing work with the book cover and for having spent several nights transforming my thoughts into images.

This work was truly 'Britalian' and European. The fact that some of this work was 'made in Italy' is an indirect thank you to my home country that financed my university education for many years. I have attempted to keep a European perspective throughout (my final period of writing in Brussels was essential for that). No researcher is an island, and I hope that UK higher education will become more involved in European debates in the next few years.

Finally, I want to thank my mother, my grandmother and my brothers (Elio, Ermes and the 'lost and found' Valerio), for their unconditional love.

To quote C. Wright Mills, 'I have tried to be objective. I do not claim to be detached.'

Introduction:
Young people's lives at university in crisis

Young people are often described as those most affected by the current European economic crisis, but what do we know about how young adults live in Europe? In the words of rapper Stromae, 'European youth's favourite misery muse',[1] European twenty-somethings embark on education to get a better job, and are then afflicted by financial pressures and by the daunting cycle of credit and debt. The life of young people in university fits well with this tale of sorrow: the pressures of studying to compete in the labour market where unpaid work and internships are increasingly mandatory, the rising costs of higher education (HE) and the issues of debt accumulated by student loans – these are all typical features of the current experience of life at university.

These are only anecdotal accounts from popular culture, however, and there are as yet no systematic studies exploring how young people embarking on university live as students in Europe. In exploring the individual experiences and living conditions of young people in university, this book shows that transitions through university tend paradoxically to enhance, rather than limit, existing social inequalities.

For policy-makers this sorry tale might appear surprising. After all, greater access to HE has been the policy mantra of the 1990s and 2000s, in an attempt both to boost employment rates and at the same time, to increase social inclusion in European societies. This double goal was behind New Labour's 'widening participation agenda'[2] in the UK, which, in the 2000s, became a constitutive part of the European Union (EU) strategy for social inclusion and economic competitiveness. For example, one of the five crucial targets of the EU 2020 strategy is to have at least 40% of 30- to 34-year-olds completing tertiary-level education by 2020.[3] The expansion of HE has, in fact, already increased all over Europe in recent years: about 50% of young people (cohort 18-29) in Europe enter HE, which means that they are embarking on university experience in increasing numbers, even if they do not necessarily finish their degree.[4]

While university education has never been so central in the lives of young adults in Europe, the continent is confronted with the 'broken promise of higher education.'[5] This refers to the mismatch between the anticipated benefits of a university education and the race to the bottom in terms of living conditions during and opportunities after university, and is essentially a consequence of the knowledge-based strategy for which upskilling represents the only way to compete in a new high-skill global environment. This strategy creates individualised competition among young people and, at the same time, declining opportunities during and after university.

While Brown and Lauder describe the broken promise of HE as the breakdown of the American dream, it can just as easily be applied to Europe. We might witness indeed the crisis of the European dream, namely, the European attempt to achieve economic growth and social cohesion in the global economy by becoming the most competitive knowledge-based society.[6] The EU 2020 strategy of making Europe the most competitive economy in the world through investment in HE clashes with the record level of graduate unemployment and under-employment.[7] While young people without education and training (the so-called NEETs, not in education, employment or training) face the harshest employment prospects,[8] even graduates wait months and send dozens of applications before landing jobs.[9] Recent European studies report that the incidence of over-qualification is particularly affecting younger cohorts of EU university graduates, with 25.2% of highly qualified young adult employees (aged 24–35) in Europe being overqualified for their jobs in 2014.[10] This is, per se, an indication that the very assumptions of HE policies need to be revised, as tertiary education is not enough to protect young people from labour market risks. But it is not only the economy that is affecting the European university dream: the cost of university is rising, and HE has become an individual social investment project to be funded by young people and their families (see Part 1 in this book).

The crucial issue here is not whether incentivising young people to go into HE has been the wrong strategy: in some respects the widening participation agenda has acted to limit inequalities by opening certain paths of transition that were once forbidden to working-class students. The compelling issue explored in this book is the striking contradiction of such policies when confronted with the fact that *equal access to university is not enough* to reach the ambitious goals of social inclusion through HE. This book shows that, on the contrary, we are witnessing a reinforcement of inequality in the paths of transition through university because of the implications of the specific preference of private sources of welfare (from the family and through young people's participation in the labour market) over public ones in supporting the lives of university students in Europe.

Student lives in crisis and the context of austerity

It is a commonplace idea that the current struggles faced by young people result from the economic crisis that began in 2007/08. As I have discussed in previous work, the context of the last economic crash and its reflection on unemployment has exacerbated and intensified the negative consequences of weak policy assumptions elaborated in previous decades.[11] The cause of student lives in crisis, however, needs to be found in the flawed assumptions behind HE policies implemented since the 1990s, which have aimed at achieving a mass expanded HE by pushing families and young people to take up the costs of this investment. As I discuss in Part 1, by focusing on 'access' and 'labour market' destinations, these policies have ultimately neglected how young people live in university. The contradictions of these policies have become more evident since the crisis started because social investment policies rely on future returns (that is, smoother graduate transitions and graduate premiums in the labour market) that are now more difficult to achieve. Furthermore, the idea that cost containment could resolve the economic crisis has resulted in austerity comprising a further trend of privatising HE costs.

Few public thinkers would now deny the struggles faced by the so-called 'Generation Y', which often feature in newspaper headlines. This cohort of young people, labelled 'millennials', face unprecedented problems of debt, housing and work[12] – similarly to what Stromae was singing about a few years ago. The envisaged solutions to this European crisis remain, however, very diverse, reflecting peculiar diagnoses of young people's problems. In mainstream media, the European crisis has been often framed as an economic crisis triggered by public debt and derived from excessive public spending.[13] The subsequent austerity policies have been justified as interventions aimed at minimising the burdens of the crisis on the entire society, young people included.

This position is best explained by the words of the European Central Bank (ECB)'s Director Mario Draghi, who, in a famous interview in 2011, pointed out that the European social model is not sustainable, and 'has already gone when we see the youth unemployment rates prevailing in some countries.'[14] For 'European social model' Draghi refers to a comparatively generous European continental way of delivering social protection in contrast with the US competitive model (of course this is mostly a myth – I will show, there is no unique social

European model). These words epitomise a widespread position in European politics, where cutting welfare state provision is perceived as a way of making government interventions 'young people-friendly'. This paradoxical idea goes as follows: given that welfare states have been very generous with baby-boomers, but have essentially failed with young people, we now need to address the economic deficit by cutting these inefficient machines (welfare states) that are penalising young people.[15] The mythology of austerity, perpetuated by Draghi's words, also implies that young people will ultimately benefit from public cuts as austerity increases the competitiveness of European economies and will eventually reduce youth unemployment – even though the evidence seems to show the opposite.[16]

This strategy neglects the contribution of the European social model to young people's lives: young people benefit in different ways from welfare state interventions in the fields of HE, housing, employment, etc.[17] While the current narrative has portrayed the crisis mainly as a youth employment crisis – creating a so-called 'lost generation' or 'generation without a future' – the context facing young people across Europe may be better defined as a social crisis. Challenges in the labour market have been accompanied by a process of worsening social conditions for young people, with declining opportunities in different areas of their lives. For young people in university, the reflection of these principles is in the reduction or abolishment of grants, the increasing reliance on loans and the rising level of university fees. The privatisation of HE costs across Europe has been actively encouraged in EU policy recommendations, suggesting also that the level of tuition fees does not have any negative socioeconomic consequences.[18] Young people's protests around Europe, which opposed the rise in the cost of HE in the UK, the change to HE support in Italy, and welfare state cuts across Europe, show that young people are aware of the real origins of this social crisis. These protests suggest that young people are not only concerned about employment rates, but also feel directly affected by policies that limit public spending and are perceived to have a negative impact on their lives.

What happens to young people's lives when the European model recedes in its capacity and responsibility to protect their lives? Does cutting the 'pro-baby-boomers welfare state machine' benefit young people? What is the effect of such policies on the level of inequality *within* the youth population? Many questions raised here prompt a consideration of the role of the welfare state in protecting young people in their transition through and out of university. This is relevant not just for young people, but also for the whole social policy discipline and practice that has traditionally focused on 'children' and 'the elderly', and has been curiously quieter about the impact of austerity on young people.[19] Young people's anger towards the rising private costs of university is hard to understand with the current analytical tools we have. As the prevailing, celebratory narrative of HE has been overshadowed by the new narrative of 'graduates without a future', the current context puts into question our own understanding of how (in)equality is reproduced in our current societies. While transitions through university are generally considered to be smooth and privileged, this book aims to bring into the debate another existing perspective: that of the difficult paths of transition at least for a certain group of young people lacking state and family support. Exploring the lives of young people in university allows us to understand how processes of social reproduction of inequality are being reshaped in the current climate. Or, in other words, if being in university is no longer a privilege, what do transitions through university consist of? How are they made sense of by young people? What does inequality within the youth population in university even mean?

The research

The date is 16 December 2012. I am in Naples and I am interviewing Maria,[20] a university student from Scampia. Scampia is internationally known as the headquarters of the local mafia (Camorra), and one of the most dangerous areas in Europe – probably the least likely 'university place' one could imagine. Before we begin the interview, Maria tells me "Today you find me in a particular moment – I've just found out I didn't get the scholarship." She is referring to state student support, which in Italy covers a minority of students (only about 10-11%, a percentage that is expected to decrease after the latest state cuts).[21] While she is telling me this, she doesn't look sad; she strikes me as being 'hopelessly angry' – she looks very critical, but at the same time, completely resigned. Maria's father has been made redundant and her mother doesn't work. They borrowed money from their relatives to pay for Maria's university fees and books. I ask her (as I ask everybody) what expectations she holds about life after university. In line with other researchers, I normally find stress and anxiety about the future to be quite common themes. However, Maria doesn't have these feelings. She tells me that she simply doesn't think about the future. Her only strategy is to focus on the present. For her the future simply doesn't exist. And she is just 22.

Maria's story is not just one of the many stories I collected for this book, but an exemplary untold story of contemporary young adulthood. This research, conducted across England, Italy and Sweden, has attempted to capture the emerging issues regarding young people and HE, and to do this by including young people from different countries and from different backgrounds. I attempted to link two aspects that normally remain separate in academia: the role of macro structures (that is, HE policies) and young people's experiences and viewpoints. While I could place most of the traditional literature within one of these two boxes (a macro or a micro approach), I analytically strived to capture the grey terrain in between by looking at 'welfare mixes' (as produced by policies and as used by the young people).

I decided to focus on three countries that, in common knowledge, would have represented very different welfare state models available to young people. This research ended up involving 84 students from six cities in England, Italy and Sweden (Bristol, Middlesbrough, Milan, Naples, Malmö and Lund). I met and interviewed 33 of those who filled in the online questionnaire in 2012/13; all of the students participated in an online survey that looked both at their objective conditions (where/how students lived and their financial resources), but also explored their views on how they lived in terms of finance, housing, education and their future wellbeing. While different 'ideal-types' of young people's experiences in university emerged from the survey, the interviews allowed me to understand how each person really experienced HE. I came across many different experiences, not necessarily determined by cross-national diversity. Many were challenging; all revealed important points in relation to how young people live and how the welfare state could help their transitions through HE. While student support systems in the three countries differ, they all suggest internal contradictions in the way welfare states aim to care for young people in contemporary society, and in particular, for those young people attempting the university route. On the one side, society puts a lot of emphasis on individual independence, and tends to frown on extended periods of dependence and semi-dependence by young people. On the other, welfare state reforms in the last few decades and the recent austerity measures have substantially cut down the welfare state sources used functionally by young people to become 'independent', reinforcing what I call here a state of 'eternal semi-dependence' among young people.

Young people have a constitutive position of semi-dependence in our societies: while they are attempting a transition to adulthood, they are not economically dependent like children, but equally they are not economically independent, like the parents who are (often) supporting them. Welfare state interventions for young people in university (that is, through grants and loans, and indirectly via fees) can support their transition to independence or reinforce the in-between position of semi-dependence. In their condition of semi-dependence, young people rely on combinations of different welfare sources from the state, the family and the labour market (what I define in this book as the 'welfare mixes'). However, access to these sources is not equally available for all young people, and this tends to vary depending on social class and educational background (what I call here socioeconomic background) and on the welfare mixes available in each country. It was for this reason that I decided to compare the 'most different welfare mixes' in England, Italy and Sweden, which reveal important dynamics in how inequalities within this generation are reinforced via the university experience.

Myth busting: looking at real-life experiences

In attempting to offer a new perspective, this book puts forward emerging ideas in the youth studies literature in order to counter some of the 'mythology' of youth transitions found in the media and wider public discourse. There are, in particular, four myths regarding young people in university that this book seeks to challenge: working-class children do not go to university; the transition to adulthood consists of linear passages from study to work; young people in university have smooth transitions; and inequality can be addressed by expanding access to HE.

Working-class children do not go to university

We are confronted with an ongoing myth regarding the relative uniformity of the types of young people who go to university. With participation rates equal to or over 50% of the youth cohort in many countries, we have reached a mass HE, and the socioeconomic background of those in university has become more heterogeneous. To put it simply, while for their grandmothers and grandfathers going to university represented a rare opportunity that signified success and social achievement, across Europe access to university has been 'normalised' for twenty-somethings from upper and middle socioeconomic backgrounds, and is increasingly possible for those from lower socioeconomic backgrounds.[22] Many studies have underlined the persisting inequalities in access to university, pointing out that while young people from lower socioeconomic backgrounds are 'catching up' with the participation rates of their more affluent peers, they still remain disadvantaged overall, as is evident in the UK. However, while the number of young people from lower socioeconomic backgrounds entering HE is still lower, relatively speaking, there are now more working-class young people than ever in university in absolute terms, as I discuss in Chapter 2. There have been a number of recent studies looking at how students from working-class backgrounds navigate university that focus on the *cultural* triggers of inequality.[23] We still know little about how these young people live in university in respect of their affluent peers, and how inequality is reproduced through university in *material* terms. This latter focus brings into question the comparative role of 'welfare mixes', as I explain more fully in Part 1.

So, how many of the total number of students can be considered 'working class'? Here I refer specifically to 'lower socioeconomic background' and not just social class, as I aim to include both the educational background (being a first-generation student) and the employment position of parents, as these are both crucial dimensions. The percentage of students with parents in manual and technical occupations is more than one would intuitively guess: 17.5% for Sweden, 19.7% for Italy and up to 32.1% for England/Wales. The share of young people from lower socioeconomic backgrounds becomes even more relevant if we compare the proportions of undergraduate students with parents who do not have a university education (the so-called first-generation university students): 40.9% of the student population in Sweden, 46.6% in England/Wales and 77.2% in Italy.

We can't really understand the inequalities of the university experience if we don't explore and compare the experiences of students from different socioeconomic backgrounds. When exploring inequality in a comparative study, it is also important to understand what inequality means in each context – in this case, in England, Italy and Sweden. For example, while in the UK the media take it for granted that young people from affluent backgrounds go to university, and statistics from Italy show that young people from affluent backgrounds may opt out of going to university, preferring instead to take advantage of their stocks of cultural capital by working in their family business.[24] Many scholars, in particular from the UK, have rightly pointed out that working-class young people who go to university often go to less prestigious universities.[25] This refers to what is called an 'institutional stratification', which is important in the UK (the division between new universities and old universities), but also in Sweden (between universities and *högskola*, or ex-technical universities), and constitutes a reflection of persisting inequalities.

So, a consistent number of young working-class people are going to university, although not as many as their peers from affluent families. They face well-reported obstacles to access, but their participation in university raises important issues. One is the implication of having new generations of young people from non-privileged backgrounds who were encouraged to go to university as a route to a good job, but who now face the prospect of graduate unemployment or under-employment.

Transition to adulthood consists of linear passages from study to work

Youth transitions are often conceptualised in policy-making in a very linear way: young people finish their studies (secondary or tertiary), and then complete their transitions by entering work. This linear path might be true for some young people, but in general, youth transitions have become more fragmented and less linear. This way of conceptualising transitions is highly influenced by the sociological contributions of late modernist theories: authors such as Beck and Giddens have played a crucial role in reconceptualising youth transitions in modern times.[26] Their ideas that transition paths are less linear and transitions more fluid have been quite prophetic of what has happened to young people in recent years. Transitions have also been expanded and postponed, creating new situations in between, such as the famous notion of emerging adulthood formulated by the psychologist Arnett.[27]

Fragmented and non-linear transitions mean in practice that young people can go back and forth between work and education, for example. This is why contemporary transitions to adulthood have been defined as 'yo-yo' transitions.[28] Following the same overall process, transitions by young people to the formation of their own families or to independent housing have been postponed. As a consequence, the landmarks of transitions to adulthood have already changed. When young people enter university they often also engage in work and seek forms of independence, as I explain more fully in Part 3. In other respects they also continue to be dependent on their families as children. This 'in-between' state is not simply a transitional phase on to something defined; it is a state of young adulthood that has specific characteristics per se, and needs to be explored as a distinct phase (a state of 'semi-dependence', as defined before).

The myth of linear transitions to adulthood needs to be challenged and replaced by a more in-depth account of what fragmented experiences of young adulthood mean in contemporary Europe.

Young people in university have smooth transitions

As a corollary of the previous myth, youth studies scholarship has for many years overlooked the experience of young people in university under the assumption that, as was the case for youth transitions during the 1990s, youth transitions through university were comparatively smooth. During this time, a division was created between troubled transitions (in particular, of the so-called NEETs) and smooth transitions via university. As a consequence, in the last 20 years most youth studies scholarship has explored 'problematic' transitions in reference to NEETs without gaining much understanding of the challenges faced by graduates. Most recently, this idea has been challenged by youth scholars pointing out the need to focus on the 'missing middle', namely, ordinary young people, with a renewed interest in those transitions.[29] Examining the reconfiguration of inequality within the current cohort of young people is a hot issue in social sciences and youth studies. Ken Roberts, an authority on youth sociology, has recently asked youth scholars to disaggregate the experiences of young people in university from different backgrounds, and to verify the emerging inequalities among young people.[30] In opposition to this focus on inequality, part of youth scholarship tends to interpret the challenges faced by young graduates as a testament of the existence of a new 'social generation' facing multiple disadvantages.[31] The title of this book suggests my attempt to reverse the terms of the debate by looking at young people's lives in university as a potential problematic issue, and by analysing the material (rather than cultural) triggers of inequality for young people in university.

When it comes to exploring the inequalities of the university experience, many will refer to the widely known studies conducted by Bourdieu in the 1970s regarding the university attendance of working-class students from France. This study provided a unique sociological insight into how cultural capital reproduces inequalities, and in short, how young people from more affluent backgrounds can mobilise their immaterial network, while young people from lower socioeconomic backgrounds cannot mobilise such cultural resources. Further studies conducted in particular in the UK have confirmed that the gap in cultural capital between students from different socioeconomic backgrounds still affects the experience of university in current times.

The element of cultural capital is a crucial aspect of the university experience, but what remains unexplored is the overall material and psychosocial disadvantages that some young people face, and this is not related to their cultural sources, but to sources of welfare. This is better analysed by looking at four aspects of young people's experience of university:

- *Financial position:* Finance has become a crucial aspect of the university experience. In order to support the mass expansion of HE, governments around Europe have introduced new instruments to make university participation more appealing and possible, expanding grants and, above all, introducing loans, which have made university a virtually accessible experience for an increasing number of young people (as I show later on in this book, the costs of HE are not directly visible to students when they take up loans). Studies increasingly show that the use of these instruments tends to disadvantage certain groups more than others.[32] At the same time, university costs have risen with the trend of privatisation and the increase in fees, although we have yet to capture one of the most dramatic effects of austerity, namely, the real-life implications of transferring the public costs of HE onto young people and their families.

- *Housing:* This is an area about which we know extremely little in relation to young people. We know even less about the specific issue of housing for young people in university, despite the fact that housing represents the greatest expense for young people in university across Europe. With the growing number of young people staying in their family home in order to make HE financially sustainable, it is pivotal to clarify the impact of this indirect use of family resources on young people's experiences, to see if staying at home during university makes the university experiences more unequal. Furthermore, it is crucial to clarify whether young people who move away from the family home during university become independent, and what the boundaries of their independence are.

- *Wellbeing:* This has been interpreted in a broad sense in order to capture the immaterial aspects of the university experience. I refer first to the reported issues of mental wellbeing that tend to affect young people in university. But I also wish to situate wellbeing in the larger debate. Wellbeing is linked to the overall issue of individualisation of youth biographies: are young people making plans for the future while in university in an individualised way, or are they confronted with structural limitations (for example, limited sources available from the state, the family and the labour market after university)? How might this sense of limitation in constructing their future biographies constrain their experiences in the present?

• *Education:* While this book doesn't cover the pedagogic side of the university experience, I am interested in how 'what happens inside the classroom' is linked to 'what happens outside the classroom'. There are two issues related to this. The first is the time budget challenges that young people face in having to combine time for study with other commitments related to the financial pressures they face during HE (for example, working while studying). The second is the record number of students dropping out, which has been reached during the process of expansion of HE: clearly many young people will never finish university, and this rate has increased in the last few years. A study on young people's lives in university tends inevitably to focus on those who have remained in university instead of dropping out. It is possible, however, to consider if and when material struggles make young people consider dropping out from university.

Emerging areas point to the increasing challenges that young people face during university following the mass expansion of access to HE and the consequences of student support policies introduced since the 1990s. The financial crisis and austerity programmes that followed have let these internal contradictions in HE policies emerge more clearly. Together they suggest that transitions via university no longer represent a smooth path. We need to explore this area and relate it more to the availability of welfare sources than to their cultural capital.

Having more people in higher education addresses inequality in society

I discuss in Chapter 1 that, while we have a record number of young people in HE, this cohort of young people is affected by more, rather than less, inequality than in the past. This in itself should suggest that the current policy focus on simply increasing access to HE in order to reduce social inequalities is short-sighted. In what respects, if any, can HE really reduce inequalities? One answer is in the sense that university represents a crucial experience for young people from all backgrounds, and one in which young people should participate equally. The contradiction is that there has been a mismatch between increasing opportunities to access HE and the trend of privatising the financial costs of university, which affects the experience that young people from certain backgrounds might have. Economist Thomas Piketty himself, a convinced supporter of social investment, recognises that the lack of social mobility in the US, where participation in university is high, could be due to the high level of fees. Student support is therefore crucial to addressing the inequality of the university experience, and Europe is becoming increasingly similar to the US in this regard. This latest trend can only reinforce the transmission of inequality across generations, when wealth and income from family are mobilised for those young people who can afford it. I am not an economist, and the definition of inequality I use in this publication refers to *the inequality of young people's lives*, assessed by looking at the areas described above (finance, housing, wellbeing and HE). I define inequality as a diversity of young people's experiences that is explained by structural factors, as socioeconomic background and welfare mixes (in academic terms, what I have just described would be called the process of *stratification*). Examining inequality during young people's experiences in university must therefore address the aspects of financial and housing support, and explore the living conditions of young people in university, not simply looking at access to HE.

Structure of the book

Before moving on to the accounts of the young people who participated in this study, Part 1 is dedicated to analysing the social implications, for young people, of the mass expansion of the university experience, showing the different social policy instruments that have sustained this, from the wide use of student loans and tuition fees, to grants, which have become much less generous and accessible to young people in university. I describe the process of privatising social risk as well as the most recent austerity trends affecting the systems of student support in Europe, which are shifting the costs incurred during university to the young people and to their families. Finally, an analysis is offered in this part of the contextual conditions of the young people in each country, and the structures of welfare available to young people in England, Italy and Sweden.

Part 2 aims to present the realities of students' university lives. The findings from the Q-questionnaire are presented, which asked participants to rank 52 statements about their experience of university. Not only do I show the ranking of the statements for each of the five profiles identified, but I also explain in depth the diversity of the university experiences of young people from these five profiles. The profiles represent 'ideal-types' of the young people's experiences in university, and they allow me to describe different models of how young people live, in material terms, during university life. I focus on the four areas already identified in this chapter: financial position, housing, wellbeing and education. The discussion in this part contextualises the different profiles in relation to the 'welfare mixes' available and socioeconomic background, discussing in what respects the different profiles of the university experience can be considered forms of inequalities. I show that the inequalities of the university experience are shaped by the interplay between the students' socioeconomic backgrounds and the 'structures of welfare' that are available to young people.

Part 3 explores in more depth the role played by the different sources of welfare and their unequal distribution through analysis of the survey and interview data collected across the three countries. The role of the family is explored as a crucial resource present in the three different countries, and as an 'inequaliser' of the experiences of the young people, enhancing or limiting their opportunities. The idea of the young people as the 'new precariat' is introduced and discussed. I show that labour market participation by young people in university is a highly structured matter, which depends on the background and welfare mixes available. The state is described in its comparative role in relation to this study, that is, 'absent' in Italy, where the needs of the students are not covered by the state; 'conditional' in England, where state provision for students is means-tested and complemented by family sources; and 'generous' in Sweden. Juggling different forms of welfare, I show here that young people live in an 'eternal phase of semi-dependence', where the availability of welfare sources is more than ever connected to their social origins.

Part 1:
University for all? How higher education shapes inequality among young people

If entering university has the magic power of decreasing inequality, why is this generation of young people, who are the most educated cohort, being affected by a rising level of inequality?

To answer this question we need to go beyond the issue of mere access to HE and look at what happens to young people once they are in university. In particular, we need to focus on the material reproduction of inequality among young people from different backgrounds.

If we analyse what happens to young people once they are in university, we can see the increasing popularity of HE as part of a broader change in young people's transitions, which makes them experience a protracted phase of semi-dependence. In a way, this phase is a 'suspension' of the transition to adulthood, as it makes young people rely on family sources, even if they try to be independent through the use of state support or by working. The way young people are able to combine and negotiate their special status of 'semi-dependence' changes across classes and societies. In addition to looking at class, this part of the book considers how the three most different systems of welfare we find in England, Italy and Sweden shape young people's destinies in university.

The first chapter deals with the social consequences of mass access in Europe – namely, what expansion has meant for inequality and social justice. Has the universal expansion of HE really changed the elitist nature of such institutions? Welfare states have a profound function in shaping young people's experiences, which is analysed in depth in Chapter 2, where the welfare systems of England, Italy and Sweden are dissected in relation to their capacity to limit inequalities, or to reproduce them by asking parents to step in. Chapter 3 explores the potential sources of inequality among young people and the way inequality can be reinforced not only by means of differential welfare state interventions, but also via the reliance on family sources and the participation of young people in the labour market.

Part Two
University for all? How higher education shapes inequality among young people

ONE

Social consequences
of mass access in Europe

As going to university becomes a 'normalised' experience for an increasing number of young Europeans, the important role that universities have for the current generation of young Europeans must be explored. Martin Trow[1] had already foreseen this revolution when he wrote how the historical passage from an elitist to a mass HE, characterised by an increase of up to 50% in the participation rate of young people going to university, was to be overthrown by the even more important passage to a *universal* system of HE with an even higher rate than 50%. By the 2000s this historical passage had become reality in most EU countries, where more than 50% of young people aged 18 to 29 entered HE.[2] When the participation rate of young people in HE goes beyond the symbolic 50%, as Trow writes, HE not only becomes an *obligation* for middle and upper classes, but also an increasingly viable experience for young people from lower socioeconomic backgrounds. However, despite the narrative of the expansion of HE as a democratising force and a symbol of the expansion of equal opportunities, HE has also become a driver for enhancing existing inequalities.

A crucial step in addressing how inequalities are reproduced through HE is to disentangle the implicit paradoxes behind the policies of mass expansion. On the one side, this mass expansion is based on a general idea of an educational path previously reserved for the elite. On the other, this access is still limited by many structural constraints that young people face while in university. A major limitation discussed in this chapter is that the democratisation agenda has not been accompanied by a change in the way of looking at universities as places that need to 'reward the successful ones'. In this competition that rewards the best students, the emphasis of policies is on access (increasing the number of young people in university) and on career destinations (the jobs that young people will get after finishing their degrees). What is missing is attention to what happens in between, namely, while young people are in university; this would shift attention towards the inequality of young people's experiences.

Paradox of higher education policies: democratisation through inequality

The historical passage that made universities change from being 'places for the elite' to central places for democratisation and social inclusion in modern society has left profound contradictions that are embedded in HE policies.

The first contradiction is that the process of democratisation and social inclusion through the expansion of HE has occurred while maintaining elitist HE institutions across Europe, wherever they existed. Of course, not all of the countries in the EU had a profound division between HE institutions. For example, one of the countries analysed in this book, Italy, was created as essentially a unitary system, without profound differences between its public universities. However, the passage to a mass HE system in Italy has reinforced pre-existing inequalities, in particular geographical ones, between institutions in the north and in the south. In our two other countries, England and Sweden, the varying levels of prestige enjoyed by different HE institutions remain intact and relate to having a system with two types of institutions (one more vocational, for the working classes, and the other more academic, for the middle/upper classes) to having a single type of academic institution.

The convergence towards a unified academic system is, however, only apparent:[3] while in Sweden many ex-vocational institutions have in many cases upgraded their status to universities, there is still a binary system of HE consisting of two types of institutions, one more academic (universities) and the other more vocational (*högskola*). England has virtually overcome this binary system by moving towards a unified system in which the division between polytechnics with vocational aims and universities has been dissolved since 1992. However, the system is still defined as a 'diversified' one, as while HE institutions are indistinctively upgraded to the status of universities, a division persists between ex-vocational and historically academic institutions.

The persistence of such a division is not just an institutional matter, and has profound effects on the experience of young adults in university. It reveals the underpinning logic that shapes the way young Europeans experience university. The most evident implication of this logic of diverse HE institutions is that it reflects existing inequality in society, and even reproduces it by making ex-vocational institutions, which were once reserved for the lower classes, the hosts to lower classes who now want to aim for an academic and aspirational type of higher education. For example, in Sweden, *högskola* are considered the natural choice of working-class students (*arbetarklass*) approaching undergraduate studies.[4] In England a division persists between the old and new universities' capacity to attract students from different socioeconomic backgrounds. In addition, studies conducted in the UK show that students in new universities and in more 'prestigious' universities (such as those of the Russell Group, a group of 24 leading universities) tend to have a different experience of university, with the ones from new universities working more and having less time to dedicate to academic-oriented activities.[5]

For those who study HE policies, this is no surprise. In fact, the expansion of HE was never meant to challenge the existing diversity between HE institutions, because such a division between institutions was in line with the 'meritocratic' agenda that informed the expansion, that is, the idea that mass expanded HE was a system that was functional to the promotion of achievement and to rewarding the best students. So, for example, the target of reaching 50% of young people (those under the age of 30) in university set by former Prime Minister Tony Blair in 1999, and the overall education agenda, was notoriously influenced by a vision of 'meritocracy' featured in numerous speeches, for which, unlike egalitarianism, 'the end is high achievement.'[6] The notion of high achievement implied drawing a distinction between young adults with and without qualifications, and also between successful transitions in 'high achievement' institutions and in less successful ones.

Meritocracy has not been at the centre of HE policies just in Anglo-Saxon countries – even in Italy, ex-McKinsey consultant Roger Abravanel published a best-seller on meritocracy in 2008 with a specific agenda to make the Italian system less egalitarian and more meritocratic. Abravanel has been a consultant to the Italian government, and his agenda directly informed the *National plan for quality and merit* of Education Minister Mariastella Gelmini (2010/11), under the government of Silvio Berlusconi. Among other measures, a Merit fund was created to award students with the best education credentials by using parts of the fund previously destined for students who did not have the ability to pay for their studies.

Ironically, while the 'meritocratic' agenda has been favourably used to expand HE in the UK, Michael Young's notion of meritocracy was created as a dystopia precisely to expose the risks of a fetishism of educational credentials. Young himself formulated a poignant critique to Blair's misleading use of meritocracy to establish an 'approval on a minority' and to express 'disapproval on the many who fail to shine' through education.[7] In some ways, while before the passage to a universal HE youth transitions were divided between successful youth transitions through university and less successful ones, after the passage to a mass/universal HE system, such divisions between successful and unsuccessful youth transitions have been embedded within HE.

The passage to a knowledge economy in which HE has been democratised might have created a situation in which grandiosity (or success) also appears to have been democratised, in the sense that 'everybody wants it and feels entitled to it.'[8] Yet it is through HE that the 'excellent sheep' are bred, and a distinction can be drawn between the privileged young adults who go to elitist institutions and the others who attend less privileged ones. The first type, the 'excellent sheep', carry what Deresiewicz calls 'a sense of entitlement'. The majority of young adults, however, will not have the experience of an elitist university, but just of a 'normal' university.[9] Rather than decreasing inequality, the mass expansion of HE has produced a system that reinforces inequalities among young adults through their time at university, not only by channelling young people into institutions that have different degrees of prestige, but by increasing the cost of HE (as will be the core of the discussions that follow), and most profoundly, by splitting the student body into different types of experiences of HE: privileged and difficult.

Features of European higher education policies: the focus on access and destination

An important feature of the modern agenda of expanding HE participation in Europe is that it has been shaped by creating a bond between the 'social' and 'economic' agendas. European and national policies since the 1990s have promoted access to HE as a policy panacea to boost employment rates and, at the same time, to increase social inclusion in European societies. This double goal is visible from the original Lisbon Strategy, launched in 2000, which aimed to make the EU 'the most competitive and dynamic knowledge-based economy',[10] but also to modernise the European social model through investment in HE 'to adapt both to the demands of the knowledge society.'[11] The same double principle can be found in the recent Europe 2020 strategy,[12] and was at the core of the EU Youth Strategy 2008-12.[13] The background to this European goal was the spirit of New Labour's agenda, which was very popular in the late 1990s and early 2000s, and assigned a central role to HE, as reported in the 2001 Labour manifesto penned by Tony Blair, to fit the overall rationale of establishing 'an even stronger bond between the goals of economic progress and social justice.'[14] New Labour's 'widening participation agenda' in the UK in the 2000s was entirely constructed around the double goal of enhancing economic competitiveness and social inclusion.[15]

Creating this bond between 'social justice' principles and economic ones responded to the overall shift in the logic and shape of welfare state interventions. HE, which has never been a central area of welfare state interventions, ended up assuming a central role in contemporary welfare states, while in the previous welfare state settlement it was not so central. Why is this the case? This is explained by looking at the way in which HE is understood in contemporary social policy-making – as one of the main areas of social investment to improve the competitiveness of young workers in the labour market. A very popular idea, both in policy-making and in social policy academic circles, is that modern welfare states should become social investment welfare states, that is, welfare states that focus not on spending for social protection, but on facilitating and enhancing the active role of the individual in the labour market. The passage from a Keynesian welfare state (KWS) to a Schumpeterian welfare state (SWS), in which welfare functions are restructured to respond to the focus on supply-side market policies, has already occurred in HE.[16] What distinguishes the new paradigm of the social investment agenda from the old paradigm of the welfare state for redistribution and social protection is the focus on economic returns. Put simply, while in the old KWS the state had an active role in job creation, in the SWS model the state limits its intervention in equipping individuals with the necessary skills to compete in the labour market.[17] In this new framework, welfare state spending is not justified if it doesn't lead to economic returns (if it only addresses social inequalities, without leading to growth). HE plays a central role in the social investment agenda, as it represents a perfect example of spending leading to (perceived) high economic returns via the labour market.

The effects of this social investment agenda on the individual lives of young people and their families are tangible. The shift towards a social investment welfare state and an individualised approach to investing in HE implies a 'privatisation of social risk',[18] where young people and their families have to meet the increasing costs, in particular, living and HE costs, individually. The rise in private contributions to funding HE across Europe is not only reported as a fact in EU policy documents, but is also actively encouraged in EU policy recommendations, suggesting that the level of tuition fees doesn't have any negative socioeconomic consequences.[19] Clearly the best way to explore the effects of those policies is to look at what happened to the lives of young people in university in this environment, but this has never been a major concern of HE policies. In line with this way of conceptualising HE, HE policies have focused not on the issue of *participation* in HE, that is, on how policies can facilitate the lives of young adults once they are at university, but rather, on young people's *access* to HE and on their *destination* to the labour market.

The whole issue of equality in HE has been reduced to a problem of equity in accessing HE. In particular, *access* to HE for young people from different socioeconomic backgrounds is framed in current policies as a proxy for equity in HE. The existing academic scholarship has, in turn, responded to these assumptions by focusing on access and destination, and suggesting that barriers to widening participation and access remain;[20] but part of academia has admitted that this focus on access has meant little attention has been paid to what happens to young people once they are in university.[21]

The other corollary of the social investment agenda is that participation in HE in itself is assumed to have a positive effect on young people's lives, as it improves their *destinations*, due to the supposed potential higher returns in the labour market.[22] This was, for example, the idea informing the EU Youth Strategy 2008–12, reflecting a human capital approach to HE, where investment in education is assumed to have positive socioeconomic implications given the returns of HE in the labour market.[23] Piketty's *Capital in the twenty-first century* refers directly to the participation of people in university as one key policy to address growing inequalities.[24] This is a reasonable stance, as participation in HE can be considered one of the key drivers of social mobility. At the same time, what is the real success of HE policies in addressing inequality?

If HE carries an economic value, there is an inherent fallacy in the idea of creating more social mobility by turning intrinsically elitist institutions – which universities are, despite their name – into institutions for the masses. It is a bit like trying to award the prize for a race not to the top 10 people, but to the top 50, expecting that winning will then have the same meaning and will be considered equally prestigious. Following this metaphor, policies (and theories) of social investment in HE have not taken into account that the marginal utility of degrees, that is, the economic and social gains of winning (having a graduate education), would have declined with the expansion of HE.

This economic fallacy was first noted by Fred Hirsch in *Social limits to growth*,[25] and is the problem of positional goods such as education:

expanding access to HE qualifications doesn't increase their economic value. What happens, in fact, is that with the development of higher qualifications (see, for example, the expansion of postgraduate education), the value of lower qualifications (undergraduate degrees) declines. This explains why, despite having the largest number of students in HE in its history, the EU is increasingly affected by the issue of graduate unemployment and under-employment. Although the expansion of HE has been flagged up as an economic panacea, it has also resulted in a decline in the economic value of qualifications in the labour market.[26]

Higher education also has a very important role in shaping the modern dynamics of social mobility. This aspect is outlined by the work of Ainley and Allen, who explain that the social class structure has become pear-shaped:[27] after the democratisation of HE, instead of having a large portion of young people in the middle, the social class structure has become polarised, with a minority of young people on top and the vast majority at the bottom. The function of HE is to protect young people from 'climbing down the ladder', in other words, from being disadvantaged compared to their educated peers in finding a job. If access to HE becomes widespread, having a degree is not a substantial gain, but at the same time *not* having a degree represents a disadvantage in the labour market.

HE qualifications therefore represent a 'hygiene factor', a factor whose presence will not improve the situation of young people, but whose absence will affect their position in the labour market. Young people are put in competition with each other in a labour market in which jobs are becoming increasingly scarce and in which employers can pick their staff from an ever-larger number of qualified candidates, thereby penalising the least qualified. A recent empirical confirmation of the inherent inequality in graduate destinations comes from a recent study conducted by the Institute for Fiscal Studies in England.[28] This study shows that, even after completing the same degrees from the same universities, graduates from a higher-income background earn more (about a 10% income premium) than their peers from an 'average' background.

In this race to gain more and more qualifications in the labour market, the family plays a very important role. The role of the 'cultural capital' deriving from the family in the experience of young people in university has been widely explored since Bourdieu and Passeron's study conducted in the 1970s in France.[29] However, at that time, the French HE system was elitist and not a mass system, and things have changed since then. Despite the changes, van de Werfhorst and Shavit[30] note that families are aware that the value of education in the labour market is positional, and that their children compete with their cohort to stay ahead of the rising level of educational qualifications required in the labour market. As they point out, the issue of inequality in relation to HE becomes even more important in relation to degrees that are more selective, such as postgraduate courses, where families can mobilise additional resources so that their children can maintain their social advantage over their peers. The paradox is that educationally expanding societies offer more, not fewer, possibilities of inequalities through HE.

Part of the literature (the educational literature that has studied processes of marketisation in HE) has concentrated on the 'institutional consequences' of the processes described above. There is a story that they leave untold: the impact of those reforms on young people themselves, and on their families, while at university. If destinations are not the responsibility of HE policies, what, then, are the real benefits of HE in terms of addressing inequality during HE? In other words, who are the losers and winners in a system in which HE is an economic good?

Students as young adults in a protracted phase of semi-dependence

In order to establish an analytical shift in the debate, it is crucial to consider that the vast majority of people in HE are, in fact, young people, and not simply students. There is an important difference between considering the individuals as simply engaging in their studies and considering the overall experience of young people during university outside of the lecture room. The latter view takes into consideration the 'social position' of young people, that is, what happens to young people as a cohort; it looks at the implications of being 'young' in this society, and considers what happens to this generation of young people compared to others. The expansion of HE is intrinsically intertwined with the changes in young people's transitions to adulthood. Youth scholars in particular have emphasised how the current transitions of young people 'in late modernity' (in particular, after the 1980s) are different from those of the baby-boomer generation, as they imply more fragmented and less linear paths.

Traditionally, Coles has identified three main transitions:[31] from school to work, from family housing to independent housing, and from family of origin to the formation of young people's own families. Current cohorts of young people have more complex transitions characterised, for example, by passing back and forth from education to work. Furthermore, these transitions are less linear and are intertwined; the passage from school to work is not the only possible transitional path, and it might happen as a temporary moment. This is, for example, the case of young people working during university. In this context, entrance into the labour market is not necessarily a 'signpost' of having transitioned to adulthood and having begun a stable career path, especially if the young person is working during HE in order to fund it. The mass expansion of HE has greatly contributed to extending the transitional moment, to the point that 'being young' doesn't have to be considered a transitional moment per se, but can be seen as a discrete period of the life course. The 'emerging adulthood' described by Arnett depicts well the experiences of young people still in university (in fact, the greatest number of participants in Arnett's study are university students).[32] While Arnett interprets the changes to the emerging adulthood as a new phase in which young people choose to suspend their decisions, this phase of emerging adulthood can be directly linked to the changing nexus between labour market and education, and to the passage to the knowledge economy, which has made participation in university so important in contemporary society.

The changing conditions of young people in contemporary society concern not only the labour market, but also the formation of the family. So, for example, young men and women stay longer in education, and this has postponed the formation of their own families, as well as the patterns of independent living.[33] Rather than establishing independent households after school, young people who stay in university look for other forms of cohabitation in order to save on housing costs, either with their partners, with their families or with their peers.

This position of young people 'in-between' is not simply a choice, as Arnett writes, but is a consequence of a structural condition that doesn't provide young people in university with a full condition of independence via, for example, state sources. What emerges is best described by the notion of 'semi-dependence'. This notion was first used by Bob Coles to describe the distinctive position of young people in the life course, and how they were transitioning from a dependent state during childhood to the independent status that characterises adulthood.[34] As pointed out by Coles, young people have a specific phase of semi-dependence in welfare states: they are in an in-between position in respect to childhood dependence and adult independence. This implies a specific position of young people vis-à-vis their use of welfare sources – while during childhood they rely completely on family sources, semi-dependent young people use a variety of sources, not only from the family, but also from the state, given their partial entitlements to social provisions, and from their own participation in the labour market. Young people's position of semi-dependence derives from the fact that states assume a specific combination of rights and responsibilities for people that have passed their childhood, but who are not yet fully into their adulthood.

The concept of semi-dependence is particularly central in exploring the case of young people in university who are experiencing a protraction of their semi-dependent state due to both living costs and HE costs. Young people in university are not completely independent as working adults, but neither are they completely dependent on their families as children. As explained earlier, current generations of young people have been increasingly encouraged to participate in HE, but this extended participation implies material and financial costs. Part of the costs linked to the development of HE has been met by welfare instruments supporting young people in HE, which include welfare state interventions outside pedagogical purposes, not only in student finances (for example, the introduction of scholarships and expansion of loans), but also in student accommodation and other services. After the mass expansion of HE, welfare state interventions to support young people in HE can be considered social policy interventions, in the sense that they provide indirect forms of support to part of the population that would otherwise be significantly affected by unemployment, and that is not necessarily protected in areas other than education by the welfare state, given the earnings-related nature of benefits in labour market protection.

Arnett, who has conducted extensive research on young adulthood in the US, has found that a crucial signifier of the current transition to adulthood is reaching the psychological notion of 'independence', which is equivalent to taking responsibility and making decisions, and also to becoming financially independent. The importance of 'economic independence' for reaching a psychological condition of adulthood is not, however, equal across countries. The 'welfare systems', and the different availability of family, state and labour market sources, are crucial factors that contribute in shaping young people's positions in a certain society. Studies conducted across Europe (which represents an excellent laboratory for the exploration of the diversity of such 'welfare mixes') show that there is a constellation of 'semi-dependence' models across countries, which also depend on young people's characteristics, such as gender, ethnicity and socioeconomic background.[35] If we look at the data on students' social conditions in

Europe, it is clear that young people across Europe use a combination of the different sources of welfare (the welfare mix presented in Figure 1), but that this welfare mix is likely to change across countries and depending on their socioeconomic background.

The variation of 'welfare mixes' is clear if we look at our case studies. England is best described as a system of 'social investment',[36] where young people receive support from the state, and also a contribution from private sources (from the young people themselves and their families). The role of private sources has increased in recent years: in England, a state of semi-dependence on family sources until the age of 25 was institutionally established as a consequence of the adoption of the Social Security Act 1986.[37] Indeed, after this policy change, young people, in particular students, were assumed to use family social support, as the automatic right to state support had been withdrawn.[38] Furthermore, the reliance on means-tested loans policies for students' families means that there are assumptions about students' reliance on private forms of dependence on the labour market or on their families – state support is present but depends on parental income, and makes an assumption that the remaining support would come from parents.[39]

Italy is a system of minimal intervention, which implies a lower form of public dependence and a higher use of private sources of dependence. In Italy the role of 'private contributions is maximised' – young people rely almost exclusively on the family, which reflects the assumption of the centrality of the family in young people's transitions.[40] These differences reflect norms about intergenerational support embedded in the 'Southern transitional regimes',[41] that is, contexts in which the family represents a crucial component of the welfare mix. The opposite example is that of Sweden, a system of

Figure 1: The triangle of welfare sources supporting young people's semi-dependence

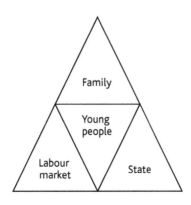

'public responsibility' that assumes a form of public dependence and entails a lower role of private sources of welfare. In Sweden young people's dependence on their families is expected before their twenties, but with entrance into HE the existence of generous grants is meant to create a 'state responsibility' in supporting young people, which replaces family responsibility during childhood.[42] In this case, therefore, the passage to university is characterised by a shift from family dependency to a sort of functional dependency on the state, before young adults reach economic independence through labour market participation.

These three forms of semi-dependence are not set in stone and are likely to be influenced by the current austerity trends affecting European welfare states, which are reconfiguring the boundaries of private and public interventions, and show a shift in the use of private and public sources of welfare by young people. The effects of these reforms for the three countries analysed in this research are explored in the next chapter. Furthermore, relying on different 'welfare sources' is related to young people's socioeconomic background and has different implications, which is the focus of Chapter 3, looking at the way in which inequality is reproduced or limited in HE through the use of the different sources.

Beyond access and destination: how young people live in university

To identify the real winners and losers of HE, it is pivotal to study what happens to young people once they are in university. However, the exclusive attention on the politics of *access* and *destination* has resulted in limited attention being paid to the *politics of living* at university as a defined period where inequalities can be reproduced through social policy interventions oriented towards individual investment, for example, by increasing tuition fees. How can we get a holistic picture of how young people live in HE? Being in HE involves many aspects of young people's lives, but the four main areas that emerge in the literature as being crucial are the financial issues that young people face while in university, their housing conditions, their 'wellbeing' and educational outcomes.

The economic aspect is crucial to the understanding of young people in university, as participating in HE implies covering extended living costs (and therefore implies an extension of young people's semi-dependent state) and HE-related costs. An issue emerges, therefore, regarding the financial pressures that young people and their families face. The economic aspect of living while at university is the one that is most directly related to the issue of inequality: evidence from the UK shows that young people from working-class backgrounds have a disadvantaged experience of university that is profoundly linked to their financial circumstances.[43] In general, finances are increasingly at the centre of young people's experiences of university,[44] as I wanted to suggest with the image used for this book cover.

The material condition of young people is always affected by the issue of housing, which represents the main cost for young people in university and one of the central costs associated with the transition to independence. For young people who stay with their family during HE, housing represents an indirect form of dependence on family sources. Two broad topics are connected with housing and young people in university: the quality of student housing and the issue of semi-dependence.

First of all, housing can be explored as an outcome of young people's experiences in university by analysing their satisfaction with student housing, that is, the quality of housing and its capacity to cover young people's needs. Regarding this first aspect, previous studies conducted on young people in university show that 'student housing' represents a 'substandard' housing arrangement that is accepted by young people due to its temporary nature.[45] Longitudinal studies, in particular, show that 'leaving home' is not a linear process but a fragmented one, characterised by temporary solutions. In other words, the quality of housing arrangements drops remarkably with the entrance to HE in the case of independent housing, but this is accepted by young people as it is (assumed to be) only for a short period. The expansion of HE has also created a separate housing market for students, which varies greatly according to the local area.[46] While in the past the housing market for students was a privileged one, most recent studies show that as a consequence of the mass expansion of HE, student housing markets present increasing challenges in relation to the possibility of meeting young people's housing needs during university.[47] While this tends to vary across national and local areas, typically students in HE have to navigate through the perils of the renting sector, mobilising savings and family sources to sustain housing solutions that are sustainable only in the short term.

The second broad topic linked with housing and young people concerns the relationship between housing and the notion of semi-dependence introduced above: the transition to independent housing is a crucial step in the transition to adult life. However, not all young people make the housing transition during their university studies, as some remain at home. A number of studies are starting to explore the difference between living at home and living independently in relation to youth semi-dependence, pointing to the fact that different housing arrangements, for example, staying with parents, might represent suboptimal solutions that appear to be influenced by structural factors, such as social class.[48] If only young people from low socioeconomic backgrounds remain at home, the research says, they will miss out on their university experience compared to their privileged peers who can transition to independent housing early on. But even for those who transition to independent housing, leaving the parental home would not be a radical passage, as student housing implies cohabitation with other students, as well as the coexistence of different housing arrangements at the same time.[49] This is, for example, the case for young people in university who live in shared accommodation during the academic year, but return home during the summer, or even at weekends.

Young people face not only 'material struggles', but also immaterial ones, which have to do with their psychosocial condition. The third crucial area of young people's experiences is wellbeing, which has emerged in recent years as a challenging topic for young people in university. If being at university represents a 'socially privileged' position, why are young people in university challenged in their mental health? A study of seven UK institutions concluded that the level of psychological problems faced by students, in the form of stress and anxiety, is relatively high, and called for university administrations to be more aware of the issue and to promote the wellbeing of students.[50] But the responsibilities seem to lie beyond UK institutions, as even in a comparative research on wellbeing and students,[51] scholars found remarkably low levels of wellbeing that, according to the scholars, could be transitional effects of the stress experienced during university. Transition seems to have an effect on students' wellbeing, proved by the fact that the first year experience is a particularly vulnerable moment for young people in university, thereby showing that entrance into academic life is a challenging moment.[52]

However, wellbeing struggles faced by young people in university are not purely psychological phenomena, and could be linked to socioeconomic factors. The stress appears to be related to *some* young people's need to undertake part-time work[53] (typically less privileged students, as will be analysed extensively in Chapter 3), but the effects of socioeconomic circumstances, financial issues and debt also seem to play a role.[54] In addition, this generation of young people might be more affected by mental health issues due to what sociologists have defined as the role of 'individualisation' in the risk society, that is, how individual young people deem themselves to be responsible for planning and constructing their future biographies. Such a degree of individual responsibility is challenged by the structures available for future planning, but as young people fail to consider these constraints and limits, and deem themselves to be solely responsible for such planning,[55] they can enter into a trap of self-blaming that could affect their wellbeing. This aspect is particularly relevant for young people in university, as they are surrounded by expectations regarding their transitions from university to work that clash, as discussed earlier, with the reality of graduate unemployment and under-employment. The effects on wellbeing of this mismatch between expectations and labour market realities are partially new.

Finally, young people not only study while they are in university, but education is a core aspect, and one of the main outcomes, of their experiences. While this book doesn't focus on the purely pedagogic aspects of young people's experiences in university, there is an interesting relationship between life outside and life inside the classroom.[56] The current surveys measuring young people's satisfaction make an assumption about the separation between the educational satisfaction of students and their lives outside the classroom. In other words, they assume that young people's educational experience is separated from the rest of their lives during university. These surveys tend to get significant media attention in the UK in particular,[57] and they inform university rankings, which influence HE institutions' funding. As has been underlined by other scholars before me, measuring the student experience without acknowledging the diversity of young people's experiences in university across gender, social class and ethnicity reflects a very narrow understanding of the student experience.[58]

In reality, research regarding students' experiences show that the educational side of the student experience in HE is connected to what young people do outside university, and in particular to the resources they have to sustain themselves while at university. Two good examples of this are the perception of workload (the balance between work and education) and student retention (how likely students are to continue with their education). Regarding the first theme, previous studies show that workload in university is perceived as negative by young people who work during university, who tend to be young people from low socioeconomic backgrounds.[59] In other words, the 'student satisfaction' ranking across UK universities might hide the fact that a higher percentage of the student population in some universities (typically new universities, as shown by previous studies in this area) need to work while studying, and therefore the final level of satisfaction might be severely affected by this additional burden.[60] The other important link between what happens inside and what happens outside the classroom is represented by student retention and attrition, that is, the probability that students will stay in university after the first year. This is a particularly important issue in Italy, where young people's participation in HE has increased in the last decade, but where the percentage of graduates has not increased as sharply due to high drop-out rates. Previous studies in this area conducted by US scholars have pointed out how success in HE, and the chances of staying on in HE, depends on the financial situation of students and on the structural conditions around them.[61] It is therefore plausible to think that the specific situation around young people in university in Italy and the welfare sources that are available to them, discussed in the next chapter, are behind the high drop-out rate that we find in this country. Overall, work–life balance and retention rate can be connected to what we have defined above as the availability of welfare sources – those from the state, the family and the labour market.

Conclusion

Understanding how young people live in university means going beyond the paradigm of access or destination to the labour market, and entails a more holistic understanding of what young people do, beyond the lecture room, once they are in university. This chapter has discussed how the mass expansion of HE has been described as a process of 'democratisation', but has, in fact, taken place within the pre-existing unequal structure of HE. One important explanation for this is that the focus of policies has been on increasing the number of people entering HE (focusing on access), or smoothing transitions to the labour market (graduate destinations). Less policy interest has been devoted to smoothing and addressing young people's experiences during university. A crucial step in changing the policy shift is to consider the social implications of mass access to HE, that is, the protracted phase of semi-dependence that this implies for young people. If we look at what happens beyond the classroom, young people in university face a number of challenges, regarding their finances, their housing, their wellbeing and also their educational outcomes. These areas are the focus of the empirical work presented in Part 2, that discusses how these challenges are faced by some groups of young people in university, determining a fundamental inequality in young people's experience of university.

TWO

How welfare influences the lives of young people in university

Any society that seriously wants to foster human capital
formation at the tertiary level must provide arrangements
that help students from middle and low-income families
to carry the cost of living during extended periods of
educational study. (Pechar and Andres, 2011)[1]

No society, no matter how rich, can afford a system of
higher education for 20% or 30% or 40% of the relevant age
group at the cost levels of the elite higher education that it
formerly provided for 5% of the population. (Trow, 2006)[2]

The development of welfare for young people in university was
essential for putting forward the dual logic described in Chapter 1, as
this was the key policy convincing middle- and low-income groups
to go into HE. Together with these 'carrots' (the development of new
systems of student support), the system of HE presents other 'sticks'
underlined by Trow, namely, the fact that while the elite system of
HE was paradoxically very generous to the privileged young people
who joined it, student support for the expanded HE system could
not have been equally generous for reasons of financial sustainability
(unless, of course, it involved expanding the welfare state, which was
not a popular idea in the 1990s). For example, in the UK in the 1970s,
the system of student support was far more generous than the current
system given its provision of grants, housing support and coverage of
fees for the privileged young people going into HE. In other words,
they were the symbol of middle-class welfare, funded by the taxpayer
to support (mostly) middle-class young people. The modern systems
for student support had to support another goal – they had to be
generous enough to convince those from the middle and lower classes
to engage in HE, but also not be so costly as to be unsustainable. So
how have systems of student support struck this balance across Europe?
And how has austerity changed these systems?

Comparing 'welfare mixes' in England, Italy and Sweden

Two strategies have been followed across Europe to convince people to join engage in HE and to maintain a financially sustainable system: first, increasing public funding of universities and charging relatively low fees; and second, charging higher fees, but offering grants and loans.[3] The first strategy represents the cases of Sweden and Italy, which, respectively, have no fees and low levels of fees, although the generosity of the support systems tends to vary greatly, as I discuss later. The second case exemplifies the route followed by England under New Labour between 1997 and 2007, when the strategy of having at least half of the youth cohort (young people aged 18-30) in HE was supported by the introduction of fees of up to £3,000, means-tested grants and loans, together with a general shift towards co-contribution.[4]

In other words, what has happened in HE reflects what I have described in Chapter 1 as a privatisation of social risk:[5] young people are increasingly expected to enter HE, but the assumption is that they have to meet the costs of this new protracted phase of semi-dependence privately. Despite this general trend, the interesting outcome of this process has not been a process of harmonisation of welfare for young people in university. On the contrary, the studies covering welfare state support for young people in HE[6] report that the systems have developed in line with the historical traditions of the countries, and show the presence of three worlds of student support that have led to the existence of three highly diverse welfare mixes available to young people to manage social risks during university. At first glance, these systems are reminiscent (but are not entirely reflective of) the famous 'worlds of welfare' introduced by Esping-Andersen about 25 years ago:[7] they represent three ways of delivering student support for young people in university that follow three different historical traditions. However, contrary to Esping-Andersen's worlds of welfare, contemporary systems need to look at what I called in Chapter 1 'welfare mixes' – while young people receive, in different ways, state support to be in HE, the welfare system itself assumes that they will combine this support with private sources of welfare, that is, family sources or their own participation in the labour market. Yet the specific way they combine private and public sources tends to vary across the three countries I focus on in this study, which represent three very different welfare mixes:

- A system of 'public dependence' found in Nordic countries, exemplified by the case of Sweden. An important contribution is made to young people's independence in these countries by the elimination of university costs (no tuition fees) and the provision of the same support to nearly all students. These countries are relatively 'generous' in terms of tools (providing grants and loans that should be sufficient to live while in university) and the least costly (with no fees). As I show later, however, the reality of young people's lives in Sweden shows that this system of student support is not as generous as it is considered. The interventions for young people in HE would broadly confirm, in this case, the presence of a welfare mix with a higher level of state intervention in supporting young people's semi-dependent state.

- A system of 'social investment' principally found in Anglo-Saxon countries, as in our case study of England. This has been defined as an 'investor model',[8] as young people are considered investors in their future career, and they have to co-contribute privately to fees that are higher compared to the rest of Europe. At the same time, student support is also relatively generous, and is transferred directly to the young person in HE, who is asked to invest in their own education. At the macro level this model shows high levels of both public and private spending: the present levels of fees are high, but the 'negative effect of high tuition fees in the liberal countries is largely offset by the high per capita amount of grants and loans awarded to students.'[9] The comparatively high level of spending is considered a form of investment in the knowledge society. This system is more closely related to the idea of private investment in HE, but it also provides forms of public support through grants, and it is therefore likely to create a variegated welfare mix for young people, with the presence of both public and private welfare sources.

- A system of 'minimal public intervention', found in continental and southern European countries, as in the case of Italy in this research. This is the model of 'children sheltered by their families', which indicates the total dependence that young people in university have on their families.[10] In these countries fees are normally charged, and support is limited to those in the greatest need. While continental welfare states are relatively generous for adults, they are not necessarily generous for young people: in these countries the welfare state intervenes the least in this area (even less than in liberal welfare states), although it also assumes a lower individual contribution demanding a low level of fees. In other words, this welfare mix is likely to be shaped mostly by private sources of welfare, in particular through the family, which intervenes in covering young people's living costs in particular (as educational costs are relatively low).

In the following pages this chapter compares the welfare systems available to young people in university by looking at the different dimensions – generosity, level of individual contribution, the role of loans and inclusiveness. The way the three systems perform is summarised in Table 1 below, which shows that the English system puts an emphasis on individual contributions, while the Italian system does not intervene, leaving the responsibility to the family. Sweden has the most generous and inclusive system of the three.

Degree of individual contributions: the level of fees

The first element of the comparison across the three countries is the level of fees (see the third row in Table 1), which determines the degree of private and individual contributions by students to the cost of HE. The comparison between England, Italy and Sweden in this book permits an exploration of three different solutions regarding private contributions through fees: England relies on private contributions to high tuition fees; the level of fees in Italy is maintained at a comparatively low level, but depends on institutions and family

Table 1: Comparison of welfare systems for young people in HE in England, Italy and Sweden

	England	Italy	Sweden
The welfare mix	High role of both public spending (for 'investing') and private sources of welfare	Predominant role of family sources, low state support	Predominant role of state sources and 'independent' private sources (labour market participation)
Sufficiency	Developed student support system (loans and grants)	Less developed student support system (only grants)	Generous student support system (loans and grants)
Individual contribution (fees)	High	Low	Non-existent
Role of loans	Covering fees and living costs	Absent	Covering living costs
Inclusiveness	Means-tested	Highly residual	Quasi-universal

income; and finally, Sweden epitomises the model of 'free university' education without fees.[11]

Both in Italy and in England in recent decades there has been a progressive trend towards increasing the level of individual contributions through fees. While in Italy this increase depends on the lack of funding of HE from the state to regions, in England there has been an increase in contributions from students and their families since the 1990s. Fees were introduced in England after the report issued by the Dearing Committee (1997),[12] which was commissioned by the Conservative government but had an important impact on the Labour government that came to power in 1997, by establishing the idea that students had to meet the costs of HE privately through fees.[13] These were introduced through the Teaching and Higher Education Act 1998 in a means-tested way, and initially at a relatively moderate level (up to £1,000). This form of private contribution has progressively increased. The Teaching and Higher Education Act 2004 established variable, but non-means-tested fees of up to £3,000 a year to be monitored by the new Office for Fair Access, and introduced the principle of using loans to sustain the costs of the increasing fees.[14] Important reforms regarding fees have occurred in the last few years, which are covered in the last section in this chapter on austerity.

How sufficient are the provisions to cover young people's needs in university?

A comparison can be made across the three case studies regarding the presence of grants and/or loans to cover the young people's needs during university in relation to the four areas described above (financial costs, housing, wellbeing and housing). In reference to the presence of student support, which can take the form of grants and loans, Sweden shows a higher level of intervention by the state, and has been defined by the OECD as an example of a country with a 'generous student support system.'[15] The system of student support in Sweden consists of a mix of loans and grants, and because of its comparatively lower cost, it attracts an average entry rate into university that is higher than the OECD average.

I define this system as sufficient rather than truly 'generous'. Even in Sweden the balance between grants and loans has changed substantially in the last few decades in the direction of increasing the component of loans as a private contribution: while the original proportions were 25% of non-repayable grants over total support and

75% of loans, the proportion of grants has decreased substantially, reaching a minimum of only 6% of the total of student support in the 1980s.[16] This balance has been reviewed since 1989, when the share of grants reached 28% of the total of student support, accompanied by an increase in the interest rate, with the overall goal of restoring the attractiveness of student support.[17] According to data for the academic year 2012/13, for which there was an increase in the debt component that had been approved in July 2011, non-repayable grants (*studiemedel*) constitute a historically high percentage of support, offering 31.6% of the total support that students receive in Sweden, while 68.4% of student support is constituted by repayable loans.[18] Supplementary grants are also available but only to special cases: students who are below 25 and unemployed, who are older than 25, or who have childcare responsibilities. Furthermore, while the Swedish system is comparatively generous, it still implies a co-contribution of private sources of welfare, as it is paid for nine months per year.[19] This creates an assumption that young people in university must still contribute with private sources of welfare during the summer recess.

Italy is an example of a 'less-developed student support system',[20] which offers partial support in the form of a (partial) grant (nowhere sufficient to cover costs) to a minority of students, and where loans are basically not used. The underdevelopment of the system of student support found in Italy is mostly the consequence of having historically managed student support at the regional level since the 1970s, something that led not only to different regional solutions, but also to a disparity in the distribution of resources across regions. The introduction of a centralised 'state fund' (*Fondo statale integrativo*) and a 'tax for the right to study' from regions to redistribute resources across the student population partially addressed the problems in the 1990s. However, especially in the south, the system of student support remains massively underfunded. The anomaly of the Italian situation is represented by the increasing number of students who are eligible for student support according to the set threshold, but who do not receive student support due to a lack of availability of regional funding. These students who are 'eligible but not beneficiaries', as they are called by the system, are far more likely to be resident in the south – while in 2005 70% of students could effectively receive student support, only about half of eligible students received the support in southern Italy.[21] For those who are eligible but not beneficiaries, and for all others who are not eligible, the system of student support in Italy assumes that young people will find the resources to support themselves through their families or their participation in the labour market.

England has traditionally had a 'developed system of student support',[22] given that the share of public expenditure on student support for university-level education in the UK is higher than the OECD average. However, the system of student support in England has been subjected to a considerable degree of reform in recent decades. This has been intended to strengthen the contribution of individuals and the role of private sources of welfare, passing from the use of grants to the means testing of grants and the increasing use of loans to cover students' living costs. Originally the system offered means-tested grants, and students could also use the social security system and access housing benefits.[23] The paradox, as pointed out at the beginning of this chapter, is that the system of student support during the elitist form of HE was far more generous: reported in the prices for 2003, between 1975 and 1987 students from England had the highest levels of state support, which provided more than three times the level of grants than the system introduced in 2003.[24] The system became more residual after the third re-election of Margaret Thatcher in 1987, when the real value of maintenance grants was reduced, the principle of co-contribution from students and parents was introduced, and the ability of students to access social security was withdrawn, removing their eligibility for unemployment and housing benefits.[25] After the introduction of loans to pay living costs in 1989, the radical change introduced with the Teaching and Higher Education Act 1998, during Labour's time in office, consisted of a total abolition of grants, to be replaced by loans to cover living costs. Grants were reintroduced in the Teaching and Higher Education Act 2004, during the second Labour term, in response to criticism, but in a very targeted way, as the (parental) income threshold for receipt of a full maintenance grant was only £17,500.[26] As discussed later on, grants have once again been abolished, and will not be available to students in England from the academic year 2015/16.

What role do loans play?

The introduction of loans represents one of the most important elements behind the mass system of HE. Loans have been introduced with the aim of making university truly accessible and sustainable, but without changing the principles of a welfare system that was 'retrenching' from the lives of young people. While loans have been introduced as a 'democratic tool', they were also transferring HE costs directing to students. As such, loans have been introduced in most European countries and have been effectively used to incentivise young people who could not otherwise afford it to enter university.

However, in a few countries considered particularly debt-averse, such as Italy, the many attempts to introduce a loan policy for students since 1991 have not been successful – loans were used in Italy in the early 2000s by only 0.1% of the student population.[27] Through a loan project (*Diamogli Credito*) arising from an agreement between the Ministry of Education and ABI (the Italian Banking Association), there was a recent attempt to introduce a loan system for ad hoc interventions (for example, to cover fees) rather than to cover general living costs. Even after this attempt, loans are still used by a negligible number of students.[28] How is it possible to explain the anti-loans sentiment in Italy? In essence, the conditions of the loans proposed in Italy can hardly be defined as a form of public intervention, considering the 6% interest rate to be paid back to banks, and the fact that families, together with the young person, are responsible for this debt. It is most likely that young people prefer to sustain some form of debt with their family rather than incur other forms of private debts for which the family is responsible.

The way loans have been implemented in Sweden and England has led to a significant difference between these two systems. An important distinction needs to be drawn between the use of loans to cover living costs and to cover fees. The use of loans to cover fees in England has the potential to stratify young people's experiences in university, not only by enhancing individual contributions to HE, but also by increasing the level of debt of young people from lower socioeconomic backgrounds, creating adverse effects. While the presence of loans in the Swedish system of student support reflects a privatisation of the costs of HE, loans are not attached to fees and have been a part of the Swedish system of student support since its creation in 1918. Loans in Sweden have been promoted in particular since the 1960s as an economically sustainable instrument to reach universal coverage of student support.[29] The aim of their introduction has been to increase student participation in university, in particular by protecting disadvantaged students.[30] These loans offer repayment at an interest rate below the market price, and at the same time, the repayment system starts only a year after students conclude their studies, and continues for 25 years. The system takes into account the ability to repay, which is measured through means testing.[31]

On the contrary, in England, loans ended up being used by the state to encourage private contributions towards HE, that is, not just for maintenance, but also to pay fees. Loans had been introduced in

1989, when the Conservative government established the principle of individual contribution by introducing a non-means-tested loan system repaid with a five-year plan, but only if incomes were above 85% of average national salaries.[32] At this stage the loan system was not meant to be a contribution to the cost of HE, but a supplementary form of support for living costs in addition to grants, whose real value was frozen and whose function progressively decreased. A radical change occurred after the Dearing Report (1997),[33] which introduced a principle of co-payment for which the system had to reflect the higher individual gains of students from university. To reflect this principle, the Teaching and Higher Education Act 1998 abolished grants and replaced them with loans to cover all living costs. The Teaching and Higher Education Act 2004 established a new principle of co-contribution where loans were used to cover fees, whose level has since then increased considerably, until reaching a market orientation as a result of the last reforms during austerity, described below.

How inclusive are the systems?

The systems of student support in the three countries vary not only in relation to the policy tools employed and the balance between fees, grants and loans, but also in respect of the degree of inclusiveness of the system, that is, the universal or means-tested nature of student support. In this respect, the three countries represent three very different solutions, from the most universal system of student support in Sweden, to a highly means-tested system in England, and a very residual system in Italy.

Sweden offers a quasi-universal system of student support, and means testing doesn't involve assessment of parental income. The only means-testing principle present in the Swedish system is in relation to the income of the student – the fact that students in university cannot earn more than a certain amount of money to be eligible for the system of student support.[34] Students who earn more than set thresholds are not eligible for student support, but those whose incomes are less than this threshold have access to a universal form of support, and are eligible for the same level of grants and loans (except for those who receive a premium level of grant because they have dependent children or are over 25). In any case, the income of the family doesn't matter in assessing eligibility. The quasi-universal nature of the system of support in Sweden means that inequality in young people's experiences of university is minimised. Instead, the system tends to 'equalise' the experiences of young people from different socioeconomic backgrounds who have the same resources while they are in university, despite their family condition. The assumption is that student support will cover all the needs that young people have in university, and that the family will not intervene much through co-contribution (although, as discussed in Chapter 3, this is not necessarily the case).

The Italian system, on the other hand, is an example of a highly targeted and residual system, accessed by only 10.9% of the total student population and relying on means testing parental income.[35] The division between insiders and outsiders in the Italian system is set, since its origins lie in Article 34 of the Italian Constitution, which states that student support is for 'pupils of ability and merit' but 'lacking financial resources', and should be allocated 'through competitive evaluation'. This principle has been applied by targeting students 'lacking financial resources' from the family, and excluding others. As a consequence, grants are awarded on a competitive basis and offered to a minority of students. Those who access the system are exempted from fees and receive a level of grant that varies across regions.[36] As reported above, the system doesn't provide financial support to 'eligible but non-beneficiary' students, that is, those students who are exempted from fees, but whose support is not covered due to lack of regional funds.[37]

The system of student support in Italy is characterised by an emphasis on targeting the poor and, by assuming forms of private contributions for the large majority of the student population, is the system that has the potential to make the experience of young people in university the most unequal. The residual nature of the system of student support in Italy has been exacerbated by the system's lack of adaptation to the mass expansion of HE occurring in Italy in particular during the 1990s and 2000s.[38] While the absolute number of students accessing the system of student support has increased from 65,352 in 1996/97 to 133,714 in 2003/04, the percentage of those who have access to grants in relation to the total student population has remained the same, and regional disparities have become more pronounced.[39] As a consequence of the mass expansion of HE, in Italy only a section of the students eligible for the targeted system of student support receive financial support in the form of grants due to the lack of regional funds.[40] The percentage of those eligible for grants who actually receive grants was only 67.7% in 2011/12 and has increased to 74.9% in 2013/14.[41] This suggests that the system of student support in Italy has not adapted to the exogenous expansion of HE, and assumes the role of individuals and families in supporting mass access to HE.

The English system lies somewhere between the very targeted nature of student support in Italy and the quasi-universal model of Sweden. While 86.2% of students in England and Wales receive a form of contribution via loans and/or grants,[42] grants and loans are distributed in a means-tested way, based on parental income and other conditions. Grants are allocated – as they were before the last reforms – on national means-testing criteria based on parental income.[43] Student loans for maintenance are both universal and means-tested: while 72% of the loan in 2011/12 was available to all students, 28% was means-tested.[44] The maximum level of maintenance loans available also depends on the housing condition of the family, that is, the fact of living at home or independently (or the fact of living in London or outside). Overall, the system of support in England is composed of several conditions and principles of means testing, and this poses issues for the capacity of the system to cover students in need, according to the assessment.

Has austerity affected the welfare systems for young people in university?

> The economic downturn has led to a decrease in public funding, while demand for higher education continues to increase, and it is now an orthodox view that this funding gap will increasingly be covered through private contributions. (Eurydice, 2011)[45]

While all three systems, as we have seen, imply the contribution of private sources of welfare, recent policy reports have not only pointed out the potential negative effects of the current economic crisis on HE, but have also deemed as inevitable a rise in the private sources of welfare that support young people while they are at university. While explicit welfare state cuts are occurring during the austerity trend in other areas of welfare,[46] policies for HE are implementing austerity in a more subtle way. What we are witnessing is not an explicit degree of cuts, as policies continue to support the idea of social investment and of having an increasing number of young people in HE. Nevertheless, there has been an equally powerful, yet more subtle, change in line with the 'privatisation of social risk' described above, which refers to the way individuals are expected to meet increasing costs or emerging risks. The impact on the three 'welfare mixes' analysed in this book is diverse, with Sweden not updating the system to match the rising costs of living for young people in university, Italy making the system even more residual and England demanding an increase in private contributions from young people and their families (which is likely to take the form of 'debt').

Sweden: a lack of adaptation to the new challenges faced by young people

In Sweden we haven't witnessed a revolution in student support policies, at least for nationals. The bill passed in 2009 in Sweden establishes the introduction of fees for international students and signals a change in the funding principles of HE, by increasing the role of private contributions.[47] However, national students have not yet been affected by this change, and the reforms have been more subtle.

In line with the trend of increasing private contributions, in 2011 (effective from the academic year 2012/13) the proportion of loans in relation to total support increased, while the percentage of grants used in relation to total contributions decreased from 33.1% to 31.6% for students who receive support[48] While this reform doesn't radically change the principles of the system, it signals a trend towards improving the repayable and private component of student support over the public part. Another element that signals the trend towards the privatisation of risk for young people in university is the extent to which student support policies do not seem to cover the increasing costs of living faced by young people in university. Even if the level of grants is adjusted annually to follow inflation, in a governmental study, students have pointed out consistently since 2001 how student support, from both grants and loans, has been less and less able to cover their expenses, and the percentage of students that can meet major unexpected expenses has also decreased.[49] Among those who receive grants and loans, only 34% of students state that the support covers all of their living expenses. This is why even the governmental agency admits that the student population in Sweden is on average 'more economically vulnerable' than the rest of the population.[50] Overall, this evidence indicates that, even in Sweden, where the system of student support is comparatively generous, young people in university have to meet the increasing costs of living during university privately.

Italy: a trend of residualisation

Italy has witnessed more radical reforms regarding student support, which have made an already underdeveloped system even more residual. In 2010 the reforms of student support introduced by the so-called *Riforma Gelmini*,[51] initiated by Education Minister Mariastella

Gelmini in Berlusconi's government, established a transfer of sources from the chronically underfunded 'state fund' for students in need to a new fund, the 'fund of merit', for students with particular academic merits. This demonstrated a shift from the goal of covering needs, as established by the Italian constitution, to a principle of meritocratic award, which, as we have seen, originated in the UK but has travelled beyond its borders.[52] While the student population in Italy has demonstrated an unwillingness to use loans, there has been a further attempt to introduce a loan system with a new agreement between the Ministry of Youth and ABI, offering loans only to 'students with merits'[53] – in other words, to high-achieving students.

The most radical change to the system of student support in Italy is linked to the 'austerity reforms' implemented by Mario Monti's government with the Spending Review in 2012, which has resulted in an unprecedented cut in public spending for Italy. The reforms in student support have focused on the so-called 'undeserving students', establishing an increase in the fees paid by students who do not graduate within the legal duration of the degree (*fuori corso* students),[54] with the idea of improving co-contributions from such students. However, this policy punishes *fuori corso* students, who are often working students.[55] They are complementing the minimal state support with private participation in the labour market and, due to the scarcity of part-time degrees in Italy, they therefore take longer to complete their education.[56] Very quickly the debate on this reform escalated when the young Vice-Minister Michel Martone, in an attempt to justify the punitive nature of these reforms, defined students graduating after the age of 28 as 'losers'.[57] The representative of student unions responded by stressing the lack of respect for students who continue to attend university despite the many economic and social difficulties that they face, in particular having to work during their studies. In other words, the debate highlighted how intrinsic the issue of class is to student support in university, and showed that, beyond the veil of meritocracy, most recent reforms have negatively affected the most disadvantaged part of the student population.

Aside from the consequences of these reforms, which increase costs for working students, the austerity plans contained in the Spending Review of 2012 are likely to have a wider impact on student support, although the effects are indirect, as they depend on the lack of state contribution at the regional level. As reported by Eurydice, Italy was expecting a cut in the state transfers of student support even before the Spending Review: 'in 2011, a reduction of the State budget for the public scholarship scheme of about 75%, as compared to

2010, is foreseen.'[58] In the last few years there have been numerous and vigorous student protests opposing public cuts to the 'right to study'. Having liaised with Italian student unions to conduct the empirical part of this research (see Parts 2 and 3), I had the chance to fully appreciate the activism of student unions in denouncing the impact of cuts to student support. These cuts resulted in an even more pronounced incapacity of the system of student support to cover eligible students, and, therefore, to increase the assumed contribution from private sources. As Laudisa has correctly pointed out, the 'economic crisis' has been used to continue cutting student support from 2013 onwards.[59] Due to the latest reforms in the calculation of eligibility criteria (the so-called 'ISEE') that occurred this year (2015/16),[60] the number of students eligible is predicted to decrease. As also stated in the latest Eurostudent: 'the Italian student welfare system – which has always been underfunded and suffered from the harsh cuts to the public expense in the last few years – does not have enough resources to cover the demand for public support.'[61] The dramatic decline in student support for young people in HE has reached a point of non-return in Italy, where young people from poorer backgrounds are increasingly giving up to the idea of going to university (this theory is confirmed by the decline of student enrolments in the last few years[62]). Yet, if the alternative is youth unemployment, young people might still decide to enrol in university, and the cost of this choice will be transferred on to Italian families.

England: a sharp rise in private contributions

The reforms implemented in England since 2011 also signal a clear trend towards the privatisation of risk for young people in university by establishing the principle of an increasing private cost met by the students and their families.[63] The changing goals of the reforms can be analysed by looking at the commissioned Browne review, which anticipated the reforms and proposed several changes to the system in the direction of such privatisation:[64] a reduction of direct grants to institutions, a change in the parameters of loans, the introduction of real interest rates on loans (above inflation, when they had previously been subsidised) and, importantly, the introduction of loans for part-time students. The overall goal of these reforms has been the aim of balancing private gains with public cost to guarantee the economic sustainability of the system,[65] in line with the logic of the system of support in England since the 1980s.

After the reforms in 2010, full-time students could take higher loans. For example, for students living outside London, the maximum loan increased from £3,838 in 2011/12 to £4,375 in 2012/13 for students who live at home, and from £4,950 to £5,500 for students who live away from home.[66] However, the increasing reliance on loans, which per se is a private form of support for students, has been matched with a change to the market interest rate and changing overall conditions (for example, the write-off, repayment rate and terms and conditions), which transfer the cost of loans from the public exchequer to individual students.[67] This means that students will pay more for those loans in the long term, although it is true that the repayment threshold had been increased from just over £16,000 to £21,000,[68] suggesting an acknowledgement of the lowering economic returns of graduate jobs. One of the most radical yet overlooked changes is that, already before the abolishment of grants, it has become much harder for university students in England to access the grant system, as the threshold of parental income for accessing grants has decreased from £50,020 to £42,600. While the reform has included a sizeable increase in grant support of £27 per month,[69] it has strengthened the conditions to access grants (see Table 2, below).

The most substantial change signalling a shift to private costs being met by students has been the privatisation of HE costs through an increase in tuition fees for undergraduates. The maximum amount of £9,000 was set to be applied only in exceptional circumstances, and the maximum level was originally moved from £3,000 to £6,000.[70] However, UCAS data in 2012 showed that 85% of students were charged between £8,500 and £9,000, and 56% of students were charged the maximum level of £9,000.[71] This change reveals a deep reform at the core of the system, where young people in university

Table 2: Maintenance grant by parental income for full-time students before and after HE funding reforms in England

2011/12		2012/13	
Parental income	Grant	Parental income	Grant
£34,001-£50,020	£1,106-£50	£40,000-£42,600	£523-£50
£25,001-£34,000	£2,906-£1,106	£35,000-£40,000	£1,432-£523
<£25,000	£2,906	£30,000-£35,000	£2,341-£1,432
		£25,000-£30,000	£3,250-£2,341
		<£25,000	£3,250

Source: BIS (Department for Business, Innovation & Skills) (2011) *Future students. Paying for university in 2012/2013*. Financial support for full-time students, London: BIS (http://webarchive.nationalarchives.gov.uk/20121212135622/http:// www.bis.gov.uk/assets/biscore/higher-education/docs/t/11-789-thinking- of-uni-2012-financial-support.pdf).

are increasingly asked to meet the institutional costs of their HE in addition to their living costs, due to cuts in transfers from central government to HE institutions.

As McGettigan put it:

> [W]hen fees were introduced in 1998, and when they were increased to £3,000, this was *additional funding*. Now, it is replacement funding covering the removal of the central block grant to universities…. In so far as fees replace public funding, we see an internal privatisation of the university, even if the loan used to pay the fees is publicly backed.[72]

While most analysts have focused on the institutional implications of such reforms for the HE system, the reforms are likely to have a negative effect on young people in university, as shown by the degree of protests that followed their introduction.[73] Even before the implementation of these reforms in 2012/13, and therefore for the young people included in this study in England, students were already in net debts of £10,299 on average.[74] A recent study from The Sutton Trust, called *Degrees of debt*, points out that, after the 2012/13 reforms, English graduates face higher debts after graduating than students from other Anglophone countries, including the US.[75] According to this study, English students graduating under the £9,000 regime scheme owe an average of £44,000. In general, as we have seen, the private co-contribution that is assumed by the system of student support in England has old roots, and the last reforms have strengthened the idea that education and living costs for young people in university have to be met privately.

After the last UK elections in 2015, there have been two forthcoming changes regarding student support in England by the newly elected Conservative government that go in the direction of dramatically reinforcing the privatisation of social risk. First, from September 2016 no grant will be available for young people from families earning less than £25,000.[76] To respond to this, students will be able to take out more loans: the maximum loan increased from £4,375 in 2012/13 to £4,565 in 2016/17 for students who live at home, and from £5,500 to £5,740 for students who live away from home (not in London).[77] The Sutton Trust has predicted an increase in English student debt in excess of £50,000 after the abolition of grants.[78] Furthermore, the Chancellor announced a potential removal of the cap on fees (for institutions with high-quality teaching), which is likely to result in further fees rising in England, and in young people taking more loans to cover them. This shift from grants to loans means that young people from low socioeconomic backgrounds will take up more loans to fill the lack of grants, with consequences on the level of inequalities already present in English HE.[79] Forthcoming scholarships will need to clarify whether this radical change will also have effects on access to HE of young people from working-class families who might be deterred to take up additional loans. The reforms implemented during austerity in England have continued to apply the principles established since the 1990s, but have reached a new peak, and an unprecedented one in Europe, in terms of privatising HE costs. The potential removal of a cap on fees has now become a reality with the publication of the White Paper *Success as a knowledge economy* published in May 2016,[80] which sets the government's plan of allowing institutions with proved teaching excellence to charge more than £9,000. This reform takes the idea of HE as a form of individualised social investment to the extreme, with a further transfer of HE costs to students. Similar to what we have seen in Italy, where enrolments have started to decline, we might be close to a point of non-return in the privatisation of social risk for young adults. English young people are caught between a rock and a hard place: facing youth unemployment, or enrolling in university and taking up unprecedented levels of debt that will be very hard to repay and will have a medium-term impact on their lives in the future.

Conclusion

One of the reasons why I decided to focus on England, Italy and Sweden in my research is that they traditionally represent three different worlds of delivering welfare across Europe. This has also been confirmed in HE studies, as England, Italy and Sweden come up in the literature as representing three models of student support. This chapter has compared these three systems across five criteria, finding that there is a persisting difference among them looking at the role of fees that represent individual forms of contribution, the role of loans, the generosity of state support provided, and how inclusive the system is. These dimensions consequently determine the welfare mix available in the three countries, that is, how relevant labour market and family sources are to sustain young people's experiences in university. Yet, despite the continuous diversity, there is an ongoing common trend in Europe, which consists of privatising the costs of HE – demanding young people and their families step in to cover the decreasing role of state sources. While in England privatisation has taken the form of an increasing use of loans and a rising level of fees, in Italy this privatisation has meant making the already residual system of grants even more residual. In Sweden this process is subtler, and concerns the declining value of the grants provided by the state. The implications of the privatisation of student support for young people's lives in university, and for the level of inequality, are discussed more fully in Chapter 9.

THREE

Beyond differences?
Determinants of inequality among European young people in university

[I often tell my students] there is only one good decision
that you have to do in life: choosing your parents.
Otherwise game over. (Stiglitz, 2015)[1]

Stiglitz is correct in his view that having the right parents really matters
for young people's future, but there is another fundamental decision
for young people to take: choosing where to be born. As we have seen
in the previous chapter, the structures available in England, Italy and
Sweden are paradigmatic of the diversity in opportunities that young
people enjoy across Europe. The two elements intersect: where young
people come from, in terms of both their social class *and* their location,
does have an impact on their experience of university. If we want to
understand the changing dynamics of inequality among young people,
and in particular among young people in university, we need to look at
both. This chapter discusses the three sources of welfare introduced in
Chapter 1 and their potential for stratifying young people's experiences
in the three countries considered in this study.[2]

Economists such as Stiglitz and Piketty, who have been increasingly
interested in writing about inequality in the last few years, seem
to neglect the profound role of welfare states in shaping people's
opportunities. Welfare states are not just economic stabilisers; they
represent the main field where class divisions can be reinforced or
limited. When young people are mentioned in debates on reforming
the welfare state, it is often to refer to the issue of intergenerational
inequality, that is, the importance of reforming (or better, reducing)
the old systems of the welfare state in order to mobilise more resources
for the younger generations. As a matter of fact, young people benefit
from welfare state systems in a number of policies, such as housing,
education, labour market policies and social security.[3] Moreover, what
they can and cannot access largely shapes their dependency on the

other two forms of welfare: their protracted dependence on the family and their need to find their own resources by working while studying. The reconfiguration of the 'welfare mixes' across Europe represents the most evident factor of inequality among this generation of young people, and one that is constantly overlooked.[4]

Inequality and welfare state intervention

Social policy academics have long studied the way welfare state interventions can increase or decrease inequalities among the population. The 'bible' of comparative research, *The three worlds of welfare capitalism* by Esping-Andersen,[5] demonstrated that the welfare state is an active force in shaping social relations. In other words, the welfare state can increase or decrease inequalities according to how it is framed, constructed and designed. The welfare state applied to young people delimits the boundaries of private and public forms of dependence. For example, if the welfare state (offering a public form of dependence) decides not to intervene, this would indirectly suggest that a private form of dependence, either from the family or from the labour market, will make up for this absence. How can the welfare state increase or decrease existing inequalities? We can look at three dimensions: the stratifying effect of debt, the sufficiency of state support and the inclusiveness of the intervention.

The stratifying effect of debt

While grants offer the possibility of covering students' living costs and therefore harmonise the experience of university, loans transfer the cost of university to individuals, and thus make individual conditions much more relevant. British studies regarding the use of loans in HE not only show that the cost of HE represents a deterrent in choosing to participate in HE and limits the choice of students,[6] but also suggest that their use has an impact on students' participation during university. For example, a qualitative research conducted in England found that the decisions on loans that students take in HE are deeply influenced by parental opinions, and therefore class positions, and that they deeply affect their study strategy once young people are in university.[7] Studies also show that given the specific lack of guidance available in their families and the complexity of the system, and despite the debt aversion of students, students from lower socioeconomic backgrounds, due to their limited familiarity with financial tools, end up with higher levels of debt compared to their more affluent counterparts, who are able to benefit from the use of additional family sources.[8] All these studies emphasise how – especially in England, where the level of debt is much higher, as we have seen in the previous chapter – debt will have the most stratifying effects on young people in university. This is because loans in England have to compensate for the high level of fees, as well as having a less generous interest rate compared to what the state offers in Sweden, for example.

Yet in Sweden, too, there are elements that show how loans can stratify young people's experiences in university. The Swedish loans system could also indirectly stratify the experience and call for the use of family sources, given that loans are offered for nine months, and assume that young people will work during the summer. Also, young people from more affluent families will need fewer loans.[9] Finally, loans represent an intrinsically stratifying system for the transition after university because they assume equal returns in the labour market in a labour market structure that is highly stratified.[10]

Sufficiency of support

The sufficiency of support is assessed both by looking at the level of grants and by the presence and level of fees. This second element signals the proximity to a market-based system in which students are expected to meet the economic costs of tuition.[11] The level of fees determines the individual cost that young people have to incur: by introducing fees, the systems of student support have established a principle of cost-sharing where young people or their family have to incur part of the cost of HE.[12] A system based on fees is in line with the process of marketisation: in a context where HE becomes a commodity in a liberalised market and an investment with future returns, those who benefit (the students) are asked to contribute.

When such forms of private contribution are present through fees, studies show that young people from low socioeconomic backgrounds are the ones who are most affected.[13] In a system with a high level of fees, inequality increases due to the pressure that this puts on the family to find new resources, or to young people's own need to participate in the labour market. At the same time, a system that is not very generous with grants is assuming that living costs will be covered by young people and their families. Out of our three models, as we have seen, both England and Italy, for two different reasons, are not very generous. England offers grants and loans, but requires a high individual contribution through a rising level of fees. Italy, albeit not asking comparatively high levels of fees, offers grants only to a minority of students, assuming that the large majority of young people in university will use parental sources. In other words, both systems are structurally designed to increase the level of inequality based on parental contributions and individual circumstances. On the other side, Sweden, by not asking for any fees from national students, and by offering relatively generous support, attempts to minimise inequalities among young people in university.

Inclusiveness

The final judgement on the function of the welfare state is on how inclusive the system is, based on whether the support provided is means-tested or universal. This can also increase inequality among young people. In the classical social policy literature, means testing has been shown to lead to forms of stratification.[14] The Nordic scholars Korpi and Palme famously identified a 'paradox of redistribution' linked with means testing – a process where increasing targeting results in improving inequality rather than limiting it, as in the case of universal provisions.[15] The paradox of redistribution is even more important in the case of young people in university. Means testing applied to young people assumes that parents will support their children, and this has been proved to affect young people from lower socioeconomic backgrounds, as in their case the assumptions do not match the reality of what is available to them.[16] Compare, for example, the Swedish and English systems described in the previous chapter: while Sweden provides universal support for all young people in university (generally speaking, unless there are specific individual circumstances, everybody gets the same, and parental resources do not matter), England offers a highly means-tested system, in which state support is only supposed to top up what is offered by families. The extremely targeted and residual system in Italy offers an even more extreme application of this principle of means testing, as only the top 10% of disadvantaged families will be eligible for some form of support from the state. It goes without saying that a means-tested system indirectly confirms a protraction of dependence on family sources, which is counter-productive to the goal of HE enhancing 'equal opportunities'. This issue is even more evident when means testing is coupled with a lack of sufficiency in grants, as in this case the system won't be able to compensate for the family's low income.[17] As discussed in Chapter 2, all three systems suffer a problem of 'insufficiency' in covering young people's needs, but this is particularly acute for England and Italy.

How relying on the family can increase inequality

The welfare state can intervene to limit the influence of young people's social origins, but the first and most important source of welfare for young people in university, given their position of 'semi-dependence', is the family. The increasing relevance of family sources of support could be considered to be a general feature of contemporary young people's lives: 'young adults across the social class spectrum are now expected by policy-makers to be able to rely on the support of their parents.'[18] Against the common expectations based on policies, however, there are substantial differences in the capacities of families to respond to these expectations, which make family sources central in understanding current processes of reproduction.

Family support in the three countries can be analysed through direct contributions and indirect support via housing. Inequality is explored in this case by looking at the different use of family sources across social classes. The latest data from Eurostudent (2012-15)[19] show that even for Swedish undergraduate students not living with their family, the family/ partner provides 18.7% of monthly income for students without an HE background (first generation university students) and 19% of their monthly income to those with an HE background. For those living with their parents, this increases to 22.2% for those without an HE background and 23.3% to those with an HE background. Interestingly, the previous round of Eurostudent indicated that in Sweden the family intervened in supporting students during university by providing 7% of monthly income[20] (although this lower percentage might be due to the inclusion of 'partner' income in the new round). The role of the family is especially important in supporting Swedish students during the summer recess, given that the system of public student support only covers students for nine months. The paradox of this system is that while it assumes the sudden independence of young people during university, young people who cannot acquire such independence will end up relying on their parents during the summer.[21]

Figure 2 below presents the percentage of students living in different types of accommodation in Sweden. It shows that only a minority of students tend to live with their parents, but this percentage is higher among those with low education backgrounds (20% versus 12% of those from medium and high education backgrounds). It also indicates that students from high education backgrounds (38%) tend to live alone more than students from low education backgrounds (25%). Sadly, the latest round of Eurostudent data (2012-15) does not distinguish between low and intermediate backgrounds, but confirms that students

Figure 2: Residential status of HE students by education background (ISCED) in Sweden, 2008-09 (%)

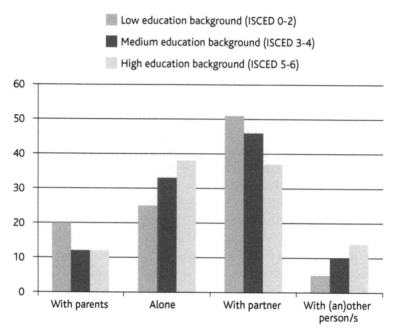

Source: Author's analysis of Eurostudent (2011) *Social and economic conditions of student life in Europe, National profile of Sweden, Eurostudent IV*, Hannover: Eurostudent (https:// eurostudent.his.de/eiv/report/data_overview.jsp?ssid=9E5B2422A2AD957CFF3D7E2C83EA 5340&sel_lang=&cnt_oid=28).

with an HE background tend to live less with parents (10.9%) than those without HE backgrounds (12.5%), and many more are in student accommodation (32.6% versus 21.1% of those without an HE background).[22] Overall this evidence signals a preference for cheaper forms of housing for students from lower education backgrounds, which suggests a potential source of stratification of young people's experiences in university, as young people from low education backgrounds have more limited access to housing independence.

As pointed out in the previous section, not only are state sources comparatively less important in Italy, but also more than half of Italian students do not work while in HE in order to fill the gap in state support. This confirms indirectly that the main provider of welfare support remains the family. Although the data on family support in Italy are limited, the latest round of Eurostudent data (2012-15) shows that undergraduate students not living with their parents receive 61.8% of their monthly income from the family.[23] This is true even for more mature students (students up to 30 years old), 80% of whom receive family support, and family help covers about two-thirds of their income. The Eurostudent analysis is very blunt in clarifying that this 'merciless picture of the difficulty that Italian students have to face to gain independence from their families' is not a product of familism, but of 'the declining trend on the youth job market, which in recent years often offered non-regular and underpaid jobs'.[24] While using family support is a general trend across Italy, the reliance on family is a factor of stratification: undergraduate students not living with their families without an HE background receive 60.5% of their income from their families, while those with an HE background receive 79.8%.[25] Family support can also be explored indirectly by looking at the support through family housing. As indicated by Figure 3 (below), in Italy the type of housing does not seem to vary greatly by social background – while a greater proportion of students with an HE background (22%) live in shared accommodation, students from different backgrounds mostly live with parents (all over 70%).

This extensive use of family housing in Italy can be directly linked to the lack of student accommodation and to the family strategy of

Figure 3: Residential status of HE students by education background (ISCED) in Italy, 2008-09 (%)

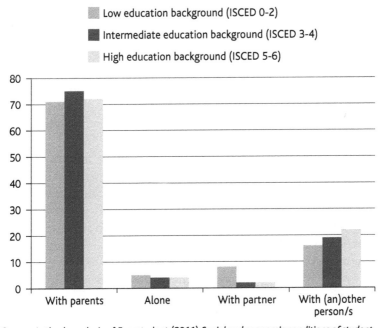

Low education background (ISCED 0-2)

Intermediate education background (ISCED 3-4)

High education background (ISCED 5-6)

Source: Author's analysis of Eurostudent (2011) *Social and economic conditions of student life in Europe, National profile of Italy, Eurostudent IV,* Hannover: Eurostudent (https:// eurostudent.his.de/eiv/report/data_overview.jsp?ssid=B16C1E22101B327AE571272751BD 0B81&sel_lang=&cnt_oid=10).

minimising living costs, the family being the main provider of welfare. This is confirmed by the fact that student halls are used by only a minority of students in Italy: by 4% of students from low education backgrounds and 2% from medium and high education backgrounds.[26] Importantly, the last round of Eurostudent data (2012/15) shows that more students with HE backgrounds tend to live outside their parental home than the 'average', as they supposedly have more financial resources to be able to move away from home.[27] A trend reported by the last round of Eurostudent is the further increase in the percentage of students living with parents (+1.8%), which can be explained by the progressive increase of study-related costs in Italy.[28]

In England and Wales the family also intervenes directly by providing on average 11% of monthly student income.[29] The Student Income and Expenditure Survey, by collecting information on student income at closer rounds than Eurostudent, detected a 'shift towards main sources of support and away from work earnings and family support' in the 2004/05 and 2007/08 surveys, a trend that continued between 2007/08 and 2011/12.[30] Are young people therefore relying less on family sources? They are, but these findings also highlight a decline in student income of 14% between 2007/08 and 2011/12,[31] and suggest not that young people are less dependent on family sources, but that their families have fewer sources to share with them. It is unclear from the report what students do when there is a mismatch between the sources needed and the sources available, although this might suggest that a role is played by private sources of debt, given that 14% of students borrowed from commercial banks and 39% of students via bank overdrafts.[32] In other words, in England young people in university continue to be dependent on their families, but the slice of the cake represented by available family support has got thinner and thinner.

Regarding indirect family support through housing, from the data it emerges that, as in Sweden, in England a greater proportion of students from low/intermediate education backgrounds live with parents (27%) compared to those from higher education backgrounds (20.8%). Social background differences also seem to matter in relation to access to student hall accommodation: only 11% of students from low/medium education backgrounds (therefore first-generation university students) live in student halls, against 24% of students with high education backgrounds.[33]

Inequality affects all three countries of interest in different ways. In Italy the vast majority of students live with their family and are assumed to be supported by family sources. Therefore, inequality in this context means looking at how the different availability of family sources can determine different experiences for young people. In other words, while most young people in university live with their parents, does this mean that all young people in university have the same experience? No: in terms of inequality, the experience they have will need to be explored in relation to the varying quality of the type of housing they have once they live with their families. In Sweden and England, the situation of inequality vis-à-vis indirect family support through housing is more immediate. Indirect support through housing is used in greater numbers by young people from low education backgrounds, suggesting that the diversity in the type of housing could stratify young people's experiences in university in those countries.

How working during university can increase inequality

Young people in university are supposed, first and foremost, to be studying. However, working while conducting university studies is a very diffused phenomenon. It is also a phenomenon that tends to reinforce inequality, as for some people there are negative implications in having to combine HE and part-time work. There are two main sources of inequality for young people in university linked to their participation in the labour market: young people from lower socioeconomic backgrounds tend to participate more in work when they are in HE, and their participation tends to negatively affect their educational experience.

Young people from low socioeconomic backgrounds tend to be over-represented among the population of young people who work during university, simply because, as the studies conducted in the UK have shown, they are more dependent on labour market sources to sustain their experience of university.[34] This is an indirect, but very powerful, way to pull 'structured inequality' into HE. In the UK, at least, this also means that the student body is 'polarised' between those who do not have to work, who have a sustainable work–life balance that allows them to take full advantage of the educational experience and to enjoy the student lifestyle, and those who need to combine study with engagement in the labour market and whose lifestyle is in between that of a worker and a student.[35] It is interesting to notice that the bulk of media reports on young people in university, for example, 'The secret life of students' broadcast by Channel 4, shows a stereotypical view of students' lives and leisure patterns that concerns only a small proportion of young people who enter university. The more challenging experiences of those who have to juggle work and education are mostly absent in those portrayals. So let's have a look at what the evidence shows about the labour market participation of young people in the three models of welfare explored in this study, and the sources of inequality that arise from them.

Labour market participation is quite diffused among students in HE in Sweden. Sweden is one of the countries where students aged 18–24 tend to participate more in the labour market compared to their European counterparts.[36] In particular, 47% of undergraduate students in Sweden work five or more hours a week during term time.[37] Furthermore, state sources are not always sufficient to cover students' monthly income: according to Eurostudent,[38] during 2009/10 the state contributed 60% of monthly income, with labour market sources providing 23%. Labour market participation in Sweden is also *expected* during the summer break by the system of student support, as the support is paid for nine months.

However, labour market participation in Sweden is not equal across socioeconomic backgrounds. As shown by Figure 4 (below) regarding the employment participation of students not living with parents,

Figure 4: Employment participation of students not living with parents during term time by education background in Sweden, 2008-09 (%)

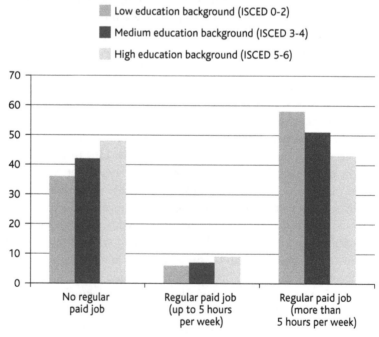

Source: Author's analysis of Eurostudent (2011) *Social and economic conditions of student life in Europe, National profile of Sweden, Eurostudent IV*, Hannover: Eurostudent (https://eurostudent.his.de/eiv/report/data_overview.jsp?ssid=9E5B2422A2AD957CFF3D7E2C83EA5340&sel_lang=&cnt_oid=28).

students with lower education backgrounds are more likely to be in regular paid jobs (jobs of more than five hours a week): 58% of students from lower education backgrounds participate in regular jobs, compared with 51% from medium education backgrounds and 43% from high education backgrounds. This suggests that students from low education backgrounds have a greater need to use private sources of welfare compared to their peers from high education backgrounds, who could potentially benefit from greater use of family sources. The latest round of Eurostudent data (2012-15), without distinguishing between low and intermediate education backgrounds, confirms that students with HE backgrounds work much less:[39] 81% of students with HE backgrounds do not work during the semester, compared to only 52% of their peers without HE backgrounds. This last round of Eurostudent was also able to explore the motivation behind working while at university, showing that 67.8% of students without an HE background work while at university to 'fund [their] living' versus 63.3% of those with HE backgrounds. This difference is relevant, but not so important, and could reflect the importance that young people from Sweden place on work to sustain their independence.[40]

The very residual nature of state support in Italy suggests that young people support their financial position by relying on private sources of welfare. However, regarding the role of labour market participation for Italian students, from Eurostat data only 5% of young people aged 18-24 in education participate in the labour market in Italy.[41] Eurostudent data, however, show a higher level, probably depending on the different measure of employment participation: according to these data, while 64% of students in Italy are not in paid jobs, 19% appear to be in regular paid jobs and 17% in occasional paid jobs, which is a comparatively low level. The data need to be interpreted with a pinch of salt, as, after conducting the fieldwork, it became apparent that data cannot help us a great deal in measuring the extent and nature of precarious jobs in southern Europe, which are often conducted on the black market.

In any case, when labour market sources are used in Italy, they tend to vary greatly across educational groups. As presented in Figure 5, students with low education backgrounds in Italy tend to participate more in regular paid jobs (of more than five hours a week) than students with an intermediate education background and students with a high education background (32%, 16% and 10% respectively). The findings also suggest that students with medium and high education backgrounds have less need to use labour market sources, probably due to a higher availability of family sources. This has been clearly

Figure 5: Employment participation of students not living with parents during term time by education background in Italy, 2008-09 (%)

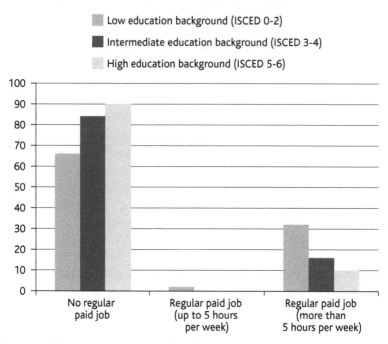

Source: Author's analysis of Eurostudent (2011) *Social and economic conditions of student life in Europe, National profile of Italy, Eurostudent IV,* Hannover: Eurostudent (https://eurostudent.his.de/eiv/report/data_overview.jsp?ssid=B16C1E22101B327AE571272751BD 0B81&sel_lang=&cnt_oid=10).

confirmed by the latest round of Eurostudent (2012–15), which asked participants to explain their motivation for working: students without an HE background were mostly motivated by the need 'to improve my living standard' (73.5% of them considered this motivation the most relevant), while students with an HE background had as the strongest motivation to work 'to gain experience on the labour market' (71.6% considered this motivation the most relevant).[42]

Finally, the data on the welfare mix in England and Wales indicate that more than a third of labour market sources in this context comes from labour market participation, supplementing the state's contribution, which does not even cover half (42%) of monthly student income.[43] However, recent data also show the declining capacity of labour market sources to sustain student income. Student income fell by 14% between 2007/08 and 2011/12. Part of the explanation for this is the decline in income from paid work, which fell by 37% in real terms.[44] Make no mistake: this doesn't mean that students in England are not working; on the contrary, they continue to rely heavily on employment participation to sustain their income. However, what is happening is a declining capacity of employment participation to cover student income due to the diffusion of casual jobs. In 2011/12, there were roughly equal proportions of full-time students in continuous work and in more casual jobs, while in 2007/08 more than twice as many students had a continuous job than a casual job. This is stated very explicitly by the report:

> [T]he decline in earnings income among full-time students appears to be related to a change in the quality and duration of job opportunities rather than in any change in the proportion of students working or the hours worked whilst studying. Instead we find more students working in casual jobs rather than in continuous jobs, and the pay in these casual jobs seems to be falling in real terms. (BIS, 2013)[45]

In addition to being 'precarious', in England and Wales student participation in the labour market is the expression of the unequal nature of young people's experiences in university. As presented in Figure 6 (below), while 44% of students from low and intermediate

Figure 6: Employment participation of students not living with parents during term time by education background in England and Wales, 2008-09 (%)

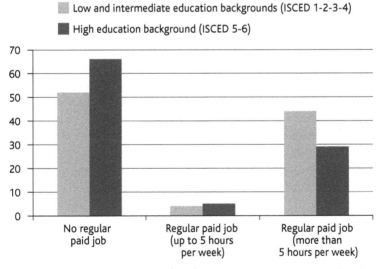

Source: Author's analysis of Eurostudent (2011) *Social and economic conditions of student life in Europe, National profile of England/Wales, Eurostudent IV,* Hannover: Eurostudent (https://eurostudent.his.de/eiv/report/data_overview.jsp?ssid=FA2AA479FEE88F3BEEAB88 B08BAE72B3&sel_lang=&cnt_oid=23).

education backgrounds participated in the labour market in a regular way in 2008, only 29% of students from high education backgrounds did so. The figure also suggests that students from high education backgrounds tended not to have regular paid jobs, which raises the issue of whether the lack of regularity could depend, as in the other countries, on a lower need to use labour market participation due to the presence of more family sources.

Overall, the analysis shows that, while labour market sources are, comparatively speaking, used more in England and Sweden, in all three countries a larger number of students from low education backgrounds tend to be in regular jobs, and are therefore more dependent on labour market sources than their counterparts with higher education backgrounds. This suggests that labour market sources are an important source of inequality and tend to 'stratify' young people's experiences across the three countries.

Conclusion

European policies have actively promoted the expansion of HE, focusing on access and destinations, but very little attention has been paid to how young people experience university. Looking at the determinants of young people's experiences in university across three different case studies (England, Italy and Sweden), it seems clear that both social class and country of origin highly influence young people's experiences. Young people stay longer in education, and in this protracted semi-dependent phase, they mix family, state and labour market sources, the availability of which depends on class and on the country where young people happen to be. All the available sources of welfare have the potential to increase or decrease inequality among young people. The state, to start with, is employing instruments (fees and loans) that tend to generate negative debt spirals for young people from low socioeconomic backgrounds. While universal provision of state sources could level the experiences of young people while in university, means-tested student support assumes a co-contribution from families. With state spending being cut during austerity, families are required to step in, but the more the family intervenes, the higher the chances of increasing inequality among young people. Young people who face a lack of both state and family sources have no other option than to look for a job while studying. In other words, the structures around young people tend to shape their individual experiences, which, as we will see in Part 2, can be described as being grouped into different 'profiles'.

Part 2:
Exploring the inequality of university lives in England, Italy and Sweden

Part 1 showed that despite more young people gaining access to university, inequality among this generation has actually increased, as structural differences persist. In particular, the welfare sources available to young people vary both across countries and also depending on the young people's own socioeconomic background. Previous studies and statistical analyses show that the university experience can actually exacerbate, rather than decrease, inequalities among young people by encouraging an over-reliance on family sources, and by forcing more young people from lower classes to work while studying. Mass HE, often depicted as a way to democratise HE by allowing the lower classes to join a path that was previously difficult to access, becomes instead a way of reproducing inequalities among young people. Inequality is not just transmitted culturally from families to young people – during university the material sources of inequality among young people are reinforced, not only due to the costs of attending HE, but also because young people have to find the resources to cope with their protracted semi-dependent state.

In order to show how young people's lives at university have been affected by the privatisation of HE costs described in Part 1, Part 2 presents the findings of the cross-national research conducted across the three countries, which involved 84 young people from different socioeconomic backgrounds. I used Q-methodology, a psychosocial method, in order to group students into different profiles through factor analysis. This is shown visually through the use of crib sheets, identifying the most relevant ranking of the statements for each of the five profiles compared to the other profiles. The results of the Q-sort, combined with qualitative material, show what the inequality of young people's experiences in university means in practice.

The research is introduced in Chapter 4, with a discussion of the young people's semi-dependent position during university life. In Chapter 5 the different 'profiles' identified are presented, showing the statements on which the different profiles agreed and disagreed, and how the five different profiles have a different university experience in the four areas identified earlier in Part 1: financial position, housing, wellbeing and education. In Chapter 6 the diversity across the different profiles is explained by discussing the function of socioeconomic background and the use of welfare sources (role of the family, state support and participation in the labour market during university). The scarcity or presence of welfare sources, which is linked to young people's social class, tends to reinforce inequalities among young people in university.

Overall, Part 2 shows that the inequality of the students' experience is shaped by the interplay between the young people's socioeconomic backgrounds and the 'structures of welfare' available to them.

FOUR

Investigating young people's semi-dependence during university

One of the most widespread misconceptions about young people's experience of university that can be found in the media (see, for example, the UK-based reality series 'The secret life of students') is that there is a single 'student life' that all young people experience once entering university. As university is considered to be a privileged path of transition, student life is also thought to be a smooth and easy experience. This study doesn't deny that this is the case for *some* young people, but the experiences are certainly more varied than the narrative of privileged and immature student lives perpetuated by the media. In actual fact, university lives in Europe have never been so diverse, partially as a consequence of the mass expansion of HE, but also because systems of student support have been developed in different ways across Europe, which also makes it difficult to assess who is benefiting and who is losing from entering university. In order to clarify the consequences of this diversity, I conducted several periods of research across six cities in the three different countries, asking young people in university first, to fill in a questionnaire, and second, to participate in face-to-face interviews.

The results of the research show that young people's experiences differ greatly in qualitative terms, with some of them being very different from the widespread image of university as a privileged and smooth path of transition. After illustrating the main aspects of conducting this research across the three countries, using the participants' own words, this chapter presents the implications of the general condition of protracted semi-dependence experienced by them during university, involving both their finances and their housing situation. It then moves on to discussing the differences among the young people, by illustrating how the five different profiles differ in terms of financial position, housing, wellbeing and education.

Researching young people in university

Part 1 of the book emphasised the need to explore the politics of living while at university, revealing the main challenges regarding young people's lives. After analysing the structures and inequality emerging from the data, it was necessary to actually describe the diversity of the young people's lives, both across their socioeconomic backgrounds and across the countries. This turned out to be a very difficult task for a single researcher – it is difficult to investigate inequality in a single country let alone conducting a comparative study on individual lives across three countries. Also, how do you ensure that you are fully exploring the diversity within each country, reflecting, for example, the diversity among HE institutions, which attracts different social groups of young people? The fieldwork conducted for this research has therefore attempted to combine the need to categorise, by using quantitative methods to construct the typology of profiles, to grasp the most important aspects of young people's experiences and to provide a narrative of the young people's lives in university. The research received ethical approval from the Ethics Committee of the School for Policy Studies (University of Bristol). In line with the policy of confidentiality, participants' original names have been replaced with invented names.

In practical terms, the research consisted of combining at-distance and in-loco fieldwork across six cities in England, Italy and Sweden:

- I initially contacted 'key actors', that is, those who have day-to-day contact with students (for example, student advisers and university professors) or student organisations, to help me recruit participants across the three countries. I also consulted them during the preliminary stage of my research to comment on the relevance of the statements that appeared in the survey.

- I travelled across the three countries to recruit 84 participants (from different socioeconomic backgrounds), who filled in an online survey in which they were asked to rank 52 statements regarding the different aspects of their experiences in university according to how much they agreed or disagreed with them. More details about how the statements were formed are included in the Annex.

- I performed a 'Q-factor' analysis of the collected data described in the Annex, which came up with eight factors. These were then reduced using statistical considerations (see the Annex).

- The factors were interpreted as profiles both by looking at the way the participants ranked the profiles and by interviewing 33 participants across the six cities.

The benefit of quantitative methods is their capacity to reduce complexity. In this case, this meant reducing the diversity, and finding commonalities, among individual experiences. After exploring the commonalities among the participants, this research devised five different profiles that summarise the young people's experiences in university. The merit of qualitative, and anecdotal, accounts of people's lives is that they prompt the development of what C. Wright Mills defined as 'sociological imagination', that is, the ability to connect our own individual experiences with what happens more broadly in society, and to change perspective by looking at the social reality from different points of view.[1] This research chose to combine these two strategies: reducing complexity and understanding young people's realities. The individual experiences of young people in university can therefore be connected to the broader structural changes described in Part 1, that is, the changing role of welfare structures and class differences among young people in university.

At this point the reader will probably wonder how representative these profiles really are of the overall experiences of young people in university in Europe. I explain my rationale for conducting a mixed methodology research more fully in the Annex. At this stage I want to stress that my choice of using Q-methodology, a specific methodology that allows one to capture people's viewpoints, implies a conscious choice of looking for new theoretical findings rather than aiming for statistical representativeness. The profiles described below must be understood as 'ideal-types' or a theoretical model, allowing us to clarify the existing relationship between social origins, welfare mixes and different university experiences. Those interested in the most methodological aspects of the research can consult the Annex, which justifies the main strategic choices made in this research in terms of sampling and the combination of different methods (in particular, the specific use of Q-methodology), and also outlines the limitations of the methods used.

Life in university as protracted semi-dependence

While young people's experiences differ in many respects, for many, entering university means a protraction of their total (or partial) dependence on family sources. The lack of independence and autonomy is often depicted in media reports as laziness or immaturity – in other words, the media portrays young people as choosing to postpone their transition to adulthood. In reality, speaking with young people in university it becomes evident that the protracted phase of 'semi-dependence' is a consequence of the structural conditions experienced by them. For example, their semi-dependent housing condition is an inevitable consequence of the way the academic year is organised, which causes them to navigate between a nine-month university life and a three-month non-university life, even in Sweden.

For young people who transition away from parental housing, semi-dependence implies the coexistence of two different living and housing conditions, one in which young people might have relative independence in living on their own, and one in which they live with their parents. For example, for Rob, who lives in a shared house and goes back to live with his parents in the summer, life is divided between these two different housing arrangements: "it seems very compartmentalised when I am in Bristol and when I am at home … I keep on forgetting the different worlds." Sasha, who shares a house during the academic year, also pointed out the "strange feeling" related to the loss of independence when going back home. When asked how it feels to live back at home, she says: "It's a bit strange, because suddenly you go from independence to live back home. I don't mind it; my mum does a lot for me because I am back. I don't mind, but it's quite different." By going to university young people implicitly accept the coexistence of these two conditions of semi-dependence.

Living at home doesn't always equal a loss of independence. Rob added that when he was living at home he was still "doing [his] things" such as "going out, making [his] own food, living independently". In the majority of cases, however, the students underlined that going back to live with their parents, even temporarily, represents a loss of independence. Stewart, from England, who goes back to live with his parents in the summer, stated: "I don't see a lot of independence. It's nice to be home because you do not have to worry about certain things, but now I have had my independence for four years … I would rather have that now." The need to go back home in the summer makes the transition to adult independence and autonomy intrinsically incomplete. This is best represented by the words of the Italian student Giuseppe, who also feels uneasy going back home due to the loss of independence: "Going back home for holidays for a longer period I start not feeling too well with my parents … due to the lack of space. I like to be by myself, I want to have one hour of silence. But I go back only once a year."

One of the difficulties faced by young people going back to the parental home is the mismatch between their old state of dependency experienced at home and their state of independence in student housing. While living in student housing indicates a transition to adulthood, going back home suggests that this transition has not yet happened. Svea, from Sweden, who goes back home for the summer, remarked on this striking difference: "When I go home to my family home I feel 13 again, it's awful.... Travelling back home is not difficult at all, but it's being there that is difficult. Because they take care of me like I am a small child." The contradiction between these two states was also expressed by Filomena, who described a similar situation that pushed her towards redefining her identity as a young person: "In the beginning it was a weight [to go back home]. Because I came here and I felt I was living by myself, but I went back home and I found two people that were taking care of me as if I had never left. I was asking myself, 'Who am I? Am I an adult person or still a child?'" In sum, there is an ongoing paradox regarding young people's experiences in university: while entering university implies achieving a certain degree of independence, in order to afford to be at university, young people are implicitly asked to rely more on their families, and in particular, regarding housing.

However, a number of students, in particular in Italy, do not transition to independent housing, and in their case their situation of semi-dependence can be better described as a situation of total dependence. Again, this is due in most cases not to choice, but to their financial dependence on their family, which, practically speaking, makes it more difficult to leave the family home. Furthermore, financial difficulties, by limiting financial independence and making it difficult to transition to independent housing, further postpones the transition to adulthood. For example, Maria, from Italy, stated:

> Psychologically at 23 I'd like to have my space, my freedom – for a sort of emancipation. I started going out at 14. The level of my freedom is the same I had when I was 14 years old.... Yes, I would like to leave [the parental home] if I could, which doesn't mean I am bad at home, it would be for emancipation. When I think about emancipation I think about being autonomous and independent.

The way different welfare mixes from different countries determines various forms of semi-dependence is explored further in Part 3. At this stage it is important to stress how semi-dependence appears shaped by structural factors rather than being a psychological condition that young adults experience. This finding echoes a view put forward in sociology that opposes the understanding of young (or emerging) adulthood as a psychological and individual condition.[2]

The importance of the housing transition to achieving independence is confirmed by all participants who moved away from the parental home during university. Furthermore, the semi-dependent young people who have transitioned to a new housing condition but are still dependent on family sources tend to attach more importance to this housing transition. For Giuseppe, from Italy, independent housing "is an important experience which allows you to mature and live with others." Alfredo, who has also moved away and is financially dependent on his family, also considers his housing transition to be a landmark of personal independence: "The distinctive trait [of becoming an adult] is to come back to your home, your family home, and not feeling it is your home anymore."

Going to university inevitably implies postponing the ambition of acquiring total financial independence, and this is particularly true for those welfare mixes (found in England and Italy) that assume family support. However, financial dependence during university is mostly described as a transitional and gradual passage to financial independence. For example, Rebecca, from England, underlined how her parents wanted her to go to university partly to have an experience of independence backed up by the security of family support: "They suggested this as also an experience to grow up but still have that security of someone keeping an eye on you a little bit, like you are not on your own." Britney, from England, also described the university experience as a transitional experience of financial semi-dependence: "that transition period where you still have the safety net to fall back on because you are still a student." From young people's narratives, it appears that this fear of becoming financially independent comes from the difficult transitions to the labour market during the recent economic crisis; in this environment, it is not surprising that families welcome young people's protracted financial dependence, especially as further study is functional to achieving better qualifications to compete in the labour market.

This semi-dependent situation that could include housing and/or financial independence is by definition temporary, as their time at university is a defined and limited portion of their life course. As I fully discuss in the illustration of profiles, expectations about the future and projections relating to different welfare mixes tend to influence young people's experiences and affect their wellbeing. Furthermore, the fear of a potential future loss of semi-dependence affects their current perception of the transition to adulthood, due to the fear of being 'relegated' to a previous condition of dependence. Pietro, from Italy, explained this eloquently:

> My parents could support me after uni, but once I finish, if I do not find a job I have to go back to live in town. This really scares me. It would mean giving up my effective independence, while now I am in a sort of fake independence, in the sense that I am socially independent, economically not, but for me this is already a lot. Going back to be dependent in all the aspects … going back home would be for me psychologically devastating. I see it with other people that are living it as well – it's not a good thing.

Overall, the students are very concerned about losing the independence they have gained during university. For example, Mark, from England, stated: "If I have to move back to live with my parents after uni I'll see it as a disappointment – [it] shouldn't happen, no one chooses to live with their parents afterwards." While a controlled loss of housing independence is considered acceptable, moving back home is perceived as a good thing only if it is something that the individual feels in control of and is for a limited amount of time. For example, for Mark: "They [his family] will let me live at home for a little bit: I left when I was 17, they owe me a little something. But if I can't find a job within three months I'll start getting worried." Rebecca, from England, is also very scared of the potential loss of independence, and while the prospect of moving back is a good plan for a period, "after that things would start getting a bit crazy". Rob, also from England, seems concerned about this possibility: "I don't think there will be an immediate loss of independence, but the more I live at home, the less I'll be independent." This fear of moving back home is also linked to the fear of not being able to achieve financial independence, due to the change in the welfare mix and to the fact that state support received during university was temporary and is expected to be replaced by labour market participation in the post-university transition.

The university experience therefore remains a transitional period, and the perception of the transition to adulthood in this phase is inevitably influenced by the young person's future prospects in terms of financial independence.

Conclusion

This chapter has introduced the rationale and logic of the empirical research conducted for this book. The main idea behind the research was to capture both individual subjective experiences and structural conditions (mainly looking at welfare sources and socioeconomic background). An original methodology was designed for this goal, combining a survey with follow-up in-depth interviews (the keen reader is invited to read the Methodological annex at the end of this book, and the very keen reader to have a look at the full methodological explanation on the website https://policypress.co.uk/ student-lives-in-crisis).

This methodology also allowed me to capture commonalities and diversities among young people, in particular, the variation in young people's experiences across the three countries and among young people from different socioeconomic backgrounds. Before moving into a discussion of the different profiles identified, I discussed in this chapter semi-dependence as a common feature among young adults, and an element that particularly reflects the lives of young people in university. Being at university, as I found in the interviews I conducted, means extending both semi-dependence in finances and housing. While one could interpret 'semi-dependence' as a unifying element among young people, this general discussion hints at the presence of a diverse condition of semi-dependence among young people. In the following chapters I will fully link the diversity to structural conditions, showing the factors of inequality. I come back to 'semi-dependence' at the very end of the book (see Chapter 9), where the different models of semi-dependence are discussed.

FIVE

The different profiles of young people's experiences in university

In order to stress the diversity of young people's experiences in university, this chapter presents the distinctive elements of the five profiles found in my research. The profiles do not have to be understood as exhaustive descriptions of all young people's experiences in university; rather, they should be interpreted as 'ideal-types' of the young people's experiences, which help to identify how similar and how different those experiences are across socioeconomic backgrounds and welfare mixes. An ideal-type consists of a hypothetical model constructed to help us to interpret the reality. This has emerged from the way the young people sorted the 52 items so it is an empirically based ideal-type (please refer to the Annex for a discussion of the methodological rationale). The interviews with the most representative young people from each profile helped not only to describe the ideal-types in the real world, but also to explain the links between different aspects of young people's lives (in other words, they helped to solve the 'puzzle' emerging from each profile).

In this chapter the typology of the young people's experiences is discussed in relation to the four areas that (as argued in Part 1) shape how good or bad young people's experiences are in university: the economic or financial aspect, housing, wellbeing and education. One of the most important findings of this research is that, in order to understand the condition of young people in university, we need to consider two temporal levels: their condition in the present and their expectations about the future. The two levels are intertwined, as future projections influence young people's wellbeing while in university. As discussed in Part 1, transitions through university are framed as a form of social investment, and consequently the returns young people expect from university influence their conditions in the present. How 'good' or 'bad' an experience is in the present will also be the product of the young people's expectations, and stating this is also a way of challenging the 'presentism' of contemporary societies (thus the obsession with 'living in the present').

In order to better illustrate the inequality behind these young people's experiences, I have ordered the profiles from the most negative to the most positive, and I present below, in Table 3, a quick comparison of the four areas. Looking at the 'outcomes' of young people's experiences, we find one profile that is particularly negative. Profile 1, 'Struggling and hopeless', captures the experience of young people who have particular difficulties in their university experience in all four areas. Profile 2, 'Facing difficulties, but with hope for the future', represents young people from all three of the countries considered who have difficulties in material terms, financially and regarding their housing, but who have a positive educational experience and a positive outlook on their future wellbeing. In the opposite position we see the situation of profile 3, 'Seeing university as a positive, but temporary, period', which represents young people who have actually improved their material condition by entering university as a consequence of additional sources being available to them, but who are particularly concerned about their future prospects. Profile 4, 'Feeling good in the present, worried about the future', is the profile of those young people (mostly from an intermediate socioeconomic background) whose condition in university is positive in the present, but who are also concerned about their future prospects. Finally, we have a profile of young people who are having an excellent experience of university and who come from upper socioeconomic backgrounds, profile 5, 'Having a great time'.

In order to make it easier to follow how my analysis has been conducted, for each profile I present the most interesting findings emerging from the way participants sorted the 52 items relating to their experiences. In order to do this, I present a 'crib sheet', an instrument proposed by Watts and Stenner, to ensure a transparent interpretation of factors in Q-methodology.[1] This is formed by comparing and putting together the most relevant rankings of statements for each profile: the highest- and lowest-ranked items in the factor array, and the items ranked higher and lower in this factor compared to the others. The crib sheet allowed an easy comparison across the factors, and enabled me to identify what was so different about a particular profile compared to the others. The crib sheet also posed a 'puzzle' for the researcher to solve: as Watts and Stenner[2] wrote, researchers using this methodology need to interpret the factors by also talking with participants and using all the ancillary information. I therefore explain how I solved the puzzle for each profile by presenting the material from the interviews. Hearing young people's voices permits an appreciation of how different circumstances lead to various experiences for young people in university.

Table 3: The five profiles of the university experience

		Profile 1: Struggling and hopeless	Profile 2: Facing difficulties, but with hope for the future	Profile 3: Seeing university as a positive, but temporary, period	Profile 4: Feeling good in the present, worried about the future	Profile 5: Having a great time
Experiences	Finance	Problematic: precarity	Challenged by the scarcity of financial sources	Satisfactory but limited	Satisfactory	Very good
	Housing	Negative (distance and quality)	Problematic (quality and choice)	Satisfactory but limited	Acceptable (independence and quality)	Excellent (quality and flexibility)
	Wellbeing	Negative, both for current situation and for the future	Mixed: present stress due to precarity versus positive expectations	Worries about the future affecting present wellbeing	Worries about the future affecting present wellbeing	Positive, with strategies for dealing with risks
	Education	Negative	Positive	Positive	Positive	Excellent

Profile 1: Struggling and hopeless

The puzzle: understanding the causes of struggling in university

This profile epitomises the situation of 'student lives in crisis'. Even before I interviewed young people from this profile, I realised that this was the case by looking at the way the items had been ranked. The negative financial situation emerged clearly from the way the young people ranked the proposed items in the Q-sort (see Table 4): students from this profile were implicitly lamenting the high cost of university studies (item 2), stating that they had experienced financial hardship during university (item 3). They disagreed more than the students in the other profiles with the items stating that they had sufficient money to cover their monthly costs (item 1) and to afford a healthy diet (item 20). In other words, the ranking of this profile underlined very clearly how young people from this profile face financial difficulties, which has a clear impact on their lives. Another negative area of the university experience is housing: this profile is the one that most agreed with the item on not having had a choice of accommodation due to financial constraints (item 1); in addition, they disagreed the most with the item on being satisfied with their housing (item 7) and its proximity to university (item 11).

Their negative experience not only concerned the material aspects of their lives, but also affected their lives in the lecture room, as educational outcome was also ranked negatively. For example, item 28 (see Table 4) on enjoying academic life was ranked lower than in the other profiles. The ranking suggests important problems in work–study balance: the students in this profile ranked lower the items regarding having enough time to get involved in the core activities of university (item 26), satisfaction with their workload (item 14) and having enough time and money to get involved in extra-curricular activities (item 27). The ranking from these students also suggests a risk of dropping out, pointing out how the university experience might have an important impact on retention: for example, item 5, 'I have never considered withdrawing from university', was negatively ranked. Finally, for young people from this profile the economic and material disadvantage not only remains an objective difficulty, but also affects the dimension of wellbeing: this is the profile that agreed the most with item 18 on the difficulties of coping with university-related stress.

The story that the ranking of the items was telling me was fairly straightforward: a bleak and disadvantaged experience of young people in university. However, there were still some issues to clarify: were

Table 4: Crib sheet for profile 1

Item no	Ranking of items in relation to other factors
	Items ranked at most like +5
2	The costs I am incurring during my studies are higher than I expected
3	I have experienced financial hardship during my time in HE
	Items ranked higher in factor 1 than in any other factor arrays
18	Sometimes I find it difficult to cope with university-related stress
30	The advice of my family has supported me during my university studies
17	I would like to acquire experience through unpaid internships but I cannot afford the loss of income
21	While at university I find it difficult to maintain relationships with family and friends outside of university because of lack of time or money
10	I did not have much choice about my accommodation during university because of financial constraints
24	I am confident that my personal wellbeing will improve after graduation
39	After graduating I expect to find a job with a higher social status than that of my parents
41	My future job choices will be influenced by the possibility of repaying my eventual debt/loans
8	Everybody who can afford it should move away from the parental home to attend university
34	My parents overestimate my future income and the type of job I will find
38	My family background might prevent me from getting the kind of job I feel that I am qualified to do
47	After graduation I do not expect to move country to find a job
	Items ranked lower in factor 1 than in any other factor arrays
5	I have never considered withdrawing from university
16	In my experience, the jobs available to university students offer an adequate rate of pay
25	The money I get from the state (loans, grants and other benefits) is enough to live well at university
1	I have sufficient money to cover my monthly costs
26	I have enough time to get involved in all the core activities required of me by the university (eg, lectures and personal study)
11	My accommodation is close enough to the university campus or buildings where I attend lectures
28	I enjoy the academic side of university life
7	I am happy with the accommodation I am living in while attending university
20	While at university I can afford a healthy diet
49	To be considered as an adult, it is important to have left the parental home
	Items ranked least like −5
14	Considering both the time I spend studying and in paid jobs, I am satisfied with my overall workload
27	I have enough time and money to get involved in any extra-curricular activities I would like to do at university

wellbeing and the quality of young people's studies affected by their negative material experience? Did young people from this profile have hopes about their transitions to work after university?

The lives of the most representative young people from this profile

I hadn't grasped the extent of young people's disadvantage in university before I met and interviewed the most representative young people from this profile: two female students from Italy (Maria and Jessica), both from low socioeconomic backgrounds, and one student from England, from an intermediate socioeconomic background (David). The diversity in their socioeconomic background in itself suggested that their disadvantage was not simply to be explained by their socioeconomic status (a topic to which I return in Chapter 6).

The most comprehensive account of what being disadvantaged in university means was provided by Maria, a student in university who lives with her parents in a poor neighbourhood of Naples (one of those from which you do not expect young people to go to university). I decided to open the book with Maria's words, as her experience epitomises the paradoxical situation for many young people from disadvantaged backgrounds: due to the mass expansion of HE, Maria had the chance to attend university, despite coming from a poor neighbourhood, but going to university did not automatically change her life; it actually had a negative material impact (at least in the short term) – Maria's family had a long history of poverty and disadvantage *even before* she entered university. Attending university in the 2010s means having to face a specific economic conjuncture, as Maria's father had lost his job when she started university. Maria's struggles are, in a way, the most extreme expression of the struggles faced by the other 'most representative' young people from this profile. The financial struggles faced by Jessica, the other student from Italy, were exacerbated by the impact of the financial crisis due to her father losing his job, and to the increasing cost of living putting pressure on her family. Maria and Jessica both described going to university as a costly choice for them and for their families, while for David it was mostly a costly choice for himself.

For Maria and Jessica, attending university meant having to push their family to face additional costs, such as buying books, commuting costs and on-campus meals, and all this with the same weekly budget they had had when in school (for Maria this amounted to €25 a week). How do families cope with these additional costs? Jessica had mobilised the family's life savings at a time of family struggle. Due to their lack of savings, Maria's parents had taken on a number of debts with their extended family and their community. This was the inevitable last resort for Maria's family, as, while she was eligible for the grant support offered by the state, she was not actually receiving any state support due to lack of regional funds. As explained in Chapter 3, Maria belongs to the category of 'eligible, but not beneficiary students', that is, a group of students who have the right to access student support, but who do not simply because support is underfunded particularly for those who attend university in southern Italian regions.

Having debt is not the only strategy to be used in this case; another direct impact of disadvantage is that students will try to cut down on their costs, which in turn may affect their personal health. One immediate consequence is that Maria skips meals when she is at university. The other way of cutting costs it is to cut out physical exercise. Not being able to afford the gym was one of the trickiest issues for Maria to explain:

> It's hard for me to explain my economic situation … take the public gym as an example: I should go to the gym and there is a public gym, but there is no way I would be able to afford all the costs associated with going to the gym, such as buying sports shoes and clothes.

Again, Maria's story is typical of what young people from this profile experience: all three mentioned that they *had* to go to the gym due to reported health issues, but they could not afford it. Jessica referred to the gym as an unaffordable activity and an exceptional treat she could enjoy only for a month after a summer of work. David also talked about going to the gym as an unaffordable option due to other financial priorities: "I would have liked to join the gym for three years for £300, but that's a month's worth of rent, so you pay the rent."

A core aspect of the lowering living standards that these young people face after entering university is a negative housing condition, which could be guessed at from the way they ranked the statements (see above), but was even more evident by speaking with them. For Maria and Jessica, their unsatisfactory housing condition was mostly the consequence of being forced to live with their parents while in university, and the fact that their family homes were not in ideal locations. Again, Maria's experience is paradigmatic of this: "I live in Scampia … obviously transport is very bad and it feels isolated … my friends are even afraid to come to visit me … most of the week I sleep at my friend's place so I can attend classes in the early mornings."

When Maria told me that she lived in Scampia, she paused, without providing any explanation of the area, as she knew that as a fellow Italian citizen, I would be aware of Scampia's reputation – Scampia is considered to be one of the most dangerous neighbourhoods in Europe, as well as the headquarters of Camorra (the local mafia). While she cannot afford to move out, she tries to 'escape' from the area by staying with friends. While Jessica does not live in such a dangerous place, she is also affected by the disadvantaged position of her family home, which is not well connected to the university, and she laments the lack of space for studying due to living in a small house and having to share a room with her brother. David lives independently, but he seemed equally troubled by the financial limits and precarity coming from moving flats several times a year in order to find the best option in terms of cost and distance. He described finding a flat as a learning process: "when you enter the housing market you have no idea how to judge a flat, then you learn." He added that he was glad not to move again for a couple of years. Interestingly, while David shares his house with flatmates and not with his family, the coping strategies these students adopt to reduce their financial problems are similar to the strategies used by their families: "we put money into a pot each week so it's a budgeted amount. We pay all our food and bills from that, which works out cheaper than paying for things individually." This replication of a family setting is a strategy for making university life more affordable.

The mental weight of being in debt and fear of the future

In the case of this profile, material problems also affect young people's wellbeing in multiple ways. I could find at least two ways in which their wellbeing was being damaged: first, the anxiety caused by not having enough financial resources – that is, the 'mental weight' (sense of guilt and general feeling of pressure) caused by having debts with the family and loans; and second, the negative projection about the future that young people from this profile have.

Regarding the anxiety coming from not having enough financial resources, Maria, for example, having found out that she would not get a studentship, fell into a phase that she defined as 'depressive'. She clearly linked her experience of anxiety to her financial constraints:

> It's more anxiety than anything else. If I think how I will be able to sustain myself in this academic year I have anxiety

> … yes, I have anxiety because I do not know how to do it.
> I am not a person who feels down easily, but since I found
> out I don't have the scholarship last week I felt really really
> bad.… In this precise moment I do not know how I will
> afford to buy books for the next semester.

There is a tendency, which I covered in Part 1, to consider psychological problems as individualised issues, and therefore to propose individual solutions (for example, counselling) in line with the pseudo-individualisation of young people's biographies. Maria did not fall into this 'individualisation trap' – she did not blame herself for the struggles she was facing, but was aware that her individual psychological struggles were due to structural material constraints. When I asked why she did not consider using psychological support to help her with concerns, she replied that she did not believe that psychological support would help:

> For this type of stress and anxiety I do not think it is
> necessary to have psychological support as it is due to
> material conditions. I know it's not my problem, but it's
> due to the conditions I live in.

Another aspect of the issues of wellbeing described above is the 'mental weight' deriving from having debts, and the negative projection of the future that results from such debts. The source of debt depends on the type of welfare available: for Jessica and Maria, it is mostly a debt with the family, while for David, the mental weight derives from having taken out loans. In all cases, however, the young people think about how they will repay the debts they have, whether these are with the family or the state. As their expectations for the future are negative, so are their hopes of paying back the debts.

Maria described in depth the anxiety and guilt emerging from having to rely on family sources *and* knowing that her family doesn't have the resources needed (which, in turn, as explained before, made her family enter a spiral of debt with their extended family and community): "As I do not have any income, I am a burden to my family. Yes, I definitely feel a great responsibility for this."

Jessica also had a negative outlook on the future, due to the fact that she didn't expect to be able to pay her parents back, who, as explained before, were mobilising their family savings. She explains the clash between her father's expectations and the reality of the labour market that she knows:

> My father has a secondary school degree and he got where
> he is now only with his own forces, so he expects that
> somebody with a degree would get a better job than he has
> with a higher wage. Maybe I am a bit more pessimistic, but as
> I see how things are going, I am not sure what I will be able
> to do, especially with a degree in humanities and languages.

During our interview, Jessica, although she had not yet graduated, was already clearly stressed by the chances of reaping any benefits from the financial resources invested by her and her family, stating: "I have no idea what will happen to me after the degree ... what if I do not find a job? Then it means that it was useless to study and to spend money. I am not really positive about this."

David expressed the same anxiety and pressure, but in his case this was due to the 'mental weight' associated with taking "a massive loan to pay off my rent". Due to the insufficiency of student support in England described earlier in Chapter 3, young people tend to take out the maximum level of loans to pay their rent.

David described an overwhelming feeling of being in debt that was linked to his future projections about housing and the labour market:

> At this point now I am about £35,000 in debt and that just
> gets to you. I don't want £35,000 of debt when I graduate
> from university. How do I enter the housing market? How
> do I pay it off? I need to get a job.

What concerns David in particular are the long-term implications for his life course of having taken on debt: "It's gonna take a very long time to pay it back. You'll never pay it off, basically, and eventually you get a mortgage, which is another loan, and then you are in debt for your whole life." When I asked him how it felt, he replied: "It's a daunting prospect!"

Maria describes how, for somebody from her background, even going to university was something "not to be taken for granted". Regarding the future, however, she still thinks her social class will prevent her from finding a job in her area: "Once I had the ambition of becoming an academic. This is an environment which is so inward looking that even thinking about it is useless. I am very realistic about this; I do not expect absolutely anything."

In general, participants from this profile pointed out that they had no resources to plan for the future and to construct their biographies, and that instead they were investing everything (using family savings, getting into debt) in the present. To go back to Maria's experience reported in the introduction, this also means, in an extreme form, stopping considering what will happen in the future. When I asked Maria how she saw herself in a few years' time, she told me:

> I do not imagine my future. If I begin imagining my future I stop here and I start working as a waitress, so I prefer not to think about it.... I have no idea what will happen to me after the degree.... The university protects me as I do not have to start seriously thinking what to do about my life … you do not have to think about it seriously while you are busy with something else. When I finish this, I will need to seriously think about what to do.

I interpret Maria's words in the following way: while some young people are stressed by the prospect of an uncertain future, Maria represents an extreme case in which she cannot picture a future at all. There is a point when young people realise that the investment they made in HE is not going to be economically repaid. Yet Maria showed no regrets about having embarked on HE, as she found her experience in university uniquely enriching from the point of view of increasing her knowledge about the world and meeting other people interested in expanding their knowledge.

Profile 2: Facing difficulties, but with hope for the future

The puzzle: how do positive expectations coexist with a difficult present?

Young people from this profile showed a mixed situation: while they were having a difficult experience in university in terms of their finances and housing situation (in a way that is comparable with profile 1), their overall experience in university is not all negative, as they have positive expectations for the future. This, in turn, seems to positively influence their wellbeing in the present.

If we look at the way they ranked the items, young people from this profile were similar to those from profile 1 in agreeing the most with the item on having experienced financial hardship during university (item 3; see Table 5). Young people from this profile also agreed the most with the item on having experienced hardship before university (item 4), which suggests a continuation between their previous condition and their current experience in university.

The peculiarity of this profile is that the material struggles do not create a demand for counselling and support: this profile is the one that most disagreed with the idea of having considered advisers and counsellors to help them cope with stress and depression (item 23; see Table 5). The sources of stress came mainly from not having enough financial resources in the present, not from their future wellbeing (as, for example, for profile 4). At the same time, the material distress experienced in the present doesn't lead to negative expectations, as

Table 5: Crib sheet for profile 2

Item no	Ranking of items in relation to other factors
	Items ranked at most like +5
3	I have experienced financial hardship during my time in HE
5	I have never considered withdrawing from university
	Items ranked higher in factor 2 than in any other factor arrays
4	I experienced financial hardship before starting university
11	My accommodation is close enough to the university campus or buildings where I attend lectures
15	Income from paid work is necessary for me to meet my living costs
39	After graduating I expect to find a job with a higher social status than that of my parents
40	I am confident that my studies will lead to a graduate-level job
44	I have self-defined objectives about my future after graduation
8	Everybody who can afford it should move away from the parental home to attend university
22	While at university I have periods of anxiety or depression due to financial constraints
49	To be considered as an adult, it is important to have left the parental home
	Items ranked lower in factor 2 than in any other factor arrays
25	The money I get from the state (loans, grants and other benefits) is enough to live well at university
43	Given the current labour market situation I have lower expectations about my future career
42	I am worried that I will only be able to find short-term, insecure or precarious jobs after I graduate
32	I am an active member of student clubs and societies at my university
34	My parents overestimate my future income and the type of job I will find
45	I am worried about not finding a job that matches my aspirations
	Items ranked least like −5
23	I have considered using advisers and counsellors within or outside the university to help me cope with stress or depression
31	My family has enough money to help me if I do not find a job soon after completing my studies

this profile had the most positive outlook regarding the construction of their future lives (item 39), and they were not worried about only being able to find short-term jobs after university (item 42). The other surprising feature of young people from this profile is their commitment to their education. Despite the material struggles they face in their finances and housing, these young people are also the ones who most agreed with the item on never having considered withdrawing from university (item 5).

The puzzle expressed above posed a few issues for me to clarify by talking with the young people: why were these young people not as concerned about their transition to work as the young people from the other profiles? Why did their present struggles in university not affect their educational experience?

The lives of the most representative young people from this profile

I found representative young people of this profile across the three countries, and they were all from low and lower-intermediate socioeconomic backgrounds. When I interviewed the young people from this profile, they were all quite vocal about the financial struggles they were facing while studying.

Mark, a student from England from a lower-intermediate socioeconomic background, was financially supported by grants and loans while working on a zero hours contract. He had gone to university slightly later (at the age of 24), and had worked before starting his studies. He told me that his standard of living had substantially decreased since going to university, and even compared to the period when he was doing A-levels and living with his mother. Comparing his current period in university with the period before, he stated: "[Back then] I didn't really need to spend any money, it was easy. It wasn't bad. I thought it was hard at that time, but in hindsight it wasn't too bad." As I discuss further in Chapter 6, his financial struggles were due to the insecure nature of his labour market income (being on a zero hours contract), and also to the delayed transfer of loans, which meant he had to borrow money from friends.

What makes it particularly difficult for Mark during university is the number of costs he has to incur, which he tries to minimise, but without success. On a number of occasions during our interview, he expressed his frustration at being unable to cut his costs down: "I don't know, I tried to work out why, I have been sitting down and writing down my budget. I don't understand.... I am losing money every month and I don't know why."

Given the mismatch between the financial sources available and what is needed to live in university, Mark tried to minimise his costs by changing his diet ("I am trying to eat a lot less meat. It's a lot cheaper if you eat vegetarian dishes") and by giving up healthy food ("you end up eating just some toast for the last days of the month"). This was not enough in the first year, and he ended up accumulating a private debt with a bank, something that he describes with shame and as a secret that he had not revealed to his parents:

> At the moment I do need financial help ... now I am trying
> to budget and I am not able to pay back this private debt,
> so I think I'll stay in debt 'till I finish university.

When I asked Sharon, from England, if she faced financial struggles, she told me: "No, but only because I shared the flat with my boyfriend." Without saving money for housing, she told me that she would have resorted to parental help or private loans.

Sofia, from Sweden, told me that she was facing financial struggles. When I asked her in what way, she said: "Every time I go shopping I have to think, 'Can I afford this? Can I afford that?' Also, not being able to go out, I go out only once in a while."

For young people from this profile, the insufficiency of their financial sources depends in large part on the cost of housing. For Mark, who shares a flat, rent is his number one financial priority: "I had my birthday ... I got £100 and that was amazing 'cause it meant I could pay my rent." Housing was also the main cost for the other students I interviewed. Sharon, from a lower-intermediate socio-economic background, stated that she was able to avoid facing financial struggles by sharing a tiny studio flat with her boyfriend, who helped to cover part of the costs, but she remarked how this option felt "claustrophobic". Sofia, who had to move five times in her first year, felt as though she didn't have any choice about her accommodation, and remarked how hard it was to find a place: "it was like you grab anything you can get". She put all her summer savings into a deposit for accommodation and still felt that this was not enough, as she ended up having to accept what she defined as "very bad accommodation". For Sofia, the periods of financial struggle were specifically associated with the anxiety of finding a place in the first year, and with getting her deposit back, which led her to call the police: "it was really hard afterwards because they wouldn't give the money back". She described this period as "really insecure" due to the fact that she had to move five times and did not know where she was going to live.

Wellbeing affected in the present, but with high expectations

The financial struggles that young people from this profile face in relation to their financial circumstances affect their present wellbeing. The sense of anxiety is due to having more costs than available resources, as explained by Mark:

> I budget quite hard but I still can't balance my account, I still come out negative. That for me is quite a shock. I shouldn't open my bank account and see negative numbers. That kind of scares me a little bit.

This feeling of anxiety becomes 'stress', which had caused Mark to try to return some of the things he had bought:

> There are periods when I do not know.... I start looking through my receipts in my wallet and think, 'Can I take any of this stuff back?' It happened last year. I attempted to give back some cleaning products.... In those moments I am already budgeting quite a lot, and that's why I get stressed, because I cannot see the solution.

However, in the case of this profile, financial hardship doesn't affect their academic experience of university, and this seems to be related to their positive projections for the future. The overall positive outlook can be explained by the fact that the students in this profile were studying a subject that they perceived as having high employability (engineering). Both Sharon (who has already secured a job that she will begin when she completes her studies) and Sofia underlined that their security comes from studying engineering. Mark's wellbeing is positively affected by his job prospects, as despite his present financial struggles, he stated: "Engineering is gonna be a relatively high employability rate and hopefully it will be a stress-free life. I should be able to get a salary where I can support myself and later on support a family."

The ranking of items from this profile indicates a mixed experience: a negative experience in terms of finance and housing, accompanied by overall positive outcomes in terms of education and wellbeing. The latter outcome seems to be linked to the (expected) high employability of the courses they were following, showing that for these young people, HE is still seen as a potentially successful path, despite the material limitations experienced in the present.

Profile 3: Seeing university as a positive, but temporary, period

The puzzle: why are young people in this profile worrying about the future?

From the ranking of items, the experience of young people from this profile was quite mixed: quite a positive experience in the present, but with many concerns about the future. Their positive experience of university emerges from their capacity to meet their monthly costs (items 1, 2 and 3; see Table 6). Young people from this profile also ranked higher than other profiles an item regarding the quality of their accommodation (item 13). However, the ranking of this profile also shows that young people have important concerns about the construction of their biographies, in particular regarding their ability to find a job, which affects their wellbeing. They agreed the most with item 42 on worries about finding short-term, insecure or precarious jobs after graduation, and with the item on having lower expectations about their future career (item 43). From a demographic point of view, it is also interesting to note that the most representative young people from this profile are young people from England and Sweden from lower socioeconomic backgrounds.

The main issue to explore in face-to-face interviews was obviously the reason why young people from this profile had a negative outlook on the future despite their positive present conditions. I was also curious to explore the extent to which young people from this profile were having a fully positive experience of university life.

The lives of the most representative young people from this profile

The interviews confirmed that the financial position of these students is not problematic, although it was somewhat constrained (more than emerged from the ranking of items). Their material condition is sustained mostly by state support (and, especially during the summer, by their participation in the labour market). In other words, young people from this profile are doing well precisely because state support has provided enough to improve their condition during university.

The first representative young person from this profile is Maja, from Sweden, from a low socioeconomic background and a single-parent family, who relies on grants and loans, and doesn't rely on her family indirectly (she lives independently in a shared flat). Maja receives

Table 6: Crib sheet for profile 3

Item no	Ranking of items in relation to other factors
	Items ranked at most like +5
42	I am worried that I will only be able to find short-term, insecure or precarious jobs after I graduate
52	Loans are a good opportunity to go into HE if your family cannot support you
	Items ranked higher in factor 3 than in any other factor arrays
1	I have sufficient money to cover my monthly costs
25	The money I get from the state (loans, grants and other benefits) is enough to live well at university
43	Given the current labour market situation I have lower expectations about my future career
6	Financial constraints might limit my opportunities to continue into postgraduate studies
13	My accommodation is a good environment to study in
46	My self-determination, rather than the ideas of people around me, is the central factor in the planning of my future
16	In my experience, the jobs available to university students offer an adequate rate of pay
44	I have self-defined objectives about my future after graduation
34	My parents overestimate my future income and the type of job I will find
	Items ranked lower in factor 3 than in any other factor arrays
3	I have experienced financial hardship during my time in HE
29	Most of my close friends and relatives go, or have gone, to university
36	I come from a middle-class background
8	Everybody who can afford it should move away from the parental home to attend university
40	I am confident that my studies will lead to a graduate-level job
2	The costs I am incurring during my studies are higher than I expected
17	I would like to acquire experience through unpaid internships but I cannot afford the loss of income
32	I am an active member of student clubs and societies at my university
9	Sharing accommodation with other students helps to improve the experience of university
19	While at university I have a supporting network of people I can count on
50	Students from poorer family backgrounds should get more support from the state than other students
	Items ranked least like −5
23	I have considered using advisers and counsellors within or outside the university to help me cope with stress or depression
31	My family has enough money to help me if I do not find a job soon after completing my studies

higher loans/grants due to her status as an independent student (for people over 25 who earn more than a certain salary), which allows her to live comfortably. However, because of her background, she is very conscious about money all the time: "It's not like I starve or I don't have money, but it's not like there's loads either, so you always feel constraints in everything you do." When I ask her about what kind of constraints she feels, she mostly mentions constraints on her diet: "there are things that I would like to eat that I don't eat because they are too expensive". The impression I get is that she might have improved her condition by entering university, but also that her expectations are quite low, as she describes having had constant financial limitations her entire life.

This was a very similar experience to the other representative young student, Mandy, from England, who is also from a low socioeconomic background and from a single-parent family. In this case she also received a higher grant compared to the other students, due to being from a single-parent family. Mandy explained that having this scholarship meant that she was actually better off once she entered university, and she could also contribute to her family budget by giving part of her grant to her mother. Exploring this issue in more depth in the interviews, it emerged that Mandy's choice of living at home was due to financial limits: "it would have been a lot harder for me money-wise if I was going to move out, as all my money would have gone on rent". Living at home, however, meant giving up the chance to join the social side of university and having to travel for long hours due to poor public transport in the area.

Wellbeing: concerns about the future

The interviews confirmed these concerns. Mandy, who had finished her studies and was already in a part-time job by the time of the interview, stated the following about the possibility of not getting a job after university: "I would have to sign on to get benefits. They [the family] couldn't support me." Maja also displayed concerns about the future that came from the pressure of having to find a graduate job in her area and the influence of her present wellbeing:

> I am worried about [not finding a graduate job]. It's probably the thing I am most worried about. I'm not that worried about what's happening next week; I am not worried about not having enough money to eat.... This is my core concern, but hopefully with life planning, and

having started to apply now.... I've got three years to go....
It should be fine ... but it's my concern.

The impression I had during the interviews was that young people from this profile entered university, by receiving additional grants, with the hope of finding better jobs that they would not be able to get otherwise, but they realised even before finishing university that this was either not possible, or the jobs were very difficult to obtain, even with a university degree.

When speaking with them, the young people from this profile expressed, despite concerns for their labour market transitions, enthusiasm for their education experience. They underlined the value of having embarked on this route, even if the benefits in relation to the labour market were not evident. Their concerns about the construction of their future biographies can be explained as an effect of the perceived low employability of social sciences degrees (in a similar way to young people from profile 2 having a positive outlook on their future biographies due to good employment prospects). In this case, this can also be linked to the temporary structure of their welfare sources, which are only available while young people are in university.

Young people from this profile show a relatively positive outcome in terms of finance and housing, but a negative outcome in relation to their wellbeing, due to the fact that their positive university experience is perceived as temporary.

Profile 4: Feeling good in the present, worried about the future

The puzzle: haw can a comfortable condition in the present cohabit with the fear of the future?

By looking at the way young people from this profile have ranked the items (see Table 7), the story seemed quite straightforward: the items on which they agreed the most (items ranked at most like and items ranked higher in this factor) almost entirely revolved around 'positive' aspects of their university experience, both outside the lecture room, as for housing (item 11), and inside the lecture room, as for their educational experience (items 26 and 28). Conversely, this profile showed no sign of financial struggle in the present (see their negative ranking of item 4). Despite what appeared to be a privileged condition in the present, the overall story was not all positive: the students from this profile expressed a certain fear of the future, regarding the match

Table 7: Crib sheet for profile 4

Item no	Ranking of items in relation to other factors
	Items ranked at most like +5
28	I enjoy the academic side of university life
45	I am worried about not finding a job that matches my aspirations
	Items ranked higher in factor 4 than in any other factor arrays
9	Sharing accommodation with other students helps to improve the experience of university
11	My accommodation is close enough to the university campus or buildings where I attend lectures
26	I have enough time to get involved in all the core activities required of me by the university (eg, lectures and personal study)
36	I come from a middle-class background
23	I have considered using advisers and counsellors within or outside the university to help me cope with stress or depression
48	To be considered as an adult, it is important to have a full-time job
47	After graduation I do not expect to move country to find a job
	Items ranked lower in factor 4 than in any other factor arrays
4	I have experienced financial hardship during my time in HE
22	While at university I have periods of anxiety or depression due to financial constraints
24	I am confident that my personal wellbeing will improve after graduation
15	Income from paid work is necessary for me to meet my living costs
32	I am an active member of student clubs and societies at my university
33	The networks and relationships I have built at university will help me to find a job
41	My future job choices will be influenced by the possibility of repaying my eventual debt/loans
49	To be considered as an adult, it is important to have left the parental home
19	While at university I have a supporting network of people I can count on
	Items ranked least like −5
35	If I needed financial help in an emergency I'd rather ask friends than my family for help
38	My family background might prevent me from getting the kind of job I feel that I am qualified to do

between their future jobs and their aspirations (see item 45), the use of wellbeing advisers (item 23), and the negative expectations on future wellbeing (item 24). To further complicate this puzzle, this profile agreed more than the others with being 'middle class' (item 36), and disagreed with the idea that their background could somehow prevent them from getting a qualified job (item 38). When looking at the way young people from this profile ranked the statements, I was interested in understanding why they were worried about the future, and to what extent this negative expectation was affecting their present.

The lives of the most representative young people from this profile

The most representative individuals from this profile were four young people from England and Italy, who all came from intermediate and upper-intermediate socioeconomic backgrounds and relied, or had the possibility of relying, on family sources. Talking with these representative young people helped to clarify the connections between their present conditions and their future expectations, as well as the role of their overall social conditions in shaping their status (their socioeconomic background and relying on family sources).

When I interviewed and met these young people, they confirmed that they have a positive financial experience in the present, mostly due to the mobilisation of financial sources by their families. This positive financial situation, however, has to be interpreted as sustainable only in the medium term. The family played a central role in smothering their transition to university life, although this varied depending on the 'welfare mix', that is, on the different welfare mixes available in Italy and England (see Part 1). Anna, from Italy, from an upper-intermediate socioeconomic background, due to the lack of state support in Italy for young people from intermediate backgrounds, relies almost entirely on family sources, both directly (through financial support) and indirectly (by living in the family home). Her condition during university is a striking continuation of her time at school: she lives with her parents, has a monthly budget and occasionally works for extra money. The fact that she relies almost entirely on family sources, however, also has some implications in terms of the 'conditionality' of this form of support, as even her choice of where to study was influenced by this:

> I have considered moving to another city, but my parents told me that since Milan has a wide choice of degrees, moving to another city for my undergraduate degree was not a worthwhile investment.

Despite sharing Anna's background (they were all from intermediate and upper-intermediate backgrounds), the other representative participants, Rebecca, Rob and Stewart, who are all from England, felt the financial pressure of having entered university more directly, as, due to the system of student support in England they combined direct state support (mostly in terms of loans) with family support. When I interviewed them, they had already accumulated about £25,000 in student loans (before the reform of £9,000 fees per year). Stewart was also entitled to a grant because of the 'retired' status of his parents, and 'only' used family support in the summer. The availability of state support for young people from intermediate backgrounds allowed the three English participants to move away from the family home and to live in shared flats during university.

They all described the need to think about life 'financially' since entering university, as in Rebecca's words:

> Before I went to uni I didn't really think about money too much, because I lived at home. Mum and dad paid for my food, and I had a monthly allowance ... a personal budget for personal use. When you go to uni, you've got to pay everything.

But they also tended to stress the safety net coming from having family sources at their disposal, as in Rebecca's words:

> I managed. I've always been sensible with money; I don't spend money I don't have. I haven't found it that difficult to stick with the budget. My parents did give me a fair amount, not loads and loads, but enough so that I could spend time with my friends and buy food without worrying.

Young people from this profile also had a satisfactory housing situation, although it was diverse, reflecting country differences between young people who live with their families during their studies (Anna from Italy) and those who live independently (Rob, Rebecca and Stewart from England). In both cases there is a sub-optimal condition for young people: a loss of independence for Anna, who lives with her family, and a loss of 'housing satisfaction' for those who moved out of the family home. Anna defines her housing condition very positively, but stressed her desire to move into independent housing at some point during her studies. When asked why this was the case, she replied: "I am okay at home, but I would like to see what's there outside."

Relying indirectly on family sources helps young people's conditions, but is perceived as a limit in terms of transitioning to independence. This is the main reason Rebecca gave for deciding to go and live in a shared flat while in university: "I love my parents, but I needed to move out. To get some independence and as proof I can live on my own." Going to live independently, however, has a price, and this was extensively highlighted by Stewart's and Rob's experiences, which provided a comprehensive inventory of the possible drawbacks of renting flats during university: "dead mice", "tiny, terrible electric radiators", "new houses are not insulated" and "mould infestations". Stewart is quite realistic about the possibility of finding good student housing, and tells me a well-known fact among students: "student flats are normally 12-month contracts so landlords don't have to deal with it too much ... they rip you off". This is perceived, however, almost as a necessary evil in order to have independence while in university. The bad condition of housing in university for Stewart "doesn't feel permanent. It's transitional: you have to deal with it in the years of university."

The impact of future expectations on present wellbeing

The present condition of young people from this profile doesn't explain their negative wellbeing, which is rather linked to their outlook on the future. As explained before, young people themselves (through loans) and their families sustain their lives in university with a social investment, which implies a 'bet' on the future, namely, the possibility of finding a well-paid job after graduation. The expectations on the social investment put forward by young people and their families create a pressure in the present to 'perform'. When I spoke with Anna, trying to investigate why she ranked wellbeing negatively, she told me that the cause of her stress was strictly linked to her family's investment: "My parents would get angry if they knew, but given how much they pay I try to work hard and finish in time." Even more important than this, Anna's sources of stress are linked to her employability after taking her social sciences degree. Talking extensively about the bad labour market situation in Italy, Anna describes her sources of stress as follows:

> I am convinced that if I do the things at my best and with a lot of determination I will do something, but my degree definitely creates a lot of perplexities, and I feel the social pressure of those who wonder what I will do in the future. There is a lot of scepticism [on the employability of the degree] and I feel it. I also wonder if I made the right choice. My degree creates objective difficulties in the labour market; I do not see the outcome for the workplace.

Anna's struggle could be interpreted as being linked to the fact that she is doing a social sciences degree, or simply the fact that she comes from Italy, but wellbeing issues were also described by the other participants, and were related to the overall issue of the mismatch between individual and social expectations (let's not forget that these are young people from intermediate and upper-intermediate socioeconomic backgrounds) and the reality of the labour market. Stewart, even though he was studying for a degree in computer sciences/engineering, which has high employability, explained that his stress came from the mismatch between doing what he likes and what is available in the labour market: "I am worried about basically finding a job which pays okay but I am just not happy there, [it doesn't] interest me or it's not exciting."

The young people from England who went to live independently during university also know that sustaining their independence after university would be entirely dependent on finding a job. It is this possibility of giving up independence, or having independence based only on labour market participation, which creates struggles:

> I am definitely gonna miss uni, because then I'll need to move back home and earn money so that I can go travelling, and that's gonna be a bit of a strain, and also I'll need to find enough things to do to use up the time and replace university as a part of my life.

Rob explained how this loss is specifically linked to a loss of financial independence: "I am fine moving back home but as long as it is a limited time period ... and that's a thing that worries me, that I'll move back home and I won't be able to find a job ... I don't know whether I'll be able to."

In general, what I perceived from interviewing these young people was a feeling of pressure coming from the fact that state and family sources had been mobilised for a short period with a particular goal: finding a qualified job. Even when state sources are used, there is an assumption that they will be returned and therefore that the job that young people find after university has the function of 'paying back'. Concerns then arise for young people about whether they will be doing a job they want to do once they enter the labour market, as they seem to be aware that the investments made will not necessarily be paid back.

Profile 5: Having a great time

The puzzle: what shapes a great experience in university?

Not all student lives are miserable; indeed, some students reported very positive experiences. The crisis of student lives also represents the way in which the university experience reinforces (rather than reduces or even keeps) socioeconomic inequalities, and it is the disadvantaged experiences that capture the headlines and allow the problem to be defined. However, the experiences of those 'who are at the top' represent the (necessary) flip-side of discourses on inequalities. Looking at the positive experience of young people from this profile closed the circle: the profile 'Having a great time' epitomises such positive (and even privileged) experiences. The peculiarity of this profile was already evident by looking at the way young people from this profile ranked the statements. It was clear that the young people in this profile have a good financial position: this is the profile that disagreed the most with the item on experiencing hardship during HE (item 3; see Table 8), and with the fact that financial constraints could limit their continuation to postgraduate studies (item 6). The ranking also indicates satisfaction with their housing and the fact that young people from this profile had a choice about their accommodation (item 10).

Young people from this profile also indicated that they enjoy positive wellbeing: this is the profile that ranked the lowest the item on the difficulty of coping with university-related stress (item 18; see Table 8). In particular, and in opposition to what I found in most of the other profiles, the students from this profile have a particularly positive outcome regarding the construction of their future biographies, showing less worries about the future than young people from the other profiles (item 45), and this also seems to have a positive influence on their wellbeing during university. In addition, the educational outcomes seemed to be perfectly positive: this profile's positive experience of university is suggested by the fact that they have ranked higher than other profiles items regarding a positive work–study balance (item 14), having time to get involved in extra-curricular activities (item 27) and never having considered withdrawing from university (item 5).

While it was self-evident that young people from this profile were enjoying a positive experience of university, the puzzle revolved around exploring the reasons why such an experience was possible, and how, unlike what happened with the other profiles, the positive experience could involve all four of the areas described above.

Confortable lives in university

I interviewed the most representative young people from this profile, who were all from upper-intermediate or upper socioeconomic

Table 8: Crib sheet for profile 5

Item no	Ranking of items in relation to other factors
	Items ranked at most like +5
5	I have never considered withdrawing from university
29	Most of my close friends and relatives go, or have gone, to university
	Items ranked higher in factor 5 than in any other factor arrays
19	While at university I have a supporting network of people I can count on
30	The advice of my family has supported me during my university studies
31	My family has enough money to help me if I do not find a job soon after completing my studies
14	Considering both the time I spend studying and in paid jobs, I am satisfied with my overall workload
36	I come from a middle-class background
51	Students with outstanding academic records should get more support from the state than other students
27	I have enough time and money to get involved in any extra-curricular activities I would like to do at university
32	I am an active member of student clubs and societies at my university
37	The students from my university have a similar social background to me
33	The networks and relationships I have built at university will help me to find a job
35	If I needed financial help in an emergency I'd rather ask friends than my family for help
46	After graduation I do not expect to move country to find a job
	Items ranked lower in factor 5 than in any other factor arrays
3	I have experienced financial hardship during my time in HE
21	While at university I find it difficult to maintain relationships with family and friends outside the university because of lack of time or money
10	I did not have much choice about my accommodation during university because of financial constraints
15	Income from paid work is necessary for me to meet my living costs
18	Sometimes I find it difficult to cope with university-related stress
17	I would like to acquire experience through unpaid internships but I cannot afford the loss of income
9	Sharing accommodation with other students helps to improve the experience of university
45	I am worried about not finding a job that matches my aspirations
	Items ranked least like −5
6	Financial constraints might limit my opportunities to continue into postgraduate studies
52	Loans are a good opportunity to go into HE if your family cannot support you

backgrounds and from Italy. As explained before, this profile should be understood as an 'ideal-type' of a positive experience of university. We can explain the fact that the most representative young people approaching this ideal-type are from Italy and are from upper or upper-intermediate socioeconomic backgrounds by considering the effects that coming from a familistic welfare model has on inequality. In a model heavily reliant on family sources, inequality is directly reproduced, and young people from wealthy families will stand out as the most privileged cohort – as I go on to discuss in Chapter 6.

Young people from this profile also remarked on the increasing costs they faced, both when they entered university and as an effect of the increasing standards of living since the financial crisis in 2008, although, unlike the young people from the other profiles, they didn't mention particular struggles in meeting those costs. These young people from upper socioeconomic backgrounds rely heavily on family sources, and therefore feel a sense of 'reciprocity' in having to return this form of family investment one day, as explained by Alfredo:

> ... it's a traditional thing, you won't abandon parents, you
> don't make money and escape. I understand the importance
> of their commitment, and certainly as soon as I will be able
> to be independent, I'll take care of my sister.

While most of the young people from the other profiles lamented negative housing experiences while in university, young people from this profile were overall very positive, even though they had different housing settings. For example, Alfredo, who lives in a private student hall, appeared very satisfied with his student accommodation, as did Leonardo, who lives with his father but who stressed that he has enough space and is in an excellent location close to his university. Giulia also had a positive experience of housing during university, although living with her parents was limiting her social life, due to the fact that she had to abide by 'parental rules'.

The striking difference with the experiences of young people from other profiles became very evident when I interviewed Federico, who is studying social sciences. Federico lives with his parents, but sometimes he rents a shared flat with his friends in the city according to his needs during the year (in particular, the need to be closer to university). He defined the quality of accommodation with his family as "fantastic" while the living standards with his flatmates were lower, although he explained that there were gains in terms of his social life. When I asked Federico why he went to live with his friends, he answered: "it was just a phase, I could afford it". This clarified for me that Federico's resources from his family allow him to be very flexible in terms of accommodation, and to pick accommodation that was most suitable according to his needs at a specific time of the academic year. From the outside, the fluid and changing nature of his housing condition could appear similar to the situation of those young people who change housing to find a cheaper flat. However, the two conditions could not be more different. It is almost as if young people from wealthy families could enjoy a sort of privileged and selected uncertainty by choice in housing, which is very different from the high turnover and precarity of the majority of student experiences of housing.

Wellbeing: affording choice biographies

In the interviews, none of the students indicated that they had particular forms of stress and anxiety associated with the student experience or with financial constraints. Alfredo, Giulia and Federico all rely entirely on family sources, and they did express in some instances a slight sense of guilt associated with being almost entirely dependent on their families, which pushed them to finish their degree on time.

While young people from the other profiles sounded very pessimistic about their future (see profiles 1 and 3) or hopeful at best (see profile 2), young people from this profile had a clear and positive vision of what to do next. As sociologists would put it, they had a clear and individualised biographical project, which has been described to be the inevitable individual strategy in response to the high diffusion of social risks.[3] While social risk sociologists have tended to interpret the construction of biographies as something that all young people do in late modernity,[4] what emerges from this study is that 'choice biographies' (in other words, being able to select your career and plan your life in the direction of achieving this result) appear to be a strategy that very few young people have. Not surprisingly, those who have it are also equipped with the resources that offered them a choice. While the students from this profile are aware of the difficulties of transitioning to the labour market, they also have specific strategies to cope with it, which are also linked to the availability of financial resources from the family and the possibility of mobilising their family capital in the right moment.

This aspect emerged very vividly when I spoke with Alfredo, an undergraduate student in business studies, who seemed very determined (even more than the doctoral student who was interviewing him, as I was struggling at that time with my postgraduate transition). He was very clear on his medium-term goal, which was a step on the way to his more long-term plan of working in consultancy:

> I set a plan of going abroad for the postgraduate degree, but as being admitted for postgraduate degrees normally requires experience, my intention is to get a qualified internship, possibly during the summer, before applying for a postgraduate degree.

Alfredo's plan had two elements that were lacking in the other young people's plans: knowledge ('cultural capital', in the Bourdieusian sense) about what one needs to enter a certain field, and the financial resources to do an unpaid internship and enrol on a postgraduate degree.

I tried to challenge Alfredo on his set plans, bringing up the potential risks he might face in the labour market after graduating, the risks he is taking in going abroad, and the fact that, overall, the labour market for young graduates is not looking good. In response, he stressed that he is equipped to cope with a risky path: "Choosing a risky trajectory would be a bet, I could lose myself, but if you have a form of protection, why not?" When I enquired about how competitive the consultancy and business sector is, he seemed determined to compete: "I am a person that doesn't miss chances. I am always getting informed about what to do better."

While Alfredo was the most 'vocal' participant talking about his future planning, the most representative young people from this profile expressed an overall sense of security coming from their possibility of mobilising connections and, above all, resources to support their post-university transitions. For Leonardo, the sense of security comes from studying medicine, which he perceives as a safe choice in terms of employability. In this sense, Leonardo doesn't even need to plan his future biography, as it has already been set.

For Federico, studying social sciences, the situation, on paper at least, is more complicated. He revealed that he is "very worried" about entering the labour market in this climate of high unemployment and under-employment. However, he is also well equipped to face the challenges of this transition, and this advantage had already started during university. Federico stated that he is "very worried" about the possibility of getting trapped in precarious jobs, but also mentioned a number of "strategies" he has to cope with this: for instance, he has the possibility of studying abroad for his postgraduate degree, given his knowledge of two languages and his insider's view of the academic world, as both his parents are academics.

Leonardo also feels secure about his future labour market position, as, after following his father's advice, he is studying medicine, which offers a "secure" entrance to employment. Finally, Giulia also seems concerned about precarious jobs, but as she had the chance to attend private schools from a young age and is fluent in two other languages, she is considering going abroad to continue her postgraduate degree studies.

Conclusion

Disproving the myth of a single, privileged experience of university, this research shows that some young people have excellent university experiences, while others worsen their situation by going to university. By looking at students' financial position, housing, wellbeing and educational outcomes, the research has identified five different experiences of young adulthood during university:

- An experience that, considering the different areas, can be defined as extremely positive, represented by profile 5, 'Having a great time'.

- Two profiles describing mixed experiences of university, as they show relatively positive outcomes regarding young people's present material conditions and educational situation (financial circumstances, housing and education), but negative outcomes in terms of wellbeing: profile 4, 'Feeling good in the present, worried about the future' and profile 3, 'Seeing university as a positive, but temporary, period'.

- Two profiles describing experiences of university that can be defined as negative: profile 1, 'Struggling and hopeless' and profile 2, 'Facing difficulties, but with hopes for the future', which show very poor experiences of university in terms of both housing and finances. These two experiences vary in relation to expectations for the future, which have an impact on present wellbeing and on educational outcomes.

The types of profiles that emerged challenge the widespread view of transitions through university as smooth and unproblematic. Furthermore, these profiles indicate that there is not a single middle in the description of young lives that is missing, but that a range of different experiences are missing – while there is an element of polarisation in the diverging experiences of profiles 1 and 5, the study also found a number of mixed experiences (see profiles 2, 3 and 4). Young people's experiences in university as described in this research don't represent a single smooth or disadvantaged path, but offer a microcosm of the overall variety of young people's experiences in current societies. In other words, some young people are gaining and some are losing. The real crisis of student lives lies in the fact that HE policies, behind their appearance of being accessible and equal, are actually reproducing existing inequalities.

The next chapter clarifies the reasons for this diversity, showing that it can be explained not only by socioeconomic background, but also by the availability of different 'welfare mixes'.

SIX

Explaining inequality: the role of social origins and welfare sources

The previous chapter underlined the extent to which young people's lives appear to be different in university. The diversity of experiences does not per se explain the inequality of young people's experiences: in order to clarify the processes of inequality, we need to explore the role of structural factors, and two dominate in my understanding of young people's inequality in university. The first is the role of social origin or 'class', which is explored here in terms of socioeconomic background. This refers to parental educational attainment (the highest educational level reached by the young people's parents) and parental occupation (the work position of the young people's parents). This typology captures where young people *come from*, but says little about the process of the reproduction of inequality. In order to examine this process, we need to look, second, at the 'welfare mix' that, as explained in previous chapters, constitutes the 'structures' around young people's lives – in other words, the availability of family, state and labour market sources influences young people's individual experiences.

At this point a disclaimer is needed regarding what I decided *not* to focus on: a traditional (and very popular) way of understanding inequality among young people in university (at least in the UK) refers to the stratification between HE institutions (young people in old versus new universities).[1] I have no doubt that this is an explanatory factor in determining different cultural experiences of university. My focus here, however, is on *material* differences in the way young people experience university. This research used a strategic sampling that takes into account stratification among HE institutions (see the Annex), but ultimately considers social origin, and in particular, welfare mixes, as the key drivers of the material reproduction of inequality in HE.

This chapter discusses the function of structural factors (class and welfare mixes) for each of the five profiles identified, providing an account of how inequality works in practice.

'Struggling and hopeless': young people without family support and working in precarious jobs

David, Jessica and Maria all come from families facing financial struggles, although their social origins are difficult to define. David's socioeconomic background is hard to define as his parents are volunteers, and although their occupations are not easy to categorise, they share the same condition as those employed in low-status occupations in terms of the availability of economic resources. On the other hand, David does come from a family with a university background, and this has influenced his decision to go to university, while the family's cultural capital has also played a role in supporting him during his studies.

For Jessica and Maria, their socioeconomic background is more clear-cut, as they are both first-generation university students in their families and have parents in lower-status occupational positions. However, Maria and Jessica's social origins are mobile rather than 'rigid': Maria defines her situation as that of "coming from a poor family", but she also describes how her family situation has progressively deteriorated over the years due to her father losing his job several times. Jessica's social circumstances also changed when her father lost his job. In terms of cultural capital, Jessica and Maria could not rely on parental support and advice in their university journey. Because of this, Jessica gathered information about university from friends and acquaintances, while Maria described her parents as supportive but uninformed: "even if they didn't fully realise what I was doing ... they blindly trusted me on all the things I shared".

Young people from this profile use a varied mix of family, labour market and state sources, with a prevalence of family sources in Italy and of state sources in England. What these students have in common is their difficulty in covering their living costs during university using only one source of welfare (the state or the family), and their attempts to use labour market sources (paid work) to complement this deficiency. In the survey, this profile expressed the highest disagreement with the item declaring state sources to be sufficient, which suggests these students need to complement their sources in other ways. Young people from this profile could not count on state support (Maria and Jessica) or on family support (David), and used labour market sources as an additional form of welfare.

All the young people from this profile remarked on the mismatch between the welfare sources they receive and what was needed to cover their needs during university. This results in a double strategy: looking for additional sources through labour market participation and/or cutting expenses. For Maria and Jessica, labour market participation had a positive effect in terms of family dependence, as it relieved the family from the burden of paying university costs. At the same time, paid employment is not a stable and reliable source of welfare for these young people, as will be fully analysed in Chapter 9.

'Facing difficulties, but with hope for the future': young people in search of additional resources

Young people from this profile come from low and intermediate socioeconomic backgrounds. However, in different respects, the students from this profile have underlined the difficulty in describing their social origins. For Mark, his status of 'independent' student and the change in his social condition due to his parents' divorce and his mother's indebtedness makes it difficult to define his background.

For Sofia, the lack of family financial support is more straightforward: "We always survive, but we haven't been travelling every year or something like that, but we always had food and clothes and things like that." For Sharon, coming from a non-university family has implications in terms of educational outcomes: "I can't really ask them questions, I can't ask for academic help and they do not really know about societies and things, but they do support me in other ways, like if I need advice on budgeting [and things like that]." Sofia is also a first-generation university student and shares the same idea: "They don't know much about engineering or maths, so they couldn't give me much advice, but they like encouraged me to do what I wanted." While Mark's parents went to university, and this should have provided him with 'cultural capital', his financial independence meant that his parents did not support him while he was at university.

In terms of welfare mixes, from the ranking of statements it was clear that young people from this profile needed to complement state sources with labour market sources: this profile was level with profile 2 in disagreeing the most with considering state support sufficient (item 25; see Table 5), and also agreed the most with the necessity of obtaining income from paid work (item 15; see Table 5). In the interviews it appeared clear that these students have in common that they are 'independent' students, as they use family sources very residually. Instead, they rely almost entirely on a mix of labour market and state sources, with a greater reliance on the labour market (by participants in England) or on the state (by the participant from Sweden). Their independence can be interpreted as a direct consequence of lack of availability of family sources.

The only indirect help that all the students get from the family is the option to live back with their family for the summer and to save the housing costs for that period. The comparative relevance of state and labour market sources is different: Sofia relies on state sources and works during the summer. However, Sharon and Mark need to complement their state sources (loans and grants) with labour market participation during the academic year, as state sources are not sufficient to sustain them independently from the family. English participants tend to underline the mismatch between what the means-tested system in England assumes parents will give them and the reality of the sources that are available.

The struggle to balance labour market and state sources came up in all three interviews. In particular, all the young people from this profile underlined the difficulty of relying only on state sources, due to the fact that working while studying during the year was very challenging. Even Sofia stressed that state sources were enough to live on, but, due to the high cost of rent, they were not enough to cover extra costs. Therefore, working during the summer in a non-graduate job (she works in a factory) was necessary for her to save money and to cover the extra costs she has for the rest of the year. While young people from this profile strive to cover their needs with their current sources, their positive outlook on the future due to their field of study can be interpreted as a more positive outlook on future sources of welfare in the construction of their biographies.

'A positive, but temporary, period': students that benefited from state support

In terms of their socioeconomic background, young people from this profile all have lower socioeconomic backgrounds. This is reflected in their subjective understanding of socioeconomic background, as this is the profile that disagreed the most with the statement regarding coming from a middle-class background (item 36; see Table 6) and with item 29 (see Table 6), 'Most of my close friends and relatives go, or have gone, to university'. The two students interviewed in this profile both grew up with a single mother and are first-generation university students. This had an impact on their experience; for example, Mandy stated clearly that her parents were not able to give her advice on university. Maja also pointed out that her choice of going to university was greeted with surprise and delight by her mother: "I think she sort of lost hope like I was never going to go [laughs] so she is very happy now, yes she is great, she is like, 'Finally!' [laughs]"

Students in this profile rely on state sources, and family and labour market sources play a marginal role. In particular, young people from this profile underlined the lack of availability of family sources. Interestingly, they believe that state support is enough to support them while they are at university. This is the profile that agreed the most with item 25, 'The money I get from the state (loans, grants and other benefits) is enough to live well at university' (see Table 6). This is also the profile that agreed the most with the item that stated that loans were a crucial tool (item 52; see Table 6) to support their university journeys. This view is linked to the fact that the students in this profile have higher state sources compared to the rest of the population, given their specific conditions. These state sources are complemented with labour market sources in both cases: for Mandy, through part-time work, and for Maja, through summer work in non-qualified positions, combined with voluntary 'graduate' jobs to acquire experience during the year.

We can link their positive experience of university in the present to the availability of state sources. At the same time, this positive arrangement with welfare sources in the present is a limited condition for young people from this profile. This is the profile that most disagreed with the statement regarding the possibility of using family sources to support themselves after university (item 31; see Table 6). This indicates that a welfare mix with state sources to cover young people's needs during university still doesn't bring the security of medium-term financial support, and its limited nature tends to affect the construction of young people's biographies in the future.

'Feeling good in the present, worried about the future': young people with (temporary) family support

Based on the objective assessment of socioeconomic background measured in relation to parental occupation and educational background, young people from this profile all come from intermediate and upper-intermediate socioeconomic backgrounds. From a subjective point of view, as also shown by the way young people ranked item 36 (see Table 7), young people from this profile self-identify as having a 'middle-class background'. We need to be wary in interpreting this 'subjective identification', as speaking with the participants it was clear that being 'middle class' was for some conflated with being from an 'intermediate' background, while for others it was a synonym of being 'upper class'. During the interviews, they all underlined the fact that their 'socioeconomic background' is the consequence of a dynamic process, and should not be understood as a permanent signifier of their family conditions. This is due, in Rob's case, to the changing nature of the occupational positions of his parents and the effects of family dissolution, or, in Anna's case, to the fact that her parents now face the double pressure of having to provide family sources for both the elderly and young members of the family. Educational background emerged as an important element for this profile in relation to their cultural experience, as all students stressed that having parents who went to university was a positive influence on their educational experience in terms of access to cultural capital. The situation of these young people might seem contradictory at first, but it is in line with what has been described elsewhere as the position of the 'squeezed middle': while intermediate classes mobilise their financial sources, in this case for HE and for financing the protracted dependence of their children, young people receiving this support are concerned about future returns.

The most interesting aspect of this profile is the function of the family in facilitating the transition before and during university, and how this interacts with the availability or lack of state sources. Young people from this profile can count (potentially or actually) on the availability of family sources – they act as a complement or as an additional contribution to state sources. Given the availability of family and/or state support, young people from this profile do not have to look for paid work. Participation in the labour market is mainly used as a source for extra expenses (as in the case of Anna and Rebecca, who have temporary work experience) or to acquire experience (as in the case of Rob and Stewart, who are looking for internships). Although family sources are available to the students from this profile, they try to reach independence from their family sources by working and/or seeking further state support. Furthermore, dependence on family sources is seen as a temporary solution, and the issues of wellbeing for this profile are also related to awareness of not being able to rely on the welfare mix during university for the period after university. In fact, young people from this profile who rely on family sources explained how family sources are mobilised during university as a short-term form of investment for families rather than as a long-term solution. This has an impact on the construction of young people's future biographies, as they have to think during university about other sources of welfare for the post-university period.

'Having a great time': young people with abundant family sources and no need to work

In terms of their objective socioeconomic background, young people from this profile come from upper-intermediate and upper socioeconomic backgrounds. This is reflected in the subjective assessment of their background, as this is the profile that agreed the most with item 36 (see Table 8) about coming from a middle-class background. Interestingly, cultural capital seemed to have played a crucial role in shaping their university choices. For example, both of Leonardo's parents went to university and, as his father is a doctor, he described studying medicine as a natural choice. Leonardo describes himself as a quite independent individual, but also remarks on the advantages of studying in the same field in which his father is employed: "In the worst case I ask my father something about anatomy, as I have to take the anatomy exam, but for the other things I have never needed particular advice." Federico also believes that his choice of going to university was related to his background: "I believe that university education is the way to train a better elite providing knowledge and, above all, because I also come from an academic family." As his father has an important academic role in his university, this enabled him to "access direct information channels". For example, since he was little he has had the chance to meet and speak with members of the faculty from his father's university. In terms of cultural capital, both Federica and Giulia had the chance to travel and learn languages from an early age, and have therefore equipped themselves to go abroad. Giulia also underlined how coming from a university family constitutes a double-edged sword. While she called going to university a "natural route, as in my family everybody has graduated", she also pointed out that her specific choice of university was criticised by her parents, who wanted her to choose the same career path as them.

Young people from this profile are almost completely reliant on family sources. Labour market sources play an ancillary role in supporting them, and they do not use state sources. In terms of welfare sources, the ranking suggested that this group does not need to enter the labour market to help them with the costs of university, as this is the profile that disagreed the most with the item on the necessity of working to meet their living costs (item 15; see Table 8). At the same time, this is the profile that agreed the most with the idea that the family has enough money to help if they do not find a job after completing their studies (item 31; see Table 8), suggesting that their positive construction of their future biographies is sustained by the possibility of relying on family sources in the future.

The distribution of welfare mixes was confirmed in the interviews where young people from this profile referred to the availability of family sources as a given. They do not need labour market sources to complement their income, and mostly consider labour market participation as a way to acquire experience. By not having to rely on labour market sources, they can direct their efforts into acquiring experience in qualified jobs, which is an important element in the construction of their biographies. This profile reflects the position of 'privileged precarity', described later in Chapter 9.

Conclusion: explaining inequality with social class and cross-national differences

To a certain degree, the participants from this study tended to be grouped according to their socioeconomic background (especially for the most polarised experiences). However, social origins, and in particular, cultural capital, did not per se explain the material process of social reproduction, which is instead linked to the availability of welfare sources. Furthermore, the analysis presented above has indicated that the categorisation of socioeconomic background is perceived by the young people themselves to provide limited explanations. They underlined the difficulty of grouping themselves into a certain background due to various factors, such as the changing occupation status of their parents, and the debts or other drains on their finances that their families have to face, which limits the availability of their sources. In terms of the *material* areas of the young people's experiences (financial circumstances, housing, wellbeing and education), welfare mixes have been able to *explain the process* of reproduction of inequality and, in particular, show how the combinations of welfare sources determine specific financial circumstances, housing conditions, wellbeing issues and educational outcomes.

Wellbeing outcomes in the present are linked to the presence of 'stretched' or 'abundant' welfare sources: young people who face the problem of 'stretched' welfare sources, which do not cover their present needs, face major issues of stress and anxiety. Conversely, more advantaged young people have a positive material experience with no forms of psychological distress. Future wellbeing seems to be influenced by future expectations about welfare sources and considerations regarding the perceived employability of students' degrees. The welfare sources that young people have are also important in terms of planning for future risks. Therefore, for example, the difference between profiles 4 and 5 is that, while young people from profile 5 can mobilise welfare sources to 'prepare' their future biography, young people from profile 4 have enough welfare sources to cover their present needs, but their welfare mixes are limited and temporary, as they are attached to their time at university. In the same but opposite way, while young people in profile 1 experience a *permanent* scarcity of welfare sources to sustain themselves and are reluctant to plan future biographies, young people in profile 2 have positive expectations that influence their present wellbeing due to the perceived employability from their fields of study, which will improve their future welfare mix. Obviously, these future considerations are just expectations. They are, however, important in respect to the effects that they have on the current wellbeing of young people. They show that the availability of welfare sources in the present is not enough for the current challenges that young people face in the construction of their biographies, which require a mobilisation of welfare sources for the future as well. This finding goes against the popular mantra of 'presentism' in neoliberal societies stressing the importance of 'living in the present'. Young people are very conscious of the importance of future planning: the focus on the future is inevitable if entering HE, and taking up loans is an individual investment to be repaid with labour market returns.

In many respects the five profiles identified reflect the differences between countries in terms of the distribution of welfare mixes. Table 9 presents a summary of the same findings, but focusing on the role of family, labour market and state sources for each profile. It indicates not only the use of welfare sources, but also their availability, for example, 'stretched' sources are sources that are used but whose availability is lacking. It is quite interesting to note, for example, that the young people in profile 5 are all students from Italy and from upper and upper-intermediate socioeconomic backgrounds. The centrality of family sources within this profile reflects the centrality of family sources in the Italian welfare mix. Similarly, the importance of state and labour market sources for profiles 2 and 3 reflects the experiences of participants from low and lower-intermediate socioeconomic backgrounds in Sweden and England. And again, the marginal role of labour market sources for profile 1 reflects the experiences of young people from intermediate and upper-intermediate socioeconomic backgrounds in Italy and England who use a mix of family and state sources.

Table 9: The profiles of the young people's experience of university and the three sources of welfare

Profile	Family	Labour market	State
1. Struggling and hopeless	Family sources 'stretched'	Necessary, insufficient and precarious	Absent or insufficient
2. Facing difficulties, but with hope for the future	Absent or indirect use (housing)	Necessary and precarious	Insufficient
3. A positive, but temporary, period	Minimal or indirect (housing)	Complementary and ancillary	Fundamental
4. Good in the present, worried about the future	Family sources as social investment	Not needed, used to limit dependence	Complementary or absent
5. Having a great time	Available	Not necessary	Absent

Crucially, participants from countries in which the family has a higher role in the welfare mix (England and Italy) tend to be pushed to opposite ends of the student experiences, while Swedish students do not emerge as particularly representative of the different profiles, probably as an effect of the universal function of the system of student support described in Part 1. Swedish participants who stand out as representative of the experiences are those from lower socioeconomic backgrounds, showing that the more generous state system cannot alleviate all social inequalities between students, even in this country. These cross-national differences matter in shaping young people's experiences, and are explored further in Part 3.

Part 3:
The 'eternal transition': young adults and semi-dependence in university

Having illustrated the five profiles of young people's experience of university, this next part of the book aims to clarify the function of the 'welfare mixes' in mitigating against, or contributing to, the contemporary social risks and uncertainties facing young people in university. This refers to the combinations of the three sources of welfare – the family, the labour market and the state. These mixes can be understood essentially as forms of protection against social risks: young people use such sources to protect themselves from the diffused social risks that characterise their transition to adulthood. In this part I want to clarify the specific function of each source of welfare in the young people's experiences in university.

While the availability of these mixes depends ultimately on individual conditions, there are some cross-national tendencies, in particular, in terms of the greater significance of certain sources of welfare in different national contexts. The comparison between England, Italy and Sweden permits an identification of the welfare mixes that differ the most – one that gives a higher role to family sources, such as that found in Italy; one that gives a higher importance to private sources of welfare, including both the family and the labour market, such as the one in England; and finally, one in which the state has a prominent role in functionally protecting young people during their university experience, as is the case in Sweden.

The young people are also confronted with an overall trend, identified in Part 1, which is making their transitions increasingly similar across the countries: the privatisation of social risks. This essentially means the progressive shift from using public sources to sustain their semi-dependency to using private sources. The trend towards using private sources of welfare has protracted the state of semi-dependency of young people. As explained in Part 1 this process started with a progressive shift towards individualised policies during the 1990s, and has been accelerated most recently by the trend of austerity. The shift towards a privatisation of social risks clashes with the reality of a declining availability of sources from the family and also the declining capacity of labour market sources to sustain young people's lives and their transition to independence. In other words, while in the past young people could sustain their independence by engaging in paid employment or through state support, they are currently confronted with the struggles of finding other sources outside those from their families to cover their needs. This creates what I call an 'eternal phase of semi-dependency' in which young people seek to become independent, but need to complement their labour market and state sources with other sources, typically from the family. When Coles introduced the notion of 'semi-dependence' in 1995,[1] he was defining a transitional period experienced by young people transitioning to an independent state during adulthood. My view is that young people now face an 'eternal phase of semi-dependence' as they juggle different forms of welfare, the availability of which depends on the young person's socioeconomic background and on the welfare mixes present in their countries.

This part explores in more depth the role of the different sources of welfare and their unequal distribution through analysis of the 84 surveys and 33 interviews conducted across the three countries. In Chapter 7 I look at the role of the family, which is a source that is present, with a different weight, in all three countries. I also discuss the role of intergenerational transfers in protecting young people from social risks: the conditioning role of family sources and the implications of their use, including feelings of a duty of reciprocity and guilt among the young people. Chapter 7 also shows how and in what ways the reliance on the family represents an 'inequaliser' of the experience of young people by enhancing the opportunities of students from upper socioeconomic backgrounds while limiting the opportunities of young students from lower socioeconomic backgrounds. Chapter 8 discusses the role of the labour market. It points to the precarious and overqualified forms of participation in the labour market widely experienced by young people in university to support themselves, and the role of internships and summer jobs. This chapter engages with recent debates on the 'precariat', showing that precarious forms of work are not just creating a new class[2] among young people, but are also intersecting with existing forms of socioeconomic inequalities. Finally, Chapter 9 discusses the role of the state, described as 'absent' in Italy, where the needs of students are not covered by the state; 'conditional' in England, where state provisions for students in university are means-tested and complemented by family sources; and 'generous' in Sweden, where the state plays a central role in protecting transitions to adulthood. Here I also discuss the role of repayable loans, which form the basis of student welfare in Sweden and in England, and the different implications associated with them.

SEVEN

The family: saviour or 'inequaliser'?

It should be no surprise to find out that the family is the primary and most important source of dependence for young people: after all, youth transitions constitute a process of progressive achievement of independence, from a state of childhood characterised by total dependence on family sources. What *is* surprising is how semi-dependence has been protracted in recent years, and how reaching a level of independence has been increasingly postponed. The phase of 'young adulthood' (or 'emerging adulthood', as defined by Arnett[1]) is not simply a psychological phenomenon, but is also (and mostly) a social one, shaped by the structural conditions around young people (the 'welfare mixes'). As discussed in Chapter 4, this phase is also characterised by a protracted state of semi-dependence linked to the progressive deterioration of the possibility of being able to survive without the use of family sources. Importantly, policies have reinforced this sense of semi-dependence in some respects, and student support policies assume young people's dependence on their parents, especially in Italy and England, as we have seen in Part 1. The systems of student support in those countries assume a co-contribution or complete reliance on family sources.

So why is reliance on family sources so problematic? Wouldn't young people be better off depending on family sources than, for example, being forced to be independent through labour market participation when they are too young and too unqualified to work? It is true that without additional sources of support from their family many young people would simply not be able to afford to go to university. While this is a fair argument against demonising 'dependence' as an intrinsically negative process – after all, we are all interdependent and fragile individuals navigating through the insecure path of life[2] – the problem with family dependence is that some young people are more dependent than others, and their capacity for independence depends on their access to unequally available resources. Young adults are often described in popular culture as those who choose to postpone their independence (that is, not wanting to grow up), as if independence was an individual choice. This is a view that has, in the last few decades, been backed up by academics, such as the notion of 'emerging adulthood' formulated by Arnett.[3] What emerges from sociological studies is, on the contrary, that dependence is a consequence of resources and opportunities available to be independent – which vary greatly across socioeconomic backgrounds.

First of all, this process affects young people from certain countries more than those from others. Specifically, the over-reliance on family sources normally affects southern European countries, where welfare state interventions are not only minimised (assuming that the family will intervene), but where they are present, they are also characterised by an intrinsic familism embedded in the policies.[4] The most recent studies have shown that there is a process of southern Europeanisation of young people's policies, in the sense of an increasing importance being assigned to family as a key driver of young people's welfare, and this familism in youth policies is affecting Europe as a whole.[5]

The second important element is that rather than standardising their experience, the use of family sources is increasing inequality within the youth population. This is why we can define the family as a potential 'inequaliser' of young people's experience of university. Evidence of this capacity of the family to make youth transitions more unequal is emerging from new studies in this area. The 'familisation' of youth social policies implies an increasing reliance on family sources, which also reinforces the reproduction of socioeconomic differences across the youth population. By looking at different sets of policies in France, Chevalier and Palier found that familisation of welfare state policies relating to young people reinforces the relevance of family sources in young people's lives, creating forms of stratification among the youth population by reinforcing the differences between the experiences of young people in different situations (HE and unemployment).[6] Gentile, who has looked at how precarity is experienced by young people, has shown that the role of family in supporting young people in Spain, financially and through housing, emerges as a crucial factor in managing instability and social risks, and in limiting the negative aspects of precarity. Pointing to the role of the family in mobilising resources for young people, Gentile suggests that precarity can be experienced either as a 'trampoline' or a 'challenge', depending on the young people's contextual situation and background.[7] These are all crucial findings in the specific sense that they challenge the widespread idea that young people in the current society are *all* losers: by mobilising family sources some young people could actually gain from risky transitions due to their comparative advantage in managing social risks.

Studies on intergenerational support have shown that the possibility of relying on the family as a source of welfare depends greatly on the individual's socioeconomic background.[8] This is basically the transposition of Piketty's argument. Piketty shows that the accumulation of capital (wealth) is the main mechanism of reinforcement of inequalities in our societies. In a similar way, inequalities are reinforced when the mobilisation of wealth and family sources is strengthened in our societies. The everyday transposition of Piketty's argument is visible in how young people have to constantly mobilise family sources, reinforcing the transmission of privilege. This occurs not only by using family income to sustain young people's transitions in university, but also by mobilising (in certain cases) the pool of intergenerational resources accumulated by families (wealth), in the form of savings, housing or other financial assets. In this framework, HE is unlikely to limit the patterns of transmission of wealth and lead to real social mobility.

Family sources might also hold consequences that are not associated with socioeconomic background, but are general weaknesses of using this specific source of welfare. In particular, the over-reliance on family sources can create a sense of guilt among young people, friction with parents and a constraining feeling of 'reciprocity'[9] irrespective of the students' backgrounds. However, as other studies show, students from lower socioeconomic backgrounds may feel more of a sense of guilt due to the negative consequences for their families of their over-reliance and the burden of familial expectations for social mobility.[10] Attending to these costs and the consequences of a greater reliance on family sources challenges the idea, formulated by Beck, Giddens and other authors of the 'risk society' literature, that young people live in a world of greater choices and freedom.[11] This is better explored by looking at how family sources affect the wellbeing of young people and can have an impact on the their psychosocial condition.

In addition to the cultural influence of the family, which has been explored by Bourdieu's studies on cultural capital and habitus,[12] in practice, the family constitutes a central source of welfare in supporting young people's semi-dependent state during university in at least two ways. First, the family serves as a financial tool to help with young people's expenses, by using income or by mobilising family wealth. Second, the family can provide essential support by offering housing during term-time or during the summer. In the next section I show how the use of family sources by young people from different profiles (identified in Part 2) reinforces existing inequalities.

Use of family sources by the different profiles

While the family is in general an important source of welfare for young people, the specific function that the family plays is mediated by socioeconomic background, by the need that young people have of this source of welfare to sustain their positions, and also by the availability of other sources of welfare. This can be better explained by looking at how the different profiles of young people in university use welfare sources.

Table 10 summarises the function of welfare sources for each profile of young people's experiences of university. Importantly, all the profiles use family sources to a certain degree, but in different ways and with different implications. The profile that uses the least family sources is profile 3. As we have seen in Part 2, these students face difficulties in the present but have a positive outlook on the future due to the specific education and career choices they have made. They are 'independent' students, as they use family sources very residually, and rely instead on labour market and state sources. This lack of use of family sources is explained by young people from this profile as a consequence not of the lack of need of these family sources (as they would be most welcome), but of the lack of family sources available. In the main these are students who come from families that cannot afford to support them, and where family sources are limited by the presence of economic difficulties. The only indirect help that all the students get from the family is the option to go back to live with their family for the summer and to save housing costs for that period.

Another profile that uses the family less than others is profile 3. Students from this profile enjoy a positive experience of university but

Table 10: The profiles of the young people's experience of university and the role of the family

Profile	Socioeconomic background	Role of the family
1. Struggling and hopeless	Low and lower-intermediate	Stretched family resources
2. Facing difficulties, but with hope for the future	Low	Absent
3. A positive, but temporary, period	Low	Minimal
4. Good in the present, worried about the future	Upper and upper-intermediate	Family sources as social investment
5. Having a great time	Upper	Abundant

face wellbeing issues due to the lack of sources that would enable them to plan for the future. These are students from lower socioeconomic backgrounds who would not have been able to afford their university experience if they had relied on their family for support. Their positive experience paradoxically derives from the lack of reliance on family sources, which would have limited their experience. In other words, the positive experience in the present of young people from this profile is due mostly to the fact that they have received state support to supplement their minimal family sources. Mandy, from England, confirms the lack of family sources: "Neither of my parents could afford to give me money; they couldn't support me financially." She does get some support from the family, as her mother supports her with accommodation and by covering some of her living expenses, although Mandy also contributes to the family budget. Maja, from Sweden, doesn't rely on family sources; she explains that this is due, first, to the fact that her mother could not afford it, and second, because she considers herself to be substantially independent, having entered university after a period of work. This is the profile that most disagrees with the statement regarding the possibility of using family sources to support themselves after university (item 31; see Table 6).

The students from profile 1 also use family sources in a limited way. They face the most important range of difficulties due to a general lack of sources to support their finances and accommodation, and rely on a variegated mix of family, labour market and state sources, with family sources being more prevalent in Italy and state sources more common in England. Coming from a lower and lower to intermediate socioeconomic background, these students experience a mismatch between what they need in order to live and what they have. What they have in common is their difficulty in covering their living costs during university using only one source of welfare (the state or the family). The use of family sources by this profile is 'stretched', and the lack of availability of family sources is solved by putting pressure on the family. This was very evident in the case of participants from Italy where, in some extreme cases, the family was taking on debt to finance their children's participation in HE. This profile also solves the discrepancy between the sources needed and those available from the family by cutting down on their expenses, both for education and for living costs.

As we have seen, the students in profile 4 enjoy a positive experience of university, but have concerns about the future. In other words, young people belonging to this profile feel that they can sustain their needs in the present, but perceive this moment as temporary.

Coming from intermediate and upper to intermediate backgrounds, they can mobilise family sources in the short term, either potentially or factually. For example, Stewart, from England, who is entitled to a full grant and a loan because his parents are retired, doesn't use family sources, but regarding his family support says: "They'd be there. If I needed money they would give it to me." In other cases, due to the structure of state support for students, it is assumed that young people will complement their sources of maintenance with family sources. For example, Rebecca, from England, who is only entitled to a maintenance loan and doesn't qualify for a grant, points out: "With the maintenance loan alone it wouldn't be enough." She explains that family sources are fundamental for living costs and paying the bills. The use of family sources has the positive effect of creating a sense of financial security for her: "My parents did give me a fair amount – not loads and loads, but enough so that I could spend time with my friends and buy food without worrying." For Anna, from Italy, who relies on family sources, this is even truer, and she feels that her parents are using a significant part of their resources to support her and her sister. In other words, for the students from this profile, mobilising family sources during university is a short-term solution that is not sustainable in the long term. Due to this lack of availability of family sources in the long term, young people from this profile face concerns about the future.

The situation is different for the young people from profile 5, who come from upper socioeconomic backgrounds. They are almost completely reliant on family sources, and the availability of family sources is likely to continue into the future. They explained that their families consider their spending on university as a form of financial investment. Family sources are provided through family income, but also in the form of mobilising family wealth (that is, savings and other financial assets), although the family don't always disclose the source of family support. For example, Alfredo, from Italy, explains that it is not clear how his parents are finding the resources: "They do not show it to me.... They hide it from me, it's a taboo topic."

Family and semi-dependence

While state and labour market sources are not always present, family sources are relevant in all the countries considered in this study. As the previous section showed, what is different is the function of family sources in each country in creating the diversity of the university experience.

Cross-national diversities were confirmed in my study: there are clearly different ways in which the family is used across England, Italy and Sweden. The role of the family is more prominent for participants from Italy where, as we have seen, a good university experience relies heavily on the use of family sources, while in England, family sources represent an important complementary source. In Sweden the family offers a starting fund or is used as an extra 'safety net' in case of need. Ludvig describes the typical situation in Sweden regarding the use of family sources:

> My parents haven't saved money for me. I don't get 5,000 Swedish kronor when I am finished. When I was younger I got 3,000 Swedish kronor to cover my driver's licence and whatever happened after high school. That was it. And then.... Now you need to find a job, so I don't get more.

However, the young people from upper socioeconomic backgrounds in Sweden who were interviewed do not have the same experience. For example, Tilde, who comes from a wealthy family in Sweden, describes her dependence on family sources in different terms:

> Let's just say that I try not to ask them, and I would rather not have money for a week just before I get the money and be like, 'Okay, I'll eat a packet of noodles,' and not ask them, because I want to be independent and I don't want to be like, 'Daddy, I need money.' But obviously if I need money they'd give me money, and I have it better than other students.

Therefore family sources are also used as an extra form of support to protect students from upper socioeconomic backgrounds from potential risks. While Swedish students are assumed to experience university equally given their use of state support, which is universal and sufficient (see Chapter 7), family sources emerge as important for some of the student population. Tilde mentions times when she has faced financial limitations, but crucially those times did not develop into hardship due to the fact that she could rely on family sources: "since I know that I have my parents there and the times I've actually needed something I've just put it up and said, 'Oh, I have no money this month,' and they were like, 'Do you want money?' 'No, I can't take your money!' 'Come on, take our money!'" The same applies to Casper, also from Sweden, who is from an upper to intermediate socioeconomic background: "Yeah, my dad helps me – if I have a hard time, I don't have any problems. If I need money I can call him – doesn't feel good but I have the social network. I don't have to use the bank." These are all accounts that challenge the widespread belief that family sources are not important in northern countries like Sweden. While young people are not entirely reliant on them, family sources seem to be relevant for some young people who can access them, in particular to cover extra expenses and to cope with risks.

The use of family sources is not limited to a form of support from the income of families. What emerged from the interviews is the way families are currently mobilising not just their income, but also their wealth, that is, the pool of resources accumulated by families across generations. For example, Rasmus, from Sweden, mentioned the possibility of using inherited sources from his family in case he doesn't find a job: "[my family] could help me because my mother, for example, has just inherited from her parents, so if I don't get a job she would help me, my brother would help me." Pietro, from Italy, also mentions inherited sources merged with those from his grandmothers who live with the family. In the case of Rosaria, too, who is also from Italy and from an intermediate socioeconomic background, the family is using its entire inheritance from a deceased grandmother to support her and her brother through university. This need to mobilise a pool of savings accumulated across generations to sustain young people's attendance in university, rather than for parental investments or needs, was not treated lightly by my interviewee – Rosaria was very gloomy about the expected returns of the family's investment from her education. When mentioning the *need* of using her grandmother's inheritance by her parents to sustain her education, she started to cry. At that point I immediately stopped the tape and suspended my interview, trying to reassure her and to limit her discomfort. I therefore avoided investigating why she was crying – if it was for the memory of her grandmother or for the sense of responsibility over exploiting her parents' resources. My overall impression from the interview was that Rosaria felt a heavy burden in using her grandmother's inheritance. Her negative outlook on her future labour market returns worsened this feeling. In other words, she clearly felt that the choice by her parents to mobilise these savings was not worth it, at least in economic terms.

The mobilisation of wealth is a fundamental trigger of inequality as not all young people have this 'stock' of economic capital they can rely on in HE or in their subsequent transitions to work. This is a real-life transposition of Piketty's argument that inequalities derive from 'capital' distribution rather than 'income'.[13] Families who are mobilising their wealth to pay for HE will also have fewer resources to support young people's labour market and housing transitions (for example, having a deposit to buy a house).

The direction of family support also depends on individuals' socioeconomic background. As state support is a residual source in both Italy and England, in the case of disadvantaged students still living with their parents the sources are transferred in the opposite direction: from the young person to their family. Maria, the only Italian participant I interviewed who received state support in Italy, has used state sources to give back money to her family:

> The first year that I had the studentship I divided it between me and my dad. It was really great – being used to living without anything, it was a big change. I gave it to my dad as I know that we have great difficulties: we have big and small debts, because in order to survive we get money from friends and relatives. My dad lives badly with this continuous dependence on others. I also had to insist on him accepting the money.

Similarly, Britney and Mandy from England give a monthly amount to their mothers to subsidise the rent and to help with overall house expenses. All these participants have low socioeconomic backgrounds and come from families that need additional sources.

The study also found that in countries that have more reliance on family sources, such as Italy and England, the availability of family sources is highly dependent on the presence of different members of the family in university. For example, the number of siblings or other dependent or semi-dependent individuals in university influences the resources that are available from the family, and therefore has an impact on the inequality of the experience. An example of this is Giulia. From a relatively wealthy family, she explains that before her brother was independent, her family was covering part of his costs, and therefore the entire family reduced its expenses. Similarly, Pietro underlines the pressure he is under to become independent due to the fact that his younger siblings have started university: "I realise it's difficult to have three kids at uni." Rosaria also points out that university "has a big impact on my parents' budget because my brother is also studying". Similarly the insufficiency of family sources for Rebecca and David, both from England, is perceived by them to be due to the presence of siblings in university, while the financial pressures that Anna's family, from Italy, are under are due to the need to care for her grandparents.

These findings reflect how young people are just one of the possible recipients of family sources making demands on the so-called 'sandwich generation',[14] the baby-boomers squeezed in between the needs of the younger and older generations in care. The over-reliance on the welfare state by baby-boomers is often discussed to be behind the struggles of 'Generation Y'.[15] The reality of intergenerational relationships shows, however, that (some) baby-boomers face the double burden of having to pay for their children's education and also having to provide care for elderly family members, when welfare state cuts have affected both HE and elderly care funding[16]

The use of family sources has specific implications on young people's subjective experiences of university. For example, the interviews have shown that over-reliance on family sources has potentially negative implications for the wellbeing of young people in university. The most extreme example is Filomena from Italy, who described her difficulties in university in relation to the overuse of family sources. Regarding issues of wellbeing, she states:

> … it's not the economic situation per se, I am not homeless, but I feel a lot of pressure because of what I asked for from my parents. Now I am feeling more comfortable, but when you know that three quarters of your parents' wage is going to pay for uni.… This is a very competitive environment and I am making my parents spend a lot of money, and what if I don't succeed?

Filomena's concerns had important psychological effects on her: "I went to a psychologist as I started having panic attacks.… I felt an enormous responsibility to my parents." She also pointed out that while her parents were trying to reassure her, it was assessing the family sacrifices that made her feel guilty: "When you go home and you see your mother goes around 10 supermarkets with voucher discounts, when you see that certain goods disappear at home, you feel the responsibility." Similarly Jessica and Maria, both from disadvantaged families, mentioned the sense of responsibility for their education outcomes, in particular the fear that they may graduate late and therefore become a burden to their family. This would seem to suggest that over-reliance on family sources causes a problem particularly for young people from lower socioeconomic backgrounds, and is emerging as a particular phenomenon in Italy, where this over-reliance is more evident.

The relationship between responsibility and the use of family sources also emerged from some participants from upper socioeconomic backgrounds who do not report significant challenges to their wellbeing, but nonetheless refer to the sense of reciprocity they feel behind the use of family sources. Giulia, for example, explains why she can't live away from home and still rely on family sources: "If I live at home my family pays, otherwise I'd need to pay. This is the way they conceive their financing: we finance you if you follow what we say." This seems to suggest that even when young people come from upper socioeconomic backgrounds, relying on family sources can be considered a sub-optimal choice for them too, as it tends to increase their feeling of responsibility and the sense of reciprocity behind the use of family sources.

Conclusion

The analysis presented here shows how profound the mismatch is between what is demanded from families and what families can effectively afford to give to the young people. This issue is becoming particularly relevant in those countries in which families have to actively intervene to sustain young people's semi-dependency – Italy – but also England. This is reinforcing inequalities among the population of young people, an aspect that is also relevant in Sweden, where young people from upper socioeconomic backgrounds are used to accessing additional sources. Family sources not only create inequalities; they also create a specific form of disadvantage, as young people will cut certain expenses when the family cannot afford to sustain them. For the young people in this study, it appears that intra-family solidarity is replacing a form of public solidarity from the state. The motto 'we're all in this together' doesn't apply to the collective, but seems to fit particularly well with the role of the nuclear family in supporting the extended transitions of young people.

Family sources play a crucial role not only in mobilising sources for the present, but also in determining sources for the future. We have seen here that the profiles that have no positive outlook for the future are also those that are aware of the limited sources from their family, and of the fact that these sources are mobilised on a temporary basis and will not be available after university. In a world characterised by social risks in which the construction of biographies is crucial, this creates problems of wellbeing in the present for young people who are constantly worried about what will happen when they finish university, and who experience guilt and a burden of reciprocity in having to rely on their families.

EIGHT

The labour market contradiction: a precarious form of dependence

The second source of welfare used by young people is the labour market. Total dependence on labour market sources is perceived as an achievement of *independence*, which characterises the state of adulthood.[1] This idea can be challenged to some degree by the fact that, in the current climate, labour market sources do not necessarily guarantee effective independence to adults. Compared to adults, young people do not rely on labour market sources to the same extent, and they are not assumed to be entirely dependent on labour market sources.

As we have seen in Part 1, transitions to work have been replaced by more fragmented and less linear transitions: young people do not necessarily enter the labour market *after* university, but start participating in it before. Exactly how many enter the labour market tends, however, to vary greatly by country. If we look at the data from Eurostudent in 2011, jobs provide on average at least 20% of students' monthly income (20% in Portugal, 28% in Germany and 24% in Belgium), 30-50% in many countries (42% in Finland, 37% in the Netherlands, 52% in Spain, 32% in France and 34% in England/ Wales), and reach peaks in Eastern Europe (72% in the Czech Republic and 92% in Slovakia).[2] This variation can be explained by the extent to which the welfare state in each country offers support to young people in university, and also by how easy it is to find a job. Labour market sources are mainly used to complement existing sources, as combining labour market participation with university studies is never easy. There is also a reported trend of more young people looking for labour market participation. This can be explained by the evaluation of the 'welfare mixes' presented in Chapter 2: given the trend of austerity that has withdrawn state sources and the increasing demands on the family, young people are under pressure to look more and more to the labour market in order to gain independence. While working might still be defined as the trademark of the transition to adulthood, the 'final' position of independence reached by getting a job has become increasingly hard to achieve, and for some young people more than others.

We know relatively little about the types of jobs that young people do while in university, although Eurostat[3] indicates that young people aged 18-24 who work while in education tend to be mostly in part-time and temporary jobs, as discussed in Part 1. It is clear, as I go on to show, that during university young people engage mostly in forms of under-employment, in the specific sense of working in unqualified positions. At the beginning of 2016 the Office for National Statistics (ONS) reported an increase in those employed on zero hours contracts, that is, contracts that are considered highly precarious as they lack any guaranteed minimum hours. About 800,000 were on zero hours contracts in the UK in late 2015, and these 'are more likely to be young, part time, women, or in full-time education when compared with other people in employment.'[4] The equivalent of this phenomenon in Italy is the widespread diffusion of another form of precarious contract, 'job vouchers'. With this system workers are not paid cash, but instead with pre-paid vouchers that can be cashed by workers after their daily work. This is clearly a strategy to generate savings for employers as there is no contract ruling workers' rights on sick pay, holidays or leave.[5] This type of contract, which risks being 'the new frontier of the precariat', according to economist Tito Boeri,[6] seems to be a popular model of employing students who work while at university.[7]

Given that young people embark on university mostly to aspire to graduate jobs – and are encouraged by policy-makers to see HE as a route to professional jobs – that so many end up working in unskilled jobs reveals the tensions and contradictions in the current role that HE plays in our societies. While this could be considered a transitional period, studies are showing that young people, especially from lower socioeconomic backgrounds, remain stuck in non-graduate jobs long after graduation.[8] Consequently, even when they find jobs, with the increasing diffusion of zero hours contracts, unpaid positions and discrepancies between working wages and living wages, young people's search for independence is not fulfilled by their labour market participation.

Young people's engagement in low or unskilled work during university – and the possible consequences of this – could be understood as characteristic of part of what Standing has called 'the precariat', the new emerging class trapped in cheap and precarious forms of labour.[9] According to Standing, young people, including students, are over-represented among this precariat. Standing's understanding of precarity is quite broad as for this term he refers not only to labour market insecurity (that is, short-term contracts and lack of protection against employment loss), but also uncertain experiences of work (what he calls 'job insecurity') and precarious patterns of income. This definition is so encompassing that young people who work for extra money while studying, although comfortably backed up by their family, would also be (in theory) part of the precariat.

Standing's view on the relationship between precarity and social class (or other traditional social divisions) is blurred and still widely discussed in social sciences.[10] On the one hand, he contends that the precariat is a new class in the making, replacing traditional class divisions. But then he also argues, 'we must remember that the precariat does not just comprise victims; some members enter the precariat because they do not want the available alternatives, some because it suits their particular circumstances at the time. In short, there are varieties of precariat.'[11] While Standing never explicitly denies the role of class, his description of precarity remains too general, and varieties of precarity (in particular, in relation to existing social divisions) are never explicitly identified and discussed.

As I go on to show in this chapter, and as other research illuminates, participating in the labour market while studying at university has a reported effect of increasing inequalities among the youth population, and it is highly stratified. It increases inequalities in the specific sense that it improves the chances of students dropping out of university, and in general, it creates pressures on the time budget of students who need to juggle both education and work. Young people's participation in work during university is also associated with socioeconomic background. A study on job participation during university in the UK shows that, due to the fact that British structures are intended to encourage a private form of dependency during graduate education, the decision to engage in part-time work during graduate studies is highly associated with socioeconomic and ethnic backgrounds.[12] This leads to social classes having a 'polarised' experience of HE.[13] The way engagement in precarious jobs during university seems to affect some young people more than others is particularly evident in the UK, where it is possible to identify two groups of students: those who enjoy a student lifestyle relatively unencumbered by the need to undertake outside employment, and those for whom immersion in the 'student lifestyle' is curtailed by the need to combine education with labour market participation.[14]

From the results of this study I have identified three types of labour market participation by young people in university, all in precarious jobs, but with profoundly diverse sociological meanings. The first refers to labour market participation undertaken solely for economic reasons: unskilled jobs that pay the bills. The second is undertaken by young people from the 'squeezed' middle (that is, families facing an increasing cost of living) in order to limit their over-reliance on the family. The third is described by the choice of embarking on qualified and graduate jobs that are not well paid. This last type is engaged in essentially in order to compete in the labour market against other young people, and not to pay the bills. It is about doing part-time work or internships that help young people accumulate capital – networks, work experience, etc – for the future.[15] It is crucial to clarify which categories of people work for the first type and which can 'afford' the third type. While Standing's narrative of the precariat offers an appealing account of the current situation of young people vis-à-vis labour market sources, the real-life experiences of young people in precarious jobs are extremely diverse and do not all exhaustively enter under the umbrella of 'precarity'.

How labour market participation changes across the profiles

Without making any claim of representativeness, the vast majority of young people in my study were participating in work while studying and were employed in 'precarious jobs', at least using Standing's definition of precarity: internships, part-time jobs, seasonal and occasional jobs (in fact, only 4 out of 84 were in full-time positions). This confirmed that, as other studies have already shown, precarious jobs are widely diffused among students.[16]

Table 11 presents a summary of how labour market participation varies across the different profiles.

Table 11: The profiles of the young people's experience of university and the role of the labour market

Profile	Socioeconomic background	Role of the labour market
1. Struggling and hopeless	Low and lower-intermediate	Necessary and insufficient
2. Facing difficulties, but with hope for the future	Low	Necessary
3. A positive, but temporary, period	Low	Complementary and ancillary
4. Good in the present, worried about the future	Upper and upper-intermediate	Not needed, used to limit dependence
5. Having a great time	Upper	Not necessary

First, we can identify the types of young people that have to participate in the labour market in order to meet their needs, and those for whom labour market sources of welfare are an essential contribution that enables them to afford to stay at university.

Profile 1 belongs to the category of those who need to participate in the labour market. Young people from this profile attempt to use labour market sources to complement the lack of sources from the state and the family. Maria and Jessica, from Italy, would like to work more, but they find it difficult to find regular work, and so they work in non-regular jobs, such as giving tuition, babysitting and summer jobs. Why do young people rely on jobs while studying? In the case of this profile, the answer is simple: because they need to. As Maria told me, "When I gave tuition I didn't receive much, but I was satisfied, as I was able to be independent from my parents." For David, from England, loans and grants don't cover his costs and his family has no support to provide, therefore: "If I didn't take work in the summer I wouldn't have any money to spend on myself. It's just living costs that I can cover by the loan."

At the same time, the students from this profile also show a negative ranking on the adequacy of payment from labour market participation. They all mentioned the precarity of labour market sources, and all cited episodes in which they were paid only after very long delays (David and Maria), or were not paid and had to go to court (Jessica).

Young people in profile 2 also need labour market sources. In terms of welfare mixes, the ranking suggests that young people from this profile need to complement state sources with labour market sources. In the ranking of statements, this profile agrees the most with the necessity of gaining income from paid work (item 15; see Table 5). As mentioned in the description of profiles in Part 2, the comparative importance of state and labour market sources is different. Sofia, from Sweden, relies on state sources and works during the summer, while Sharon and Mark, from England, need to complement their state sources (loans and grants) with working in retail during the academic year, as state sources are not sufficient to enable them to sustain themselves independently from their families. The struggle to balance labour market and state sources came up in all three interviews. In particular, they all underline the difficulty of relying on state sources alone. For Sharon, having a part-time job that enables her to cover her expenses "is just too much", given her commitments during university. The same is true for Mark, who, due to his university schedule, needs to work at weekends. Mark complained about how his life was particularly affected by lack of free time: "I only sleep six hours a night. I don't really have that much time [in between work and studying]." Sofia also remarks that state sources are enough to live on, but due to the high cost of rent, they are not enough to cover unexpected costs. Therefore, for her, working during the summer in underqualified jobs is necessary in order to form a pool of sources that can be used to cover the extra costs she has during the rest of the year. The difficulties reported by this profile can be directly ascribed to their labour market participation in two ways: first, labour market participation affects their participation in university and their time budget; and second, these students are confronted with a discrepancy between what they need to live on during their time in university, and what is provided from engaging in paid work.

Profiles 3 and 4, given the availability of other sources of welfare during university, do not need to work, but they get casual jobs in order to limit the burden on their families or for extra expenses. These young people use participation in the labour market mainly as a source of income for extra expenses (as in the case of Anna, from Italy, and Rebecca, from England, who have casual jobs) or to acquire experience (as in the case of Rob and Stewart, from England, who are looking for internships). The choice of not seeking employment during term time is due to time constraints; as stated by Rebecca, who has considered working during term time but decided not to: "I kinda realised that with the amount of time I had to spend at uni in studying and doing coursework and having a social life I couldn't really fit a job in and still have the time to sleep." However, Rebecca works during the summer to accumulate resources to use throughout the year and to limit her over-reliance on her family:

> [In the summer] I worked quite a lot. I didn't have a lot of time to relax and have a break from things – it was full on, like, all the time. But on the other hand, I earned quite a lot of money, which helped me to get through the first term of the second year without much financial support from my parents.

Their motivation for working is not as 'desperate' as that of the first two profiles, but they feel a clear pressure in having to reduce their reliance on family support by working.

Profile 5 epitomises the case of young people who do not need labour market participation and can concentrate their labour market participation on graduate jobs in order to compete in the labour market in the future. Young people from this profile (all from Italy) do not need labour market sources to complement their income, and mostly consider it as a way to acquire experience. This was proved by the fact that this profile mostly disagreed with the impossibility of acquiring experience through unpaid internships in the survey (item 17; Table 8). The interviews confirmed this idea. Alfredo, for example, told me that he didn't want to work during university and would only take jobs to acquire experience through a summer internship. Federico gained an internship that he describes as "a very qualified job" through his father's network in order to improve his CV. For these students, working during university is not a financial neccesity, and they can therefore engage in work that is about accumulating capital for the future. As shown in an important study conducted by my colleagues in Bristol (the Paired Peers project),[17] this is a mechanism through which class privilege is reproduced as young people from these backgrounds can mobilise their cultural capital to build future advantages in the labour market (for example, by improving their CVs).

Young people from this profile also tend to have non-regular sources of income for non-career purposes. These are related to their hobbies and are used to cover extra expenses – in fact, these precarious jobs, sailing for Federico and photography for Giulia, looked more like well-paid hobbies to me than the problematic experiences of precarity described by Guy Standing.

Why university students have different experiences of precarity

Labour market sources are widely used by the students interviewed in this study – almost all the young people who worked were employed in non-qualified and/or precarious jobs. While young people tend to work more while in university, labour market sources have a limited capacity to sustain their livelihoods in university. However, some young people still need to work in order to meet all their costs.

This particularly affects independent students (students living in independent housing and without family support), who, due to lack of family sources, *need* to work to complement the insufficient state sources. Given this dependence on labour market sources, the financial struggles of this set of young people are precisely linked to the precarity of labour market income. This was particularly common for students interviewed in England, where, as we have seen, students are more dependent on labour market sources. Mark, for example, works on a zero hours contract in retail. His contract makes it hard for him to budget, as he doesn't have a regular income, but working is necessary for him to cover his rent and living costs. He explains his situation as follows: "I declare no income. I earn so little. I am on a zero hours contract so it's impossible for me to predict how much I am gonna earn." This lack of ability to predict results in periods of financial stress for Mark that, interestingly, follow the same path of precarity as his labour market participation: "The periods of stress, like financial stress, I have usually only if I have a hard month or something like that, but then it will be alright after."

The irregular nature of labour market pay can have negative consequences on young people's lives *if* they are necessarily dependent on the labour market. This is the case for David, from England, who was working on a freelance contract, and described the effects of irregular income on his financial condition. The precarity of pay created a situation of economic disadvantage: "[At the] start of the summer I was paying rent in Bristol and working in Cambridge and I wasn't paid for a month. At the end of the month I was like £90 minus my overdraft, for a week I didn't have any [money]. I lived out of my Nectar points ... you can buy food out of your Nectar points. That was the closest I've been to having nothing." In these cases, when young people need to rely on the labour market to sustain their lives, the precarious nature of labour market pay generates 'lived experiences of precarity'.

Labour market participation is associated with a number of issues. The first issue that the young people had to face was the difficulty and competition in finding a job, which appears to be a crucial issue affecting all three countries. Even those who did have a job, such as Maria and Jessica from Italy, experienced problems, including delays in payment and legal problems obtaining their wages. The insecurity of the salary and lack of jobs make the labour market a source that students cannot rely on to cope with social risks, as it is a source of welfare that has itself become risky. Maria felt the pressure of combining work with her studies, and understood the impact of each one on the other: "If I do not work I cannot finish university; if I work I cannot study. This is a contradiction and I haven't found out how to solve it." Maria refers to the fact that she needs to find multiple jobs in order to sustain her university experience, but this has a negative impact on her studies. This not only confirms the negative effects that working during university has on studying, but also highlights a general paradoxical trend. The privatisation of costs during HE indirectly encourages seeking independence through labour market participation, but labour market sources have a declining capacity to sustain young people's independence.

Even Swedish students face the pressure of having to participate in the labour market, in particular to cover the gap of student support in the summer, when they don't receive state sources and are assumed to have to work. Saga, from Sweden, and from a low socioeconomic background, points out the strong competition to find jobs in the summer and during the year in the following way:

> It's still on my mind that I should look for extra work.... In Sweden having a job is very important. If you don't really have a job people may start feeling sorry for you. So it's like, if you have a job then you are doing good and paying back to the society. If you do not have a job and need welfare from the society then people might get annoyed with you and think you are not doing anything. I think it's a bit of a fear not having a job.

Students who have direct availability of family resources (that is, students from upper socioeconomic backgrounds) are also often in precarious jobs. Their reasons for working are, however, different, and so are the implications of their participation in the labour market. One reason to work for students from upper socioeconomic backgrounds is to gain some extra resources and some form of financial independence. Tilde, from Sweden, for example, explains that working for her is a way to cover extra expenses that enable her to participate in hobbies and other lifestyle choices, such as travel: "I like travelling. Sometimes I want to do something that's nicer, and then you need a bit more money to save up for that because the money I have now I feel that covers a life in Malmö that's pretty okay, but not if I want to go to Stockholm." Giulia, from Italy, also states that working is not necessary for her, although it is important to limit her over-reliance on family sources:

> I feel lucky, as I come from a wealthy family. But I try to have economic independence because it feels ridiculous to be the little girl who asks for money from mum and dad. I have trouble looking for work because, firstly, university is a priority and I couldn't do full-time work ... and part-time jobs are extremely underpaid and the conditions are those of slavery: you work six to eight hours and you get paid four euros per hour. Sometimes I try to do photography, but I am not well paid, it's not regular, it's for extra. Sometimes I do tutoring. It's not a necessity, it's because I wanted to

do it and I am lucky enough to come from a family that has the resources.

Young people from upper socioeconomic background work during HE in order to gain experience, improve their credentials and better compete in their post-university transitions. This was explained by Federico, an Italian student from an upper socioeconomic background, who, through his family connections, was able to find a qualified internship:

> I have been offered an internship from [name of the company]. My dad has worked with them as an external consultant ... it should be a good learning experience. I mean, it won't be one of those internships where they make you do photocopying.

Federico's experience in a job that is considered precarious (an internship) will be ultimately beneficial as it will enrich his CV and allow him to better compete for future graduate jobs than his colleagues who had to work in retail. This is not the only way in which family can facilitate labour market insertion. For some students, in particular in England, the family directly influences participation in the labour market, in so far as they work for the family business. This is the case for Tom, who works in his family business, and Graham, who is employed in a business run by his father during the academic year. Both students refer to their participation in these family businesses as more flexible and easier to negotiate around their schedules given the relationship they have with their parents who are in charge of the business. Graham states, for example, that it would have been harder for him to squeeze in a normal job and combine it with university and social life. Sasha also works in her father's company in the summer with the specific goal of limiting her over-dependence on family sources: "When I work in the summer I like having my own money, because it feels more grown up. I don't like depending on my parents' money – I feel bad." This suggests a specific way in which the family is present in England through facilitating labour market insertion and allowing more educational-friendly participation in the labour market. For the other students without family connections, combining labour market participation with university attendance remains a major issue. Britney, from England, for example, points out that while she works during the summer, she could not find a job during the year: "The actual time at uni I couldn't [work] because everyone I know is after a job. It is difficult to find an employer who is so flexible, so I couldn't have that flexibility."

Conclusion

Labour market sources can be defined as the most desired sources of welfare by young people in university. As we have seen before, for some profiles, labour market sources are necessary, as they constitute a vital complement to the insufficient mix of family and state sources. They were particularly described as necessary for those students who do not receive state support and who do not have sufficient family sources. In this case, labour market sources are used as a source of income by students who have no additional family resources on top of state support, and are also accumulated during the summer to cope with extra expenses during the year, in particular, for those students in England and Sweden.

Those young people for whom labour market participation is essential are confronted with the difficulty of finding jobs and with the precarious and non-regular nature of these jobs. In addition to this, because of the necessity of having to work during university, their university life becomes more difficult. A consistent number of young people look and try to find labour market sources to alleviate the burden on their families. In this case these young people are also confronted with the problem of having to combine jobs with full-time education. While the first type are those who tend to fall into the category of the precariat identified by Standing, there is also a second type of young person who has the chance to selectively participate in the labour market. To some extent the young people want precarious labour market participation in order to combine it with education, but this becomes an experience of 'precarity' when their participation in precarious jobs has a negative consequence in their lives *due to the lack of other resources*. These situations occur when the young people need to rely on labour market sources: in these cases, their power of negotiation clearly declines and they accept any type of job to sustain their semi-dependence. Guy Standing is correct in reporting a widespread diffusion of precarious jobs, but he wrongly assumes that participation in these jobs will have the same sociological meaning. Being part of the 'precariat' entails being part of a category of workers whose lives are negatively affected by being in precarious jobs. As I have stressed before, this is not always true for young students in precarious jobs, as some use qualified (albeit precarious) jobs to improve their credentials for future labour market transitions.

There are also substantial cross-national differences in the way labour market sources are used. As we have seen in Chapter 1, the structure of the system of student support in Sweden requires participation in the labour market during the summer term. In most cases, the students from Sweden tend to work in the summer, but a consistent number also try to work during the year to get additional sources. The students from Italy find it particularly hard to combine work and education due to the educational commitments required by Italian universities. Those who cannot avoid working are those who do not have the family sources to support their semi-dependence. The students from England, in many cases, need to work to complement the lack of sources from the state and the family, especially where there is a mismatch between what the state expects the family to give and what the family can actually provide.

NINE

State: generous, conditional or absent?

The function that welfare states have in shaping young people's lives at university is largely underplayed. For young people at university and in some cases for their families, the welfare state provides financial support and possible additional security benefits. From a financial point of view, European undergraduate students receive on average 22% of their monthly income from state sources,[1] although the percentage tends to vary across countries. An additional form of state intervention that influences young people's semi-dependent state is student housing policy, although this is mostly at the institutional and local level, reflecting the lack of state policy awareness on the function of student support regarding housing.[2]

As stressed in Part 1, welfare state interventions are relevant not only due to the amount of intervention provided, but also because of the assumptions they make about the role that private sources of welfare should play in supporting young people before they reach a status of independence. In other words, what the state decides to offer or not to offer to young people will indirectly influence the function that labour market and family sources have in supporting young people's lives in university, while they are still in a state of semi-dependence. Both labour market and family sources, as we have seen in Chapters 7 and 8, have a role in increasing inequality among young people's experiences in university.

Part 1 has devoted much space to stressing the different welfare state policies that are available to young people across the three countries, arguing that these influence not only young people's experiences, but also how unequal their experiences are across the countries. The system of public responsibility found in Sweden implies a higher contribution by the state. State support can be considered generous, and state sources support young people during their quest for independence. The system of social investment in England assumes that private sources contribute alongside state sources in sustaining young people's costs. Support can therefore be considered to be conditional depending on the young people's status and is highly means-tested. The system of minimal intervention found in Italy assumes that almost all financial support comes from private sources. The state can be described as absent, as it doesn't take any public responsibility for supporting young people in their transitions through university.[3]

The existence of different systems, in turn, has different implications for stratification in each country, in particular due to the links between social class and the availability of family sources, and to the higher labour market participation by students from lower socioeconomic backgrounds in all three countries. What can the state do to limit spreading inequalities among young people? It can reinforce or limit the stratification of young people in university depending on two dimensions: the generosity of the policy instruments used (the presence and level of grants and loans and level of fees) and their inclusiveness (that is, the type of intervention in terms of whether it is means-tested or universal).

The presence of state support is not in itself an instrument to decrease inequalities. There are several elements to consider in assessing how state policies can reduce inequality. The first refers to the fact that, while grants offer the possibility of covering student living costs and therefore harmonise the experience of university, loans transfer the cost of university to individuals. As shown in Part 1, loans influence HE choices, and also young people's strategies while in university. Evidence from England clearly shows that students from lower socioeconomic backgrounds, due to their limited familiarity with financial tools, end up with higher levels of debt compared to their more affluent counterparts, who are able to benefit from the use of additional family sources.[4] Even when student support is generous, as in Sweden, the system only provides support during the academic year, assuming that young people will work in the summer; this favours young people from privileged backgrounds who will need to take out fewer loans.[5] Loans carry in themselves an element of inequality, as they assume equal returns in the labour market, whereas, as we know, the labour market structure is highly stratified, and the 'graduate premium' differs greatly across degree subject and across social categories such as gender and class (we find both gender and class ceilings in the labour market).[6]

Even more than loans, the level of fees signals how generous – or not – the system is: higher fees mean that young people are expected to meet the costs of education privately. The presence of fees and the high level of debt deriving from fees also tend to affect young people from low socioeconomic backgrounds in particular, due to what has been recently called 'the class ceiling'.[7] If HE becomes a commodity in a perfect market and an investment with future returns, young people who benefit are asked to contribute. This, however, also means that the more initial investment you have to put in, the higher returns you will have from HE. In other words, this is certainly a system that encourages the role of the market, but it is also one that reinforces inequalities. The potential stratification deriving from the use of fees therefore needs to be explored in terms of the indirect pressure that having fees creates by requiring additional private sources of welfare (family sources or young people's labour market participation).

Finally, when state support is available in the form of grants, this doesn't necessarily mean that inequalities will be reduced. This largely depends on how support is provided, as there is a substantial difference, underlined by the classical social policy literature, between means testing and universal support. The famous 'paradox of redistribution' means that means testing and targeting will result in increasing inequality rather than limiting it, as in the case of universal provision.[8] The role of means testing is especially relevant for young people in university, as this form of targeting assumes a co-contribution from family sources that might not be available.[9] The paradox of redistribution for young people in university increases inequalities among young people by making student support match family sources that are highly diverse among the student population. Even when state support is provided universally, another element to assess the capacity of state support in limiting inequality is its sufficiency: can student support truly compensate for the low income of some young people's families?[10] If not, student support ends up reproducing existing inequalities. After setting out the terms of the debate, I now discuss how these theories apply to the experiences of young people in my study, starting from the differences that emerged across the five profiles.

State sources and profiles

As we have done for the family and the labour market, we can explore the variation in the use of state sources across profiles, as summarised in Table 12 below.

Not all profiles indicated that they have a need for state sources. For example, young people from profile 5 were able to draw on family sources if they needed to, and did not expect to receive state sources to support their experience in HE.

For profile 4, state sources are complementary or absent. However, this puts more pressure on the use of family sources, which are available, but are still limited, compared to those of profile 5. For example, Rebecca, from England, from this profile, underlines that the

Table 12: The profiles of the young people's experience of university and the role of the state

Profile	Socioeconomic background	Role of state sources
1. Struggling and hopeless	Low and lower-intermediate	Absent or insufficient
2. Facing difficulties, but with hope for the future	Low	Insufficient
3. A positive, but temporary, period	Low	Fundamental
4. Good in the present, worried about the future	Upper and upper-intermediate	Complementary or absent
5. Having a great time	Upper	Absent

lack of state sources implies a pressure on the resources available to her family: "If I got more support from the state it would be easier on my parents. They'd rather be saving money for retirement, given that the pension is going downhill." As we have seen in previous chapters, for this profile, lack of state sources that are available results in an intense investment of family sources.

Young people from profile 2 face a similar situation, except that no family sources are available for these young people. The pitfalls of means testing based on family income have been particularly damaging for English participants, as what the state provides depends on an assessment of need, which doesn't always reflect the availability of family sources. Sharon remarked several times on the 'disconnect' between her social origins 'on paper' and the real ability of her family to provide financial support due to the debts that her parents have:

> My parents earn a really reasonable amount of money, but because they haven't been so clever in the past, they do not have a lot to spare. So we have a nice house and I do not go without food or things, but like if I said I want to go out then they might not be able to say, 'Here's £20.'

The insufficiency of state sources is experienced in a particularly negative way by those students in profile 1, which is affected by the mismatch between what the state assumes the family will provide and the reality of the family sources that are available. The impact of this lack of state support on students' wellbeing is captured in the case of Jessica and Maria. Maria, who received a scholarship for one year but not for the following year, affirmed:

> It's more anxiety than anything else. If I now think how I
> will be able to sustain myself in this academic year I have
> anxiety.… I have anxiety because I do not know how to
> do it, I am not a person who feels down easily, but since
> I found out I don't have the scholarship last week I felt
> really, really bad.

Over-reliance on the limited family sources available becomes a form of "mortification" (Maria) and creates anxiety, stress and a sense of guilt and responsibility (Jessica). For David, who depends on state sources, the main mental struggles are related to his ability to pay back his loans and the difficulties he has in covering his monthly costs. For example, expressing his concerns about the level of loans he has accumulated, David stated: "At this point now I am about £35,000 in debt and it just gets to you. I don't want £35,000 of debt, how do I enter the housing market? How do I pay it off? I need to get a job." This suggests that David's reliance on loans has a negative impact on the construction of his biography.

Finally, there is one profile for which the availability of state sources made the difference. Young people from profile 3 underlined how the availability of state sources allowed them to improve their situation. The young people from this profile who were interviewed were receiving more state support than their peers, due to their special assessed needs. For example, Mandy, from England, receives a full grant and an additional scholarship due to the fact that she comes from a single-parent family and has a brother who counts as a dependent. Maja, from Sweden, is taking the maximum loan and has an extra loan for people over 25 who earn more than a certain salary, which she uses to pay for her accommodation. She explained that this is to encourage older students not to change their living standards: "so that you do not have to go from earning a lot of money to being poor". In general, for young people from this profile, state sources have been described as essential for raising their living standards and for allowing them to participate in HE.

Dependence on the state: grants and loans

The role of state sources has been explored in the research, particularly in Sweden and England, as in Italy only one participant was fortunate enough to receive a limited form of support. The findings suggest that universal state support in Sweden, given its capacity to cover the full costs of students without contributions from the family, has the ability to improve the situation of students who were experiencing hardship before entering university. For example, prior to university, Saga, from Sweden, was attending high school and receiving a very limited amount of money from the family and the state. This changed when she went to university:

> The entrance to university has improved my economic situation: I now have the opportunity to save money. Before I just got a small amount of money, but I had to use it so I could live well. But now I get a lot of money so I can save it. In a good way ... for the future.... I have much more money now, I feel more flexible and that I can put more money in other things, which I would not do before.... The reason why I am saving money is that I am looking for jobs for the summer but want something in case I do not find them, and, of course, sometimes you have unexpected expenses.

Therefore she also used state sources to cope with possible risks and the possible lack of other sources (labour market sources in particular) in a way that she could not before due to the absence of material family support.

In Chapter 3 I discussed how state provisions in Sweden are comparatively inclusive and provide a sufficient form of support, at least during the academic year. The *universal* nature of state sources in Sweden pushes young people to use state sources (grants and loans) instead of family sources, even if they come from families that could support them. Elvin, from Sweden, explained his choice of relying on state sources instead of using family sources in the following way:

> I talked a lot with my father how to do it. He could afford to pay me or to help me with everything right now, but he said: 'It would be good for you to feel this responsibility, to consider what you are doing with the money since it's your own money, you are borrowing from them, it's not just coming from me, and then you'll feel more independent as well.' And that's why ... why I wanted it.

The interviews with my participants from Sweden revealed that there is a process of levelling down standards of living for students from different backgrounds as a consequence of using equal state sources: Tilde, from an upper socioeconomic background and living mostly on state sources, pointed out how she lowered her standards:

> From living with my parents 'till now there is kind of
> a big difference with what I can do and I cannot do....
> The main thing is probably that you need to think when
> you buy food.... In my parents' house it was like if I want
> something it's probably there.

However, as we have seen before, young people from upper
socioeconomic backgrounds from Sweden effectively complement
their state sources with family sources to provide extra resources and
to cope with the many social risks they face during university.

In Chapter 3 I discussed how the English system of student support
assumes a co-contribution from the family and has become increasingly
residual in the last few years. The *means-tested* and *insufficient* structure
of support in England has different implications for young people, who
are assumed, in most cases, to complement state sources with family
sources, as explained by Rebecca:

> I do not get enough money from the state to support my
> studies. My loan just about covers the extortionate rent
> that we're charged as students. Luckily my family has some
> expendable income with which to support me financially and
> I manage to live within the means that they can provide me.

Assumptions underlying policy do not always reflect the reality. As
Sharon pointed out, the government assumes how much her parents
can contribute from their income, and doesn't take into account the
family's specific financial position:

> I do not get any grant from the government, only a loan,
> which barely covers my accommodation fee. For this reason
> I had to live in private accommodation in freshers' year
> rather than in halls because it was cheaper and I feel like I
> missed out. I think the government assume, based on my
> parents' earnings, that they will give me money for food,
> etc, but they do not have spare money because they have
> a high mortgage and debts, so instead I managed to apply
> and get some scholarships to cover my living costs.

In both England and Sweden state support makes extensive use of
students loans, which attracted very different opinions across the
students interviewed. Swedish students mostly expressed favourable
opinions, although some showed concerns about repaying them. For

example, Elvin expressed his mixed feelings as follows:

> Well, I didn't have any problem with my finances before university. It's from now on that I have a big-ass huge loan to pay back. Although it is a good loan and it isn't the toughest pay-back plan, it's still big.

Young people from England seem even more concerned about the possibility of accumulating debts. Although most of them talked about loans as "a good debt" as opposed to negative debts with banks, some who could not rely on family sources ended up accumulating a high level of debt. David, for example, stated:

> Up [until] to coming to uni my parents took care of my finances and then suddenly I was taking out massive loans trying to pay my own rent. It wasn't particularly difficult, but it does add a mental weight when you have all those responsibilities all of a sudden.

While young people are required to take out loans, they also use different strategies to make the dependence on loans more bearable. The first strategy is to take a lower amount of loans than they are eligible for. For example, Svea, from Sweden, following her sister's suggestion, took half of the loan available by saving on her housing costs in order to accumulate less debt. The other strategy is to take student loans and save that money to save interest from future mortgages. For example, Ludvig, from Sweden, stated clearly that he does not need all the state support: "I take loans just to save the money for an apartment in future, because the interest rate is lower on the money I borrow from the state." Ludvig explained that this strategy would allow him to put money into a deposit that he would otherwise not be able to afford: "this is not a good thing to do, but people do it and it's legal". Similarly, Saga uses loans to accumulate savings that she could use in the future and to cope with potential risks, given that she comes from a family with limited capital:

> The amount of money I get each month from my loan is a lot, which also allows me to save a lot of money each month. So I will get more financially independent in our society.

As described in Chapter 3, loans are not part of the system of student support in Italy, not because of any lack of attempts to introduce them, but because young people are reluctant to use a system of loans introduced through banks and that therefore also involve family. This is best expressed by Giulia, who stated the following about the capacity of loans to make her less dependent on family sources:

> I am not willing to get debt [loans] to be more independent, and it's not independent as it's a debt not to the individual but to the family. You get an education, you'll be forever precarious, and if you can't pay back your family will need to. So it's an additional source of dependence on your family.

Pietro expressed a similar negative view:

> I would not consider using [loans] … then if I didn't find a job my family would have needed to pay them back. I prefer to have a debt with my family: one day if I'll have a nice job, I'll pay it back to my family, I'd feel less guilty. I'd prefer it like that.

In general, all students across the countries considered loans to be a great opportunity, but also the least optimal choice. While Swedish students are able to find positive strategies to use loans as an alternative to other (more costly) forms of debt, English students seemed particularly affected by the level of debt, and Italian students were against the idea of loans altogether.

Effects of state support on young people's dependence

In Chapters 1 and 4 I discussed how the condition of semi-dependence is considered an inherent part of the current transitions of young people in university and concerns, in various respects, all the students involved in this study. The variation of 'welfare mixes' also creates substantial differences in the structures of dependence that have been mostly neglected in the literature. Those different models of dependence are based on housing transition (independent housing versus family housing) and financial situation (family dependent versus family independent). As shown in Table 13, by combining these two different dimensions, this study has identified three models of dependence.

The 'dependents' are young people in university who have not transitioned to independent housing, so they still live with their parents and at the same time are financially dependent on the family.

Table 13: Models of dependence based on housing and finances

	Independent housing	Family housing
Financial dependence on family	Semi-independents	Dependents
Financial independence	Independents	Semi-independents

The 'semi-independents' are young people in university who have one of two forms of independence, financially, or by having housing independence. Finally, there are the young people in university who are 'independent' from their family, in terms of both housing and financial dependence (therefore they use labour market and state sources to gain financial independence). While most of the participants navigate through a situation of dependence, the balance between dependence and independence veers towards one of the two limits, determining a different condition of dependence. The distribution of these models of dependence is not accidental, but is directly dependent on the socioeconomic background and mixes of welfare available. Therefore, we see a different distribution of these different models of dependence in the three countries considered.

In Sweden the structure of student support provided by the state, as a universal form of provision supporting financial independence as described in Chapter 3, facilitates housing transitions, making the majority of Swedish participants in the study 'independents'. However, as we have seen, a number of Swedish participants from upper socioeconomic backgrounds in this study have continued to complement their state sources with family sources to cope with additional expenses. In this case we are in the presence of semi-independents: young people who live in independent housing, but who are not fully financially independent. Also, Swedish independent young people in this study operate in a situation of semi-dependence, given that independent housing and financial status relate to their academic year and are suspended in the summer, when they rely on family housing and/or participation in the labour market. These findings correspond in part to the model, set out in Chapter 3, of the Swedish system of support of HE as one that fosters independent students: while the experiences of the participants show that the Swedish system is able to support, comparatively, a higher independence, young people remain dependent on family sources in different ways according to their socioeconomic background. In particular, participants from upper socioeconomic backgrounds use additional family sources, while young people from lower socioeconomic backgrounds tend to use indirect family support through housing during the summer.

In the case of the participants from Italy, where students were all financially dependent on family sources, achieving the condition of semi-dependence means living independently. The possibility of making a housing transition, however, depends on family sources. For participants from Italy reaching semi-independence depends entirely on housing independence, because financial independence from family sources is virtually impossible: state support is extremely residual and labour market participation is rarely able to sustain the young people. Therefore, in Italy, the students who are semi-independent are those who live in independent housing, while the others are entirely dependent. This is in line with the model described in Chapter 3, where the system of welfare support in Italy made young people reliant on private sources of welfare and almost entirely dependent on family sources. Compared to the general model of Italian young people in university as 'totally dependent', these findings show an important diversity within the Italian student population. The state of being semi-dependent or totally dependent is connected with the availability of family sources, which have an important function in stratifying young people's experiences.

The means-tested structure of student support in England, described in Chapter 3, results in greater variety in the models of dependence, as this is the only country where the study found that all three models were represented: independent, semi-independent and fully dependent. The degree of independence depends on the condition of the family and on the extent to which state support is able to cover gaps in familial welfare. Due to the effects of the welfare mix found in England, participants from England are independent young people who live in independent housing and are able to sustain themselves with a mix of state and labour market sources; semi-independent young people, also found in Sweden and Italy, who have left the parental home, but use family sources in addition to those from the state and, in some cases, from the labour market; and finally, a third type of semi-independents who are not found in the other two countries, namely, young people who are financially independent, as they receive state support, but for whom state support is not sufficient to transition to independent housing and who remain in family housing. These results reflect the fact that, as pointed out in Chapter 3, the system of student support in England relies on both public and private sources of welfare and is also highly means-tested. Both factors tend to stratify young people's conditions in university.

Figure 7 (below) summarises the participants' different conditions of dependence, showing their distribution across welfare mixes. The

Figure 7: Models of dependence and their relationship with welfare mixes for the young people participating in the study

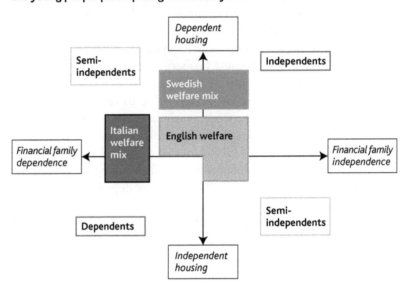

horizontal line represents the financial situation, which goes from financial independence on the right to financial dependence on the left. The vertical line represents the degrees of housing transition, from independent housing on top to living with the family at the bottom. In this framework, the welfare mix from England appears to create greater variation in the models of dependence, while the Swedish and Italian welfare mixes present two different types of dependence.

Emerging adulthood or 'eternal semi-dependence': the role of welfare states

Given the premises of welfare systems of student support, young people are increasingly expected to adopt individualised strategies, such as using family sources and engaging in paid work. The tale of the young adult who postpones her independence in order to avoid growing up could not be further from the reality of my participants. Young people in university experience an inevitable extension of their semi-dependent state (as described in Chapter 4), but they also *strive* to limit the over-reliance on the family. They struggle to become independent due to the structural boundaries around them.

National differences matter, but rather than finding three different models of semi-dependence that are worlds apart, the research has instead found three systems in which young people combine family, state and labour market sources, but in different ways. Of course, private sources are used in different ways in the three welfare mixes as a consequence of different state approaches to how to support young people in university. While for participants from Italy reliance on family sources constituted the main source of welfare and was a shared feature among the population of young people, participants from Sweden from upper socioeconomic backgrounds tended to use family sources to complement the state sources and for extra expenses. The state in this case provides support that is comparatively higher, but still cannot fully cover young people's needs. For participants from England, family sources represented a component of a more variegated welfare mix, and a way to complement scarce state sources. We are used to thinking that familism in youth policies is exclusive to southern European transitions,[11] but this is far from the reality. The presence of family sources doesn't reflect local cultural norms about intergenerational support 'embedded' in the southern European transition regime as a consequence of having a traditional society.[12] This sociological explanation is not convincing and, above all, does not provide a fair assessment of how European societies are evolving during austerity. Family seems rather to be the (unwanted) consequence of the welfare state's very residual and limited intervention in supporting young people in university, and of the limited capacity of labour market sources to sustain young people's independence. This is suggested in this study by the malaise expressed by participants from Italy using 'stretched family sources', and also by the fact that those experiences are shared with participants from England who rely on family sources.

In the context of an increasing diffusion of precarious jobs for young people who work while at university, to cope with social risks young people in Sweden and England also rely on family financial support. For example, in the absence of labour market sources, or with labour market sources showing a declining potential to sustain young people's semi-dependence, even participants from Sweden, traditionally a country with low levels of familism, have been shown to rely on family welfare sources to sustain their financial position, while family housing and financial support is a normalised strategy for participants in England. The study highlights the role of family sources in compensating for declining welfare state interventions for students. Are we witnessing a southern Europeanisation of policies for young people? It is clear that, as welfare states move towards a common strategy of privatising risk, young people's individual strategies, and problems, converge. The final point of convergence of the systems is likely to be a condition that is somewhere in the middle, between the liberal system found in England, based on individual responsibility, and the familistic system found in Italy, based on the use of family sources.

For the past couple of decades the media have portrayed a vision of young people as individualistic agents who decide to intentionally postpone their transitions to adulthood. The 'emerging adult' described by Arnett is a good example of this characterisation that has been very popular in media reports.[13] As other sociologists, I believe that this idea has neglected the role that structural factors play in postponing young people's transitions to adulthood. The latest studies from the US have begun to reconsider this: the sociologist Jennifer Silva has argued that working-class young people are 'coming up short' in their aspirations because of the dismayed conditions around them.[14] Using the amazing laboratory of social comparisons we have in Europe, I wanted to explain the ongoing *process* of semi-dependence and its implications. Where state sources are sufficient, as for many young people in Sweden, young people transition towards independence in finance and housing in a relatively smooth way. The continuous reliance on family resources makes young people's status of semi-dependence 'eternal' rather than transitional. Paradoxically, young people from families without financial resources are becoming even more dependent on their families, as they are forced to postpone their housing transitions. What is the endpoint of this continued reliance on family support? Theoretically the end point would be entering full-time employment that is able to fully sustain young people's independence. This is something that needs, of course, to be further explored in studies looking at post-university transitions.

Conclusion

By incentivising young people to enter university, European welfare states have also indirectly created a new situation for young adults, who are in a protracted phase of semi-dependence. Young people therefore combine family, labour market and state sources to sustain themselves financially while at university.

The availability of welfare sources is deeply linked to young people's social origins. The findings of this study show that family sources reinforce inequality, but that this varies across 'welfare mixes', with young people from different socioeconomic backgrounds using family sources in Italy and England, and with only young people from upper socioeconomic backgrounds using family sources in Sweden. We should not simply assume equivalence between social origins and disadvantage because this ultimately depends on how relevant family sources, and also labour market sources, are to young people. In other words, if you are a working-class student, this doesn't automatically mean you will have a disadvantaged experience of university. This highly depends on the availability of state sources, which could potentially limit the influence of social class on young people's experiences.

The ability of the state to limit such stratification depends on the generosity and, crucially, on the degree of inclusiveness of support, that is, on whether student support is universal or means-tested. In the previous pages I compared three different solutions – the means-tested (England), very residual (Italy) and universal (Sweden) systems of student support – reflected in young people's individual experiences. The means-tested nature of student support creates a mismatch between what the state assumes and what families are really able to provide. The Italian system is extremely residual and doesn't have a substantial impact in limiting inequalities. Participants from Sweden have underlined the positive effect of universal state support in 'equalising' and creating a universal experience of university, by providing at the very least a minimal but sufficient form of support. Young people from lower socioeconomic backgrounds from Sweden indicated in some cases that the state support they began to receive when they started university improved their financial situation, although the inability of state sources to cover the cost of housing also emerged, both in the survey and in the interviews.

These findings push us to a reconsideration of the 'paradox of redistribution', that is, the idea that means-tested provisions tend to reproduce rather than address inequalities.[15] Employing this idea, welfare state interventions for young people will address inequalities if they are provided universally. A public debate on the role of means testing in relation to social provisions for young people is needed, in particular in the UK, where means testing is extremely popular. By making assumptions about the co-contribution of parental income, means testing ends up reproducing pre-existing patterns of inequality and reinforces, counter-productively, the ties with young people's families.

Conclusion:
Addressing growing inequality among young people in university

The starting point of this research was the idea that we need to look at the 'social category' of young people in university, who are not just students in the lecture room, but also individuals experiencing a protracted phase of 'semi-dependence'. The idea of democratic and open access to university has shaped the aspirations and choices of the current cohort of young Europeans, as young people from modest backgrounds have been invited to join the European mass HE system. However, increasing the number of young people enrolling in university has had profound overlooked sociological implications: the current cohort of young people deciding to embark on HE are implicitly required to find the resources to pay for HE costs and also to fund the living costs of their HE experience. The corollary of the choice of entering HE for young people is, in fact, that their transition to full independence through labour market participation is postponed until they end their studies. But how are young people supposed to support this protracted semi-dependent state?

Working towards open and democratic access to HE was thought to be a key element in reducing inequalities in society, although this all depends on which type of policy supports the mass expansion of HE: is it a strategy that tackles pre-existing inequalities by providing equal support to young people, or is it a strategy that asks young people to fund their HE privately? As illustrated in this book, the policy strategies used across Europe are different. Policy strategies in England and Italy are clearly in line with the idea of extending access to HE by increasing the private sources that young people and their families invest in this experience. Sweden, instead, has traditionally devoted much policy effort to creating a virtually equal system for all young people embarking on HE, also assuming that their families will not contribute. The Swedish strategy was to propose a 'public dependence' during HE, enabling young people to experience equal transitions to independence. In the different ways described in Part 1, all three countries have been influenced by austerity, which has resulted in increasing the private contributions across the three countries. What was previously a generous contribution in Sweden, able to fully cover young people's needs in university, has become a much less sufficient system, with working-class young people struggling to find affordable housing and summer jobs, and with families actively intervening to top up state sources of support to meet the needs of the more privileged young people. While this doesn't mean that European policies in this area are all the same, it certainly provides a warning against the current policy mantra of European HE, which clearly stresses the need to increase private contributions in the future, due to lack of state spending in this area and the foreseen cuts.

After discussing the two main messages that emerge from this book, I consider the implications of these findings for broader debates about the role and nature of HE. Specifically, I challenge perspectives that HE is intrinsically elitist in nature and should remain that way – accessible to only the 'brightest' few. Countering this, I argue that the fact that current HE systems reproduce inequalities doesn't mean we should return to a situation where HE is reserved for the elite. The failures of the current systems of student support pointed out in this book underline the need to review existing policies. In particular, the case of young people in university shows the existing trade-off between configuring HE as an individual investment and having policies that address inequalities. Furthermore, while there is a common European HE strategy behind the economic use of HE, the same cannot be said for European solutions involving the 'social dimensions' of young people's experiences in university. This area is entirely left to national member states. Yet the challenges faced by young people in university during these times of austerity are common across Europe, as is the difficulty they have in sustaining their independence through the labour market. The European integration project doesn't imply a harmonisation of the social side of HE, but indirectly affects its social dimension through austerity policies that reduce state spending. Even before changing policies, the challenge is to redefine the terms of the debate: arguing against the idea that young people in university have smooth and privileged experiences, the political message of this book is that HE is the battleground where inequalities are most reproduced for young people in European societies at present.

Two messages

The research presented in this book aims to put forward two messages. First, university can be a very difficult experience for some young people, while it continues to be a smooth and great experience for others. Second, the way young people have to rely on family and labour market sources to fund their university experience creates one of the most pervasive mechanisms of the reproduction of inequalities in contemporary societies.

Diversity of young people's experiences

By presenting the accounts of the young people who participated in this research, this book has shown that young people's experiences in university are not uniform, but can be disaggregated into different profiles. Young people have a negative, mixed or positive experience in university, depending on their present condition and on their wellbeing, which is influenced by their expectations regarding their future transitions to the labour market. Their diverse experiences reflect the persistence of inequality, one explained by structural conditions, that is, the provision of welfare sources and young people's socioeconomic background.

To begin with, young people's experiences are diverse because, outside the lecture room, they have profoundly different financial and housing circumstances. This research has found polarised experiences – at the extreme, between those of profile 1 ('Struggling and hopeless') and profile 5 ('Having a great time'), which reflect in particular financial circumstances and housing conditions. The challenges that some of the profiles face are also connected to young people's psychosocial wellbeing. For example, the difference between young people from profile 1 and those from profile 2 ('Facing difficulties, but with hope for the future') is that while the first have a negative outlook on their future transitions, the latter have positive expectations about life after university, based on the perceived employability of their degrees. For some disadvantaged groups of young people, even the educational experience itself is affected by external conditions.

Welfare mixes and inequalities

The effect of each welfare source on the stratification of young people's experiences has been explored by looking at how experiences are explained by the effects of three highly different welfare mixes in England, Italy and Sweden. Regarding the function of welfare state sources, young people's experiences in relation to the three structural conditions described in Chapter 3 show that the reproduction of inequality in young people's experiences is more evident in welfare mixes where private sources of welfare are more relevant, such as in Italy and England, and less so in Sweden, where the universal system of state support intervenes in 'equalising' young people's experiences in university, but also implies the contribution of private sources of welfare. I have shown how the family is increasingly intervening across the three countries to protect young people by covering the gaps left by the retrenchment of the state.

The reliance on family sources has a direct effect on the reproduction of inequality. Despite the general trend of privatisation, which makes the use of private sources of welfare increasingly important, a cross-national diversity persists: in England and Italy, which assume a higher function of private sources of welfare, the family has a more evident role in stratifying young people's experiences, while in Sweden, where state support is more prominent in protecting young people, the families of young people from higher socioeconomic backgrounds are more likely to provide additional sources to cope with unexpected risks.

The findings show that state financial support has an important effect in limiting the reproduction of inequality among young people, but only when welfare state sources are universal, as in the case of Sweden, rather than means-tested, as in the case of England. On the other hand, the lack of state sources, as in the case of the Italian welfare mix, explains the over-reliance on family sources, and therefore in familistic contexts there is a clear link between young people's backgrounds and their current conditions.

The trend towards the privatisation of social risk for young people in university also makes sources from the labour market very important. The findings show that labour market sources reproduce inequalities, as young people from low socioeconomic backgrounds, across the welfare mixes, need to rely more on precarious jobs, and this affects their experiences in university. Young people who are more 'dependent' on labour market sources are those who lack sources from the state and the family, and the presence of precarious labour market participation for young people in university negatively affects young people's experiences. Given that the labour market is showing a declining capacity to sustain young people's conditions, young people in university who need to rely on precarious short-term jobs are often captured in lived experiences of precarity. Their experience is substantially different from the strategy of their peers who are supported by family sources, who can cherry-pick qualified unpaid experience in the labour market, which will allow them to compete more effectively in the labour market after university.

University was never for everybody?

The findings of this research broadly confirm the idea of the 'broken promise of HE' coming from debates in the US, but also show that in Europe this promise is broken for *some* young people for whom university is very far from being the easy path assumed by HE policies. While this research only explores what happens during university rather than young people's post-university transitions, the strain put on some young people and their families during university is highly likely to have an effect after they graduate. This would make sense given the current difficult reality of graduate labour markets in Europe, where under-employment and youth graduate unemployment are a common experience.[1] The fragmented transitions to the labour market, as shown by existing evidence, are also linked to young people's socioeconomic background, with working-class young people being particularly affected.[2] A recent study from the Institute for Financial Studies conducted in England shows, for example, persisting inequalities in terms of post-graduation income between graduates from high or average income backgrounds.[3]

If university is such a bleak experience for young people from the working classes, why should we still encourage these young people to go to university? The conservative way to interpret these findings would be to argue, as the journalist Julia Hartley-Brewer has in an article for the UK's *The Telegraph* newspaper,[4] that university was never meant for everybody, and that young people deserve more than the lie of 'university for all'. According to Brewer, young people deserve a university system for the few, which selects only the brightest and guarantees them a future. While rightly criticising the naivety of New Labour's policies and showing that graduates are not always, in fact, employed in graduate jobs, this critique is also rooted in a nostalgic about a past in which universities were truly for the elite. Selecting the elite was, after all, the purpose of universities, according to this view. Absent from this yearning for the past and evocation of the 'meritocratic' principles of education is a recognition that the reservation of HE places for the elite reinforced inequalities by excluding people from working-class backgrounds. In terms of access, mass expanded HE systems have at least diminished some previous class barriers. The problems facing young people today, however, are not in removing barriers to accessing HE, because widening access is not enough to tackle existing inequalities. Even if academia was reserved only for the brightest members of the student population, the elitist approach to HE conflated academic excellence with the middle class. In that system, 'meritocracy' was used simply as a way to confirm the already privileged positions of young people from upper to intermediate and upper socioeconomic backgrounds.

Policies have largely overestimated the capacity of HE to generate returns in the labour market. The other problem is that the systems in many respects still operate to confirm existing inequalities, rather than being platforms for 'changing mobility', as the liberal view seems to suggest. The way inequalities are reproduced is a bit more subtle now: when Bourdieu and Passeron conducted their studies on the reproduction of inequality in university, there were a relatively smaller number of working-class young people accessing university.[5] The problem emphasised by the scholars at that time was in the cultural reproduction of inequality, and in how young people from the working classes had a lower cultural capital to mobilise. In many respects, HE culture has become more open to the idea of non-traditional students entering university. The mechanism of reproduction of inequality doesn't really entail the issue of transmitting culture across the privileged sections of society, but concerns the material transmission of inequality, a process created when some young people have fewer resources to properly participate in HE.

Social investment or addressing inequalities?

The specific policies behind HE expansion explain why current welfare states are not addressing the rise of inequality. As pointed out in Part 1, university is increasingly being promoted as a form of social investment in human capital. European and national policies consider HE to be an individual investment, which implies a private co-contribution from young people and/or their families.

The trend of austerity affecting European welfare states since the crisis of 2008 has reinforced these trends by enhancing the privatisation of risk. If risks have to be managed at the individual and family level, this creates patterns of stratification among the youth population. The research presented in previous pages has pointed out the crucial role that private sources of welfare play in shaping young people's lives in university at present and in reinforcing existing inequalities, in particular for participants from England and Italy, where welfare state interventions are, respectively, highly means-tested and extremely residual. For participants in Sweden, universal welfare state support limits the potential effects of stratification that derive from a reliance on private sources of welfare, although it doesn't eliminate them, and other sources are increasingly used to complement state sources. The social investment strategy has already been criticised for its lack of focus on stratification and class by scholars who look at poverty policies.[6] This criticism also holds for the effects that social investment policies have on young people in university. In the area of HE, few policies seem to currently acknowledge the existence of a trade-off between enhancing individual contributions in HE and diminishing inequalities.

It is interesting to note that this fallacy is also present in Piketty's work, which addresses the current rise of inequality across Europe. Among the solutions proposed by the French scholar, one is enhancing social investment in HE, as student funding is rightly described as one of the crucial areas through which rising inequalities can be tackled. While the analysis is correct, the proposed solution of enhancing social investment in HE[7] neglects the negative effects of an individualised approach to HE. Even though Piketty's analysis shows that the intergenerational transmission of family wealth increases inequality, his policy proposals largely underplay the role that welfare states could play for young people who rely on family sources during HE. One could argue that there are different versions of social investment. If policies genuinely want to address the increasing inequality among young people, investment in HE should be framed as a *public* form of investment from the state, rather than an *individual* investment required by young people and their families to secure economic returns from the labour market. Unfortunately the recent agenda for a social investment welfare state put forward by part of the European social policy community seems to neglect the negative effects of previous social investment policies on young people, which have been illustrated in this study.[8] Another leading progressive scholar, Jacob Hacker, has instead discussed how the privatisation of university costs increases inequalities in the US.[9] The policy strategy of pre-distribution he developed aims at tackling inequalities before entrance to the labour market, and stipulates that interventions for young people in university are a crucial area in this respect.

European problems and national solutions?

The findings of this study add to these debates by pointing out the negative effects of the overall privatisation of welfare in HE that reproduces young people's inequalities, and by identifying the universal system of student support in HE as a tool that is able to limit the reproduction of inequalities for young people in university.

One of the limits of the current policies framing HE as a form of investment in human capital is that they imply an artificial separation between social policy interventions and HE policies. This research shows that young people have specific needs in university that concern the social policy of university and not simply the area of intervention in education policy. Due to the extended phase of semi-dependence in their housing and finances reported in this study, it is possible to argue that social policy interventions in HE are 'a vehicle' to address the welfare of young people, just as school policies have been a way to address children's needs beyond education.[10] Policies that aim to limit inequalities in youth transitions today have to 'rebalance' the distribution of welfare sources by intervening in different areas.

There are several recommendations for policy that emerge from the findings of this study:

- Employment precarity should be tackled by increasing the stability and security of wages to improve the capacity of labour market sources to sustain young people's semi-dependence. Young people in university are in the paradoxical position of being asked to contribute privately to finance their participation in HE by working, but also of being excluded by many existing forms of labour market protection due to their student status. Internships are good examples of such instruments. Including young people in university in existing forms of labour market protection would limit the diffusion of precarity among this category of workers.

- As discussed in Part 3, the best way to limit the reproduction of inequalities among young people in university is to provide a generous and universal form of support. As recently suggested by activists working on unconditional income, young adults in HE could be entitled to a form of unconditional income[11] This would be a much-needed addition to the current focus of EU youth policies in improving skills and training (for example, through the Youth Guarantee).[12]

- If explicit youth policies are largely non-existent across Europe, the lack of attention in housing policies to student housing represents one of the most evident policy gaps. Student housing has developed in recent years without being guided by national or European regulations. This research shows clearly that housing costs contribute in determining very different experiences among young people, and policy interventions in this area could substantially address the issue of inequality among young people in university.

- Young people in university are not only affected by material concerns, but also seem to be particularly interested in issues of wellbeing. Yet welfare services and wellbeing counselling are sharply separated in HE establishments. New policies should address a possible integration of welfare services and wellbeing counselling offered by HE institutions, under the premise that, as shown in this study, there is a link between wellbeing and overall socioeconomic conditions.

Many of the challenges described in this research affect young people cross-nationally. Yet the 'social dimension' of HE is considered to be a national matter in the European HE area. While there is strict European legislation in economic affairs that affects HE spending, HE policies are curiously left without a solid hard law basis to non-binding EU cooperation.[13] Surely a common European approach in tackling these issues would be welcome. However, this requires careful thought, as the current state of EU affairs seems to promote a very specific view of HE and youth policies that is centred on being more economically competitive, rather than on tackling inequalities. For example, the recent report from the European Commission supporting a reform of student support in the direction of an increasing contribution to HE costs from young people and their families epitomises the European trend of cost-containment, and goes in the opposite direction to what should be done to address inequality.[14] There is a serious risk that transferring competences to the EU on student support could result in a race to the bottom for those systems that tend to be more generous, such as the Swedish system. European social policy interventions are actually occurring in the field of youth policy, but it is the shape that they are taking which is puzzling: the Youth Guarantee (2013), implemented through the EU's Youth Employment Initiative (YEI), by targeting NEETs and providing assistance in the form of training and education if a job is not available, is in line with the weak notion of social investment described above, and with a conceptualisation of rigid transitions from education to work. This view tends to exclude forms of protection for young people in university despite the many struggles they face.

Inequalities and 'Generation Y'

While I am writing, *The Guardian* has decided to dedicate a special report on the struggle faced by the so-called 'Generation Y', the same group of young people who participated in this study.[15] The coverage of their struggles in housing and the labour market resonates with *some* of the experiences of the participants of my study. As struggles become more diffused among the youth population, it is inevitable to consider these processes as 'generational characteristics'. Some colleagues even talk about the current cohort of young people as a new social generation with new features.[16] Young people face unprecedented struggles, and yet inequalities within this generation are also rampant. How can these two processes cohabit? There are two processes at stake that tend to be confused when examining Generation Y. The first is a reconfiguration of the positions of the intermediate classes, the so-called 'squeezed middle', or families of ordinary workers, whose cost of living is increasing while the value of their wages decreases.[17] As I have shown in this study, young people from this squeezed middle (that is, from intermediate socioeconomic backgrounds) often need work to compensate for the decrease of family sources, and feel the pressure on their family finances.

The second process in place (neglected by the narrative of 'social generation') is the spreading level of intragenerational inequality that benefits those at the top. Considering the sociological implications of Piketty's work,[18] I have illustrated how young people from upper socioeconomic backgrounds, even if in precarious jobs, are backed up by family resources in the shape of both wealth and income. Having spent most of the last five years of my life reflecting and writing on differences among young people, I find it misleading to place all young people's experiences under the umbrella of 'Generation Y'. Furthermore, I do not think that writing about young people's struggles as generational offers a realistic analytical depiction of the re-configuration of inequality occurring in Europe, which is profoundly influenced by intergenerational relations.

Capturing the zeitgeist to change the terms of the debate

My colleague and mentor Rob MacDonald has correctly warned scholars against exaggerating the effects of the crisis on young people in line with the fashion of 'newism': youth studies scholarship has, after all, witnessed and reported cyclical crises affecting young people for several decades.[19] There are new elements involving young people in university that deserve to be reported: the fact that young people in university (once considered to be a smooth path of transition) are increasingly featured in the reports on young people in crisis constitutes a new element that has only recently started to trigger academic attention. But there is more to that story: my book shows that European policies are ultimately failing young people. Behind the façade of open and fair HE, HE policies have shifted the financial costs of this experience to young people and their families, creating a major driver of inequality.

When my academic journey started in 2009, students (or 'graduates without a future', as they have been dubbed by the media) had not yet taken to the streets of Europe to protest against the austerity reforms affecting the rising costs of HE, as occurred in 2010.[20] I remember having had conversations with an internationally renowned scholar at the London School of Economics who was puzzled by my decision to research this category of young people, hinting at the fact that they were a privileged part of society who did not deserve social policy attention. For anybody who has had direct experience of HE, there was already a palpable feeling that young people's 'smooth transitions' through university, as they were once described by the literature, were starting to be challenged, and deserved scholarly and media attention.

The time has now come to finally change the terms of the debate. If media reports tend to stress that young students are lazy and enter HE to postpone their transition to adult life, this picture seems to be quite far from the reality captured in this book. The delay to independence implied by going to university is a consequence of the current nexus between HE and the labour market, for which young people are expected to gain additional education credentials to compete in the labour market. The level of debt that young people accumulate even before entering university is an element that is entirely new, and is destined to increase. The reality is that even scholars do not know what the implications of the intense personal investment that young people and their families are currently having to make will be for them in a few decades' time.

Possibly the most striking finding of this research is the mismatch between what young people in university told me, and how young people are framed in policy papers. This mismatch is evident reading the latest White Paper setting out the forthcoming HE reforms in England that perpetuates the narrative of HE as individualised social investment.[21] The policy agenda of *Success as a knowledge economy* is designed around an imaginary social world detached from the reality of the demand crisis in the labour market and the struggles faced by the latest cohort of over-indebted English students. European and national policies continue to describe young people as rational individuals who compete in skilled labour markets and enter university in order to gain future returns in the labour market. Certainly the discourse of employability has been internalised by young people, but what I found while collecting data and interviewing young people across the countries is that young people in university have highly benefited from this experience. There isn't the space in this book to cover the role of politics, but through my research, I met many young people who had become critically aware and politically active during university. I concluded all my interviews, asking, 'Was higher education worth it?', a question that challenged young people with financial problems more than the others. Yet, even young people for whom HE did not appear to have been a good 'economic investment' told me that attending university had changed their lives for the better and improved their understanding of the world. Making this experience sustainable from a material point of view and achieving a viable condition of dependence from different sources were some of the top concerns of young people in university. It is, of course, the young people who lack welfare sources who have to spend much of their energy and effort on making HE sustainable from a material point of view, making them paradoxically less able to focus on their *educational* experience. Considering the importance that HE plays in European societies, it would be a destructive policy choice to maintain only the façade of open systems of HE, which masks the existing reality that causes universities to reinforce inequalities.

Notes

Introduction

[1] Poirier, A. (2013) 'Stromae: European youth's favourite misery muse', *The Guardian*, 27 October (www.theguardian.com/music/2013/oct/27/belgian-rapper-stromae-eurozone-disaffected-youth).

[2] Naidoo, R. (2009) 'The "Third Way" to widening participation and maintaining quality in higher education: lessons from the United Kingdom', *The Journal of Educational Enquiry*, vol 1, no 2, pp 24-38.

[3] European Council (2011) 'Council conclusions on the role of education and training in the implementation of the "Europe 2020" strategy', *Official Journal of the European Union*, 2011/C 70/01.

[4] Bohonnek, A., Camilleri, A.F., Griga, D., Mühleck, K., Miklavic, K. and Orr, D. (2010) *Evolving diversity: An overview of equitable access to HE in Europe*, The EQUNET Consortium, Brussels: MENON Network.

[5] Brown, P. and Lauder, H. (2010) *The global auction: The broken promises of education, jobs, and incomes*, New York: Oxford University Press.

[6] Sapir, A., Aghion, P., Bertola, G., Hellwig, M., Pisani-Ferry, J., Vinals, J. and Wallace, H. (2003) *An agenda for a growing Europe: The Sapir report*, Oxford: Oxford University Press.

[7] For an economic discussion about graduate unemployment and under-employment during the recent financial crisis, see Bell, D.N.F. and Blanchflower, D.G. (2011) *Youth unemployment in Europe and the United States*, Bonn: IZA (Institute for the Study of Labor). As I wrote a few years ago, youth unemployment should not just be discussed by presenting youth unemployment rates: Antonucci, L. (2012) 'More than rates: putting youth unemployment in context', *Social Europe*, 30 July (www.socialeurope.eu/2012/07/more-than-rates-putting-youth-employment-in-context/). In Chapter 1 I place youth unemployment within the broader context of social policy reforms and changes to youth semi-dependence.

[8] Eurofound (2014) *Mapping youth transitions in Europe*, Luxembourg: Publications Office of the European Union (www.eurofound.europa.eu/sites/default/files/ef_publication/field_ef_document/ef1392en_0.pdf).

[9] Sedghi, A. (2013) 'Survey lays bare European graduates' hopes and fears', *The Guardian*, 2 July (www.theguardian.com/world/datablog/2013/jul/02/survey-european-graduates-hopes-fears).

[10] Cedefop (European Centre for the Development of Vocational Training) (2015) *Skills, qualifications and jobs in the EU: The making of a perfect match? Evidence from Cedefop's European skills and jobs survey*, Cedefop Reference Series 103, Luxembourg: Cedefop.

[11] Hamilton, M., Antonucci, L. and Roberts, S. (2014) 'Introduction: Young people and social policy in Europe', in L. Antonucci, M. Hamilton and S. Roberts (eds) *Young people and social policy in Europe: Dealing with risk, inequality and precarity in times of crisis*, Work and Welfare in Europe, Basingstoke: Palgrave Macmillan, pp 3-12.

[12] *The Guardian* (2015) 'Millennials. The perfect storm of debt, housing and joblessness facing a generation of young adults – and what is to be done' (www.theguardian.com/world/series/millennials-the-trials-of-generation-y).

[13] On the construction of the economic crisis, see Clarke, J. and Newman, J. (2012) 'The alchemy of austerity', *Critical Social Policy*, vol 32, no 2, pp 299-319.

[14] *The Wall Street Journal* (2012) 'The Euro Crisis. Q&A: ECB President Mario Draghi', 23 February (http://blogs.wsj.com/eurocrisis/2012/02/23/qa-ecb-president-mario-draghi/).

[15] Willetts, D. (2010) *The pinch. How the baby boomers took their children's future – And why they should give it back*, London: Atlantic Books.

[16] David Blanchflower has been very vocal in showing how austerity is damaging youth employment; see, for example, Blanchflower, D. (2015) 'David Blanchflower: Young people are suffering from austerity in the UK as well as in Greece', *The Independent*, 1 February (www.independent.co.uk/news/business/comment/david-blanchflower/david-blanchflower-young-people-are-suffering-from-austerity-in-the-uk-as-well-as-in-greece-10016988.html).

[17] Antonucci, L., Hamilton, M. and Roberts, S. (2014) *Young people and social policy in Europe: Dealing with risk, inequality and precarity in times of crisis*, Work and Welfare in Europe, Basingstoke: Palgrave Macmillan.

[18] European Commission (2014) *Do changes in cost-sharing have an impact on the behaviour of students and higher education institutions? Evidence from nine case studies, vol 1*, Luxembourg: Publications Office of the European Union (http://ec.europa.eu/education/library/study/2014/cost-sharing/comparative-report_en.pdf).

[19] I address some of these limitations in my co-edited book (see note 17).

[20] Maria's real name has been changed, as for all the other participants in this study (in line with the confidentiality policy described in the 'Ethics' section of the Annex).

[21] Laudisa, F. (2015) 'Diritto allo Studio Universitario: non si chiede mica la luna (nella Stabilità)', *ROARS: Return on Academic Research*, 23 November (www.roars.it/online/diritto-allo-studio-universitario-non-si-chiede-mica-la-luna-nella-stabilita/).

[22] Trow (2006) op cit.

[23] The 'cultural capital' approach has dominated classical studies of inequality in HE, such as Reay, D., Crozier, G. and Clayton, J. (2010) '"Fitting in" or "standing out": working-class students in UK higher education', *British Educational Research Journal*, vol 32, no 1, pp 1-19; Reay, D., David, M.E. and Ball, S.J. (2005) *Degrees of choice: Class, race, gender and higher education*, London: Trentham Books; Archer, L., Hutchings, M. and Ross, A. (2005) *Higher education and social class: Issues of exclusion and inclusion*, London: Routledge; Thomas, L. and Quinn, J. (2006) *First generation entry into higher education*, Maidenhead: Open University Press. There are also most recent studies applying a cultural understanding of inequality in HE, notably, the Paired Peers project conducted by colleagues: Bradley, H., Abrahams, J., Bathmaker, A.-M., Beedell, P., Hoare, T., Ingram, N., Mellor, J. and Waller, R. (2013) *The Paired Peers project year 3 report: A degree generation?*. And finally, Finnegan, F., Merrill, B. and Thunburg, C. (eds) (2014) *Student voices on inequalities in European higher education: Challenges for theory, policy and practice in a time of change*, London: Routledge. My focus in this book is on the material, rather than the cultural, triggers of inequality.

[24] Mele, S. and Sciclone, N. (2006) 'Le ragioni economiche, un problema di pari opportunità', in L. Biggeri and G. Catalano, *L'efficacia delle politiche di sostegno agli studenti universitari*, Bologna: Il Mulino.

[25] A comparative discussion of institutional stratification in HE is provided in Shavit (2007) op cit.

[26] Two books by these authors have been particularly influential in youth theory: Giddens, A. (1991) *Modernity and self-identity: Self and society in late modern age*, London: Polity Press/Basil Blackwell; Beck, U. (1992) *Risk society: Towards a new modernity*, New Delhi: Sage.

[27] Arnett, J. (2000) 'Emerging adulthood: A theory of development from the late teens through the twenties', *American Psychologist*, vol 55, pp 469-80.

[28] du Bois-Reymond, M. and Lopez Blasco, A. (2003) 'Risks and contradictions in young people's transitions to work: yo-yo-transitions and misleading trajectories: towards integrated transition policies for young adults in Europe', in A. López Blasco, W. McNeish and W. Andreas (eds) *Young people and contradictions of inclusion: Towards integrated transition policies in Europe*, Bristol: Policy Press, pp 19-41.

[29] See, for example, Roberts, S. and MacDonald, R. (2013) 'Introduction for special section of *Sociological Research Online*: The marginalised mainstream: Making sense of the "missing middle" of youth studies', *Sociological Research Online*, vol 18, no 1, p 21, and the whole issue introduced by the article.

[30] Roberts, K. (2013) 'Education to work transitions: How the old middle went missing and why the new middle remains elusive', *Sociological Research Online*, vol 18, no 1, p 3.

[31] Woodman, D. and Wyn, J. (2014) *Youth and generation: Rethinking change and inequality in the lives of young people*, London: Sage.

[32] Callender, C. (2006) 'Access to higher education in Britain: The impact of tuition fees and financial assistance', in P.N. Teixeira, D.B. Johnstone, M.J. Rosa and H. Vossensteyn (eds) *Cost-sharing and accessibility in higher education: A fairer deal?*, New York: Springer, pp 105-32.

Chapter 1

[1] Trow, M. (2006) 'Reflections on the transition from elite to mass to universal access: forms and phases of higher education in modern societies since WWII', in J.F. Forest and P. Altbach (eds) *International handbook of higher education*, New York: Springer, pp 243-80.

[2] Bohonnek, A., Camilleri, A.F., Griga, D., Mühleck, K., Miklavic, K. and Orr, D. (2010) *Evolving diversity: An overview of equitable access to HE in Europe*, The EQUNET Consortium, Brussels: MENON Network.

[3] Shavit, Y., Arum, R.T., Gamoran, A. and Menahem, G. (2007) *Stratification in higher education: A comparative study*, Stanford, CA: Stanford University Press.

[4] Trondman, M. (1994) *Bilden av en klassresa: Sexton arbetarklassbarn på väg till och i högskolan*, Stockholm: Carlsson; Holmström, O. (2000) *Tre utbildningsberättelser. Arbetarklass-och invandrarstudenters väg till och upplevelse av universitetet*, SOU 2000:47, Stockholm: Statens Offentliga Utredningar (SOU).

[5] Forsyth, A. and Furlong, A. (2003) *Losing out? Socioeconomic disadvantage and experience in further and higher education*, Bristol: Policy Press.

[6] This is stated by Tony Blair himself in BBC News, 'Tony Blair talks to Newsnight – Part 3' (http://news.bbc.co.uk/1/hi/programmes/newsnight/archive/1988874.stm).

[7] See Young. M. (2001) 'Down with meritocracy', *The Guardian*, 29 June (www.theguardian.com/politics/2001/jun/29/comment).

[8] Alvesson, M. (2013) *The triumph of emptiness: Consumption, higher education, and work organization*, Oxford: Oxford University Press, p 8.

[9] Deresiewicz, B. (2014) *Excellent sheep: The miseducation of the American elite and the way to a meaningful life*, Los Angeles, CA: Simon & Schuster.

[10] European Council (2000) *Conclusions of the European Council of March 2000*, Brussels: European Council, Articles 25-27.

[11] Ibid.

[12] European Council (2011) 'Council conclusions on the role of education and training in the implementation of the "Europe 2020" strategy', *Official Journal of the European Union*, 2011/C 70/01.

[13] European Commission (2012) *Draft 2012 joint report of the Council and the Commission on the implementation of the renewed framework for European cooperation in the youth field (EU Youth Strategy 2010-2018)*, Brussels: European Commission.

[14] Blair, T. (2005) 'Preface', in *2005 Labour Party manifesto*, London: Labour Party.

[15] Naidoo, R. (2009) 'The "Third Way" to widening participation and maintaining quality in higher education: lessons from the United Kingdom', *The Journal of Educational Enquiry*, vol 1, no 2, pp 24-38.

[16] Ball, S.J. (1997) 'Policy sociology and critical social research: a personal review of recent education policy and policy research', *British Educational Research Journal*, vol 23, no 3, pp 257-74.

[17] Jessop, B. (1993) 'Towards a Schumpeterian workfare state? Preliminary remarks on post-Fordist political economy', *Studies in Political Economy*, vol 40, pp 7-40.

[18] This was first formulated in Hacker, J.S. (2004) 'Privatizing risk without privatizing the welfare state: The hidden politics of social policy retrenchment in the United States', *American Political Science Review*, vol 98, no 2, pp 243-60.

[19] European Commission (2014) *Do changes in cost-sharing have an impact on the behaviour of students and higher education institutions? Evidence from nine case studies, vol 1*, Luxembourg: Publications Office of the European Union (http://ec.europa.eu/education/library/study/2014/cost-sharing/comparative-report_en.pdf).

[20] Skilbeck, M. and O'Connell, H. (2000) *Access and equity in higher education: An international perspective on issues and strategies*, Dublin: Higher Education Authority.

[21] Basit, T. and Tomlinson, S. (eds) (2012) *Social inclusion and higher education*, Bristol: Policy Press.

[22] European Council (2011) op cit.

[23] Bessant, J. and Watts, R.W. (2014) '"Cruel optimism": a southern theory perspective on the European Union's Youth Strategy, 2008-2012', *International Journal of Adolescence and Youth*, vol 19, suppl 1, pp 125-40.

[24] Piketty, T. (2014) *Capital in the twenty-first century*, Cambridge, MA: Harvard University Press; Piketty, T. (2014) *The future of inequality: Making progressive politics work*, London: Policy Network.

[25] van de Werfhorst H. and Shavit, Y. (2015) 'The limits of education's impact on equality', World Education Blog, 22 January (https://efareport.wordpress.com/2015/01/22/the-limits-of-educations-impact-on-equality/).

[26] Keep, E. and Mayhew, K. (2010) 'Moving beyond skills as a social and economic panacea', *Work, Employment & Society*, vol 24, no 3, pp 565-77.

[27] Ainley, P. and Allen, M. (2010) *Lost generation? New strategies for youth and education*, London: Continuum; Ainley, P. and Allen, M. (2013) 'Running up a down-escalator in the middle of a class structure gone pear-shaped', *Sociological Research Online*, vol 18, no 1, p 8.

[28] IFS (Institute for Fiscal Studies) (2016) 'What and where you study matter for graduate earnings – but so does parents' income', Press release, 13 April (www.ifs.org.uk/uploads/publications/pr/graduate_earnings_130416.pdf).

[29] Bourdieu, P. and Passeron, J.D. (1977) *Reproduction in education, society and culture*, London: Sage.

[30] van de Werfhorst and Shavit (2015) op cit.

[31] Coles, B. (1995) *Youth and social policy: Youth citizenship and young careers*, London: UCL Press.

[32] Arnett, J.J. (2006) *Emerging adulthood: The winding road from the late teens through the twenties*, Oxford: Oxford University Press.

[33] Berrington, A., Stone, J. and Falkingham, J. (2009) 'The changing living arrangements of young adults in the UK', *Population Trends*, vol 138, no 1, pp 27-37.

[34] Coles (1995) op cit.

[35] Biggart, A. and Walther, A. (2006) 'Coping with yo-yo transitions: young adults' struggle for support, between family and state in comparative perspective', in C. Leccardi and E. Ruspini (eds) *A new youth? Young people, generations and family life*, Aldershot: Ashgate, pp 41-62.

[36] This is based on three sources: Pechar, H. and Andres, L. (2011) 'Higher education policies and welfare regimes: International comparative

perspectives', *Higher Education Policy*, vol 24, no 1, pp 25-52; Willemse, N. and de Beer, P. (2012) 'Three worlds of educational welfare states? A comparative study of higher education systems across welfare states', *Journal of European Social Policy*, vol 22, no 2, pp 105-17; Schwarz, S. and Rehburg, M. (2004) 'Study costs and direct public student support in 16 European countries – Towards a European higher education area?', *European Journal of Education*, vol 39, no 4, pp 521-32.

[37] Furlong, A. and Cartmel, F. (1997) *Young people and social change: Individualization and risk in late modernity*, Buckingham: Open University Press.

[38] Jones, G. and Wallace, C. (1992) *Youth, family and citizenship*, Milton Keynes: Open University Press.

[39] Furlong, A. and Cartmel, F. (2009) *Higher education and social justice*, Maidenhead: Open University Press.

[40] van de Velde, C. (2008) *Devenir adulte. Sociologie comparée de la jeunesse en Europe*, Paris: Presses Universitaires de France; Micheli, G. and Rosina, A. (2010) 'The vulnerability of young adults on leaving the parental home', in C. Ranzi (ed) *Social vulnerability in Europe: The new configuration of social risks*, Basingstoke: Palgrave Macmillan, pp 189-218.

[41] Leccardi, C. and Ruspini, E. (eds) (2006) *A new youth? Young people, generations and family life*, Aldershot: Ashgate; Moreno, A. (2012) 'The transition to adulthood in Spain in a comparative perspective: The incidence of structural factors', *Young*, vol 20, no 1, pp 19-48.

[42] Laaksonen, H. (2000) *Young adults in changing welfare states: Prolonged transitions and delayed entries for under-30s in Finland, Sweden and Germany in the '90s*, MZES Working Papers 01/2000, Mannheim: Mannheimer Zentrum für Europäische Sozialforschung (MZES).

[43] Forsyth and Furlong (2003) op cit.

[44] This is a topic that has been overlooked, but Claire Callender has done excellent work in this area. See, for example, Callender, C. (2003) *Attitudes to debt: School leavers and further education students' attitudes to debt and their impact on participation in higher education: A report for Universities UK and HEFCE*, London: Universities UK.

[45] Aassve, A., Billari, F.C., Mazzuco, S. and Ongaro, F. (2001) *Leaving home ain't easy. A comparative longitudinal analysis of ECHP data*, MPIDR Working Paper, Rostock: Max Planck Institute for Demographic Research (MPIDR).

[46] Rhodes, D. (1999) 'Students and housing', in J. Rugg (ed) *Young people, housing and social policy*, London: Taylor & Francis, pp 65-85.

[47] Rugg, J., Rhodes, D. and Jones, A. (2002) 'Studying a niche market: UK students and the private rented sector', *Housing Studies*, vol 17, no 2, pp 289-303; Clapham, D., Buckley, K., Mackie, P., Orford, S. and Stafford, I. (2010) *Young people and housing in 2020: Identifying key drivers for change*, York: Joseph Rowntree Foundation.

[48] Holdsworth, C. (2006) '"Don't you think you're missing out, living at home?" Student experiences and residential transitions', *The Sociological Review*, vol 54, no 3, pp 495-519; Holdsworth, C. and Morgan, D. (2005) *Transitions in context: Leaving home, independence and adulthood*, Buckingham: Open University Press.

[49] Thomsen, J. (2007) 'Home experiences in student housing: about institutional character and temporary homes', *Journal of Youth Studies*, vol 10, no 5, pp 577-96; Cairns, D. (2011) 'Youth, precarity and the future: undergraduate housing transitions in Portugal during the economic crisis', *Sociologia, Problemas y Praticas*, vol 66, pp 9-25.

[50] El Ansari, W., Stock, C., Snelgrove, S., Hu, X., Parke, S., Davies, S. et al (2011) 'Feeling healthy? A survey of physical and psychological wellbeing of students from seven universities in the UK', *International Journal of Environmental Research and Public Health*, vol 8, no 5, pp 1308-23.

[51] Christensson, A., Runeson, B., Dickman, P. and Vaez, M. (2010) 'Change in depressive symptoms over higher education and professional establishment – a longitudinal investigation in a national cohort of Swedish nursing students', *BMC Public Health*, vol 10, no 1, p 343.

[52] Yorke, M. and Longden, B. (2008) *The first year experience of higher education in the UK*, York: Higher Education Academy; Fisher, S. (1994) *Stress in academic life: The mental assembly line*, Milton Keynes: Open University Press.

[53] Cotton, S.J., Dollard, M.F. and de Jonge, J. (2002) 'Stress and student job design: Satisfaction, well-being, and performance in university students', *International Journal of Stress Management*, vol 9, no 3, pp 147-62; Tobin, P. and Carson, J. (1994) 'Stress and the student social worker', *Social Work and Social Sciences Review*, vol 5, pp 246-55.

[54] Roberts, R., Golding, J., Towell, T. and Weinreb, I. (1999) 'The effects of economic circumstances on British students' mental and physical health', *Journal of American College Health*, vol 48, no 3, pp 103-9.

[55] Furlong, A. and Cartmel, F. (2006) *Young people and social change: New perspectives*, Maidenhead: Open University Press.

[56] Jones, J.R. (2010) 'So just what is the student experience?', Society for Research into Higher Education (SRHE) Annual Research Conference,

Newport, Wales; Brennan, J. and Osborne, M. (2008) 'Higher education's many diversities: of students, institutions and experiences; and outcomes?', *Research Papers in Education*, vol 23, no 2, pp 179-90.

[57] Grove, J. (2014) (2014) 'National Student Survey 2014 results show record levels of satisfaction', *Times Higher Education*, 12 August (www.timeshighereducation.com/news/national-student-survey-2014-results-show-record-levels-of-satisfaction/2015108.article).

[58] Ainley, P. (2008) 'The varieties of student experience – an open research question and some ways to answer it', *Studies in Higher Education*, vol 33, no 5, pp 615-24.

[59] Humphrey, R. (2006) 'Pulling structured inequality into higher education: the impact of part-time working on English university students', *Higher Education Quarterly*, vol 60, no 3, pp 270-86; Metcalf, H. (2003) 'Increasing inequality in higher education: The role of term-time working', *Oxford Review of Education*, vol 29, no 3, pp 315-29.

[60] Forsyth and Furlong (2003) op cit.

[61] Tinto, V. (2006) 'Research and practice of student retention: what next?', *Journal of College Student Retention: Research, Theory and Practice*, vol 8, no 1, pp 1-19; Tinto, V. and Pusser, B. (2006) *Moving from theory to action: Building a model of institutional action for student success*, National Postsecondary Education Cooperative (NPEC), Washington, DC: Department of Education.

Chapter 2

[1] Pechar, H. and Andres, L. (2011) 'Higher education policies and welfare regimes: International comparative perspectives', *Higher Education Policy*, vol 24, no 1, pp 25-52, p 32.

[2] Trow, M. (2006) 'Reflections on the transition from elite to mass to universal access: forms and phases of higher education in modern societies since WWII', in J.F. Forest and P. Altbach (eds) *International handbook of higher education*, New York: Springer, pp 243-80, p 266.

[3] Salmi, J. and Hauptman, A.M. (2006) *Innovations in tertiary education financing: A comparative evaluation of allocation mechanisms*, Education Working Paper Series, Washington, DC: The World Bank, p 2.

[4] McGettigan, A. (2013) *The great university gamble*, London: Pluto Press.

[5] Hacker, J.S. (2004) 'Privatizing risk without privatizing the welfare state: The hidden politics of social policy retrenchment in the United States', *American Political Science Review*, vol 98, no 2, pp 243-60.

[6] Callender, C. (2006) 'Access to higher education in Britain: The impact of tuition fees and financial assistance', in P.N. Teixeira, D.B. Johnstone, M.J. Rosa and H. Vossensteyn (eds) *Cost-sharing and accessibility in higher education: A fairer deal?*, New York: Springer, pp 105-32.

[7] Esping-Andersen, G. (1990) *The three worlds of welfare capitalism*, Cambridge: Polity Press.

[8] Schwarz, S. and Rehburg, M. (2004) 'Study costs and direct public student support in 16 European countries – Towards a European higher education area?', *European Journal of Education*, vol 39, no 4, pp 521-32.

[9] Willemse, N. and de Beer, P. (2012) 'Three worlds of educational welfare states? A comparative study of higher education systems across welfare states', *Journal of European Social Policy*, vol 22, no 2, pp 105-17, p 13.

[10] Schwarz and Rehburg (2004) op cit.

[11] OECD (Organisation for Economic Co-operation and Development) (2013) *Education at a Glance 2013*, Paris: OECD Publishing, p 229.

[12] National Committee of Inquiry into Higher Education (1997) *Higher education in the learning society* (the Dearing Report), London: HMSO.

[13] Lunt, I. (2008) 'Beyond tuition fees? The legacy of Blair's government to higher education', *Oxford Review of Education*, vol 34, no 6, pp 741-52, p 744.

[14] Callender (2006) op cit.

[15] OECD (2013) op cit, p 228.

[16] Reuterberg, S.-E. and Svensson, A. (1987) *Studiemedel-medel för jämlikhet? En granskning av studiemedelssystemets effekter under en tjugoårsperiod*, Stockholm: UHÄ.

[17] Eurydice (1999) *Key topics in education: Financial support for students in higher education in Europe, Trends and debates*, Luxembourg: European Commission.

[18] CSN (Centrala studiestödsnämnden) (2013) 'Beviljning av studiestöd 2012/13' (www.scb.se/sv_/Hitta-statistik/Publiceringskalender/Visa-detaljerad-information/?publobjid=23055+).

[19] Government of Sweden (2013) 'Financial aid for studies', Stockholm: Government Offices of Sweden (www.government.se/sb/d/2098/a/69849).

[20] OECD (2013) op cit, p 229.

[21] Prato, F. (2006) 'Il sostegno agli studenti universitari: gli strumenti e le risorse', in L. Biggeri and G. Catalano (eds) *L'efficacia delle politiche di sostegno*

agli studenti universitari. L'esperienza italiana nel panorama internazionale, Bologna: Il Mulino, pp 69-90.

[22] OECD (2013) op cit, p 228.

[23] Blanden, J. and Machin, S. (2004) 'Educational inequality and the expansion of UK higher education', *Scottish Journal of Political Economy*, vol 51, no 2, pp 230-49.

[24] Goodman, A. and Kaplan, G. (2003) *'Study now, pay later' Or 'HE for free?' An assessment of alternative proposals for higher education finance*, London: Institute for Fiscal Studies.

[25] Blanden and Machin (2004) op cit.

[26] Callender (2006) op cit.

[27] Laudisa, F. (2012a) 'I prestiti universitari in Italia: le ragioni del fallimento passato (e futuro)', *ROARS: Return on Academic Research*, 4 June (www.roars. it/online/i-prestiti-universitari-in-italia-le-ragioni-del-fallimento-passato-e-futuro/#_ftn2).

[28] Laudisa, F. (2012b) 'I prestiti universitari in Italia: le ragioni del fallimento passato (e futuro)', *ROARS: Return on Academic Research*, 4 June (www.roars. it/online/i-prestiti-universitari-in-italia-le-ragioni-del-fallimento-passato-e-futuro/#_ftn2).

[29] SOU (1963a) *Studentrekrytering och studentekonomi. Studiesociala utredningen II*, Stockholm: Statens offentliga utredningar (SOU); Reuterberg and Svensson (1987) op cit.

[30] Svensson, A. (1984) *Vad skall vi göra åt studiemedlen?*, Stockholm: UHÄ; SOU (1963b) *Rätt till studiemedel. Studiesociala utredningen IV*, Stockholm: Statens offentliga utredningar (SOU).

[31] Government of Sweden (2013) op cit.

[32] Callender (2006) op cit.

[33] National Committee of Inquiry into Higher Education (1997) op cit.

[34] CSN (2013) op cit.

[35] Eurostudent (2011) *Social and economic conditions of student life in Europe, National profile of Italy*, Hannover: Eurostudent (https://eurostudent.his.de/eiv/report/data_overview.jsp?ssid=9E5B2422A2AD957CFF3D7E2C83EA5340&sel_lang=&cnt_oid=10).

[36] Laudisa, F. (2006) 'Il diritto allo studio universitario e la riforma costituzionale: verso i livelli essenziali delle prestazioni', in L. Biggeri and

G. Catalano (eds) *L'efficacia delle politiche di sostegno agli studenti universitari. L'esperienza italiana nel panorama internazionale*, Bologna: Il Mulino, pp 45-68.

[37] Prato (2006) op cit.

[38] Bohonnek, A., Camilleri, A.F., Griga, D., Mühleck, K., Miklavic, K. and Orr, D. (2010) *Evolving diversity: An overview of equitable access to HE in Europe*, The EQUNET Consortium, Brussels: MENON Network.

[39] Prato (2006) op cit., p 72.

[40] Laudisa, F. (2012b) 'Spending review e tasse universitarie: quale relazione?', *ROARS: Return on Academic Research*, 30 July (www.roars.it/online/spending-review-e-tasse-universitarie-quale-relazione/).

[41] Laudisa, F. (2015) 'Diritto allo Studio Universitario: non si chiede mica la luna (nella Stabilità)', *ROARS: Return on Academic Research*, 23 November (www.roars.it/online/diritto-allo-studio-universitario-non-si-chiede-mica-la-luna-nella-stabilita/).

[42] Eurostudent (2011) *Social and economic conditions of student life in Europe, National profile of England/Wales*, Hannover: Eurostudent (https://eurostudent. his.de/eiv/report/data_overview.jsp?ssid=9E5B2422A2AD957CFF3D7E2C 83EA5340&sel_lang=&cnt_oid=23).

[43] BIS (Department for Business, Innovation & Skills) (2011) *Future students. Paying for university in 2012/2013. Financial support for full-time students*, London: BIS (http://webarchive.nationalarchives.gov.uk/20121212135622/http://www.bis.gov.uk/assets/biscore/higher-education/docs/t/11-789-thinking-of-uni-2012-financial-support.pdf).

[44] BIS (Department for Business, Innovation & Skills) (2013) *Student Income and Expenditure Survey 2011/12*, London: BIS (www.gov.uk/government/uploads/system/uploads/attachment_data/file/301467/bis-14-723-student-income-expenditure-survey-2011-12.pdf).

[45] Eurydice (2011) *Modernisation of higher education in Europe: Funding and the social dimension*, Brussels: Education, Audiovisual and Culture Executive Agency, p 12.

[46] Taylor-Gooby, P. (2013) *The double crisis of the welfare state and what we can do about it*, Basingstoke: Palgrave Macmillan.

[47] The government bill, 'Competing on the basis of quality – tuition fees for foreign students', passed in 2009, establishes that HE remains free of charge for Swedish citizens and citizens of an EU/EEA state or Switzerland, but that tuition fees have to be paid by third-country students as of the autumn term 2011. See Government of Sweden (2009) *Konkurrera med kvalitet – studieavgifter*

för utländska studenter [*Competing on the basis of quality – tuition fees for foreign students*], Prop 2009/10:65, Stockholm: Government Offices of Sweden.

[48] CSN (2013) op cit.

[49] CSN (Centrala studiestödsnämnden) (2012) *Studerandes ekonomiska och sociala situation 2011* (www.csn.se/polopoly_fs/1.1246!/Rapport%20-%20 Med%20framsida.pdf).

[50] CSN (2012) op cit., p 5.

[51] 30 December 2010, no 240 (2010) 'Norme in materia di organizzazione delle università, di personale accademico e reclutamento, nonché delega al Governo per incentivare la qualità e l'efficienza del sistema universitario', *Gazzetta Ufficiale.*

[52] Antonucci, L. (2011) 'University students in transition to adult age. Comparing Italy and England', *Italian Journal of Social Policy*, vol 15, no 3, pp 271-89.

[53] CONSAP (Concessionaria Servizi Assicurativi Pubblici) (2011) *Fondo per lo studio – 'Fondo per il credito ai giovani'*, Rome: CONSAP (www.diamoglifuturo. it/%C2%A7en-US/fondo-studio).

[54] 7 August 2012, no 135 (2012) 'Disposizioni urgenti per la revisione della spesa pubblica con invarianza dei servizi ai cittadini', *Gazzetta Ufficiale.*

[55] AlmaLaurea (2011) *XII Profilo dei laureati italiani: l'istruzione universitaria nell'ultimo decennio: all'esordio della European higher education area*, Bologna: Il Mulino.

[56] Laudisa (2012b) op cit.

[57] Squires, N. (2012) 'Italian minister under fire for saying students who drag out degrees are "losers"', *The Telegraph*, 25 January (www.telegraph.co.uk/ news/worldnews/europe/italy/9038146/Italian-minister-under-fire-for-saying-students-who-drag-out-degrees-are-losers.html).

[58] Eurydice (2011) op cit, p 78.

[59] Laudisa, F. (2013) 'Borse di studio: è vero che il governo Letta ha «invertito la tendenza»?', *ROARS: Return on Academic Research*, 15 November (www. roars.it/online/decreto-istruzione-si-torna-a-investire-sul-dsu/).

[60] Laudisa (2015) op cit.

[61] Eurostudent (2015) Eurostudent database, 'Public support and payment of fees to institutions of higher education for Bachelor students (Italy)' (http:// database.eurostudent.eu/87#countries%5B%5D=13).

[62] Laudisa, F. (2014) 'Istruzione universitaria: lasciare o raddoppiare?', *ROARS: Return on Academic Research*, 8 May (www.roars.it/online/istruzione-universitaria-lasciare-o-raddoppiare/).

[63] Barr, N. (2012) 'The higher education White Paper: The good, the bad, the unspeakable – and the next White Paper', *Social Policy & Administration*, vol 46, no 5, pp 483-508.

[64] Browne, J. (2010) *Securing a sustainable future for higher education: An independent review of higher education funding and student finance* (www.gov.uk/government/uploads/system/uploads/attachment_data/file/31999/10-1208-securing-sustainable-higher-education-browne-report.pdf).

[65] McGettigan (2013) op cit.

[66] BIS (2011) op cit.

[67] McGettigan (2013) op cit.

[68] BIS (2013) op cit.

[69] BIS (2011) op cit.

[70] BIS (2011) op cit.

[71] UCAS (2012) *How have applications for full-time undergraduate higher education in the UK changed in 2012?* (www.ucas.com/sites/default/files/ucas_how_have_applications_changed_in_2012.pdf).

[72] McGettigan (2013) op cit, p 25.

[73] See Walker, P. and Paige, J. (2010) 'Student protests – as they happened', *The Guardian*, 9 December (www.theguardian.com/education/blog/2010/dec/09/student-protests-live-coverage).

[74] BIS (2013) op cit.

[75] The Sutton Trust (2016) *Degrees of debt, Funding and finance for undergraduates in Anglophone countries*, April (www.suttontrust.com/wp-content/uploads/2016/04/DegreesofDebt.pdf).

[76] BIS (Department for Business, Innovation & Skills) (2015) *Higher education: Student finance equality analysis – The Education (Student Support) (Amendment) Regulations 2015*, London: BIS (www.gov.uk/government/uploads/system/uploads/attachment_data/file/482110/bis-15-639-student-finance-equality-analysis.pdf).

[77] BIS (2015) op cit.

[78] The Sutton Trust (2016) op cit.

[79] Garner, R. (2015) 'Budget 2015: Universities will be allowed to raise fees beyond £9,000, says George Osborne', *The Independent*, 8 July (www.independent.co.uk/news/uk/politics/budget-2015-universities-will-be-allowed-to-raise-fees-beyond-9000-says-george-osborne-10375910.html).

[80] BIS (Department for Business, Innovation & Skills) (2016) *Success as a knowledge economy. Teaching excellence, social mobility and student choice*, London: BIS (www.gov.uk/government/uploads/system/uploads/attachment_data/file/523396/bis-16-265-success-as-a-knowledge-economy.pdf).

Chapter 3

[1] Stiglitz, J.E. (2015) 'The great divide', video presentation, 19 May, London School of Economics and Political Science (www.lse.ac.uk/newsAndMedia/videoAndAudio/channels/publicLecturesAndEvents/player.aspx?id=3085).

[2] In conducting this analysis I am presenting the results of the IV Round of the Eurostudent survey, the last comparative source of data. When possible, and relevant, I refer to the latest round of the Eurostudent (Eurostudent V, published in 2015). This last round has not been used in the analysis as, first, it does not include England; second, this round does not distinguish between the three educational backgrounds of students; third, there is a disclaimer on the comparability of the European data; and fourth, it only presents students' sources of income for students not living with their parents.

[3] Antonucci, L., Hamilton, M. and Roberts, S. (eds) (2014) *Young people and social policy in Europe: Dealing with risk, inequality and precarity in times of crisis*, Work and Welfare in Europe, Basingstoke: Palgrave Macmillan.

[4] Swedish Government (2013) 'The Swedish financial aid system for studies' (www.government.se/sb/d/2098/a/69849). See also Shildrick, T., MacDonald, R. and Antonucci, L. (2015) 'Focus: Hard times for youth?', Discover Society, 5 May (http://discoversociety.org/2015/05/05/focus-hard-times-for-youth/).

[5] Esping-Andersen, G. (1990) *The three worlds of welfare capitalism*, Cambridge: Polity Press.

[6] See Connor, H. (2001) 'Deciding for or against participation in higher education: the views of young people from lower social class backgrounds', *Higher Education Quarterly*, vol 55, no 2, pp 204-24; Callender, C. and Jackson, J. (2005) 'Does the fear of debt deter students from higher education?', *Journal of Social Policy*, vol 34, no 4, pp 509-40.

[7] Christie, H. and Munro, M. (2003) 'The logic of loans: students' perceptions of the costs and benefits of the student loan', *British Journal of Sociology of Education*, vol 24, no 5, pp 621-36.

[8] Callender, C. and Kemp, M. (2000) *Changing student finances: Income, expenditure and the take-up of student loans among full- and part-time higher education students in 1998/99*, Research Brief no 213, London: Department for Education and Employment (http://webarchive.nationalarchives. gov.uk/20130401151715/http://www.education.gov.uk/publications/ eOrderingDownload/RB213.pdf); Callender, C. and Wilkinson, D. (2003) *2002/03 Student Income and Expenditure Survey: Students' income, expenditure and debt in 2002/03 and changes since 1998/99*, London: Department for Education and Skills.

[9] Cook, T.D. and Furstenberg, F.F. (2002) 'Explaining aspects of the transition to adulthood in Italy, Sweden, Germany, and the United States: A cross-disciplinary, case synthesis approach', *The Annals of the American Academy of Political and Social Science*, vol 580, no 1, pp 257-87.

[10] Woodrow, M. (1999) 'Student finance: Accessing opportunity', in Independent Committee of Inquiry into Student Finance (ed) *Student finance: Fairness for the future*, Edinburgh: Independent Committee of Inquiry into Student Finance, pp 374-88.

[11] Furlong, A. and Cartmel, F. (2009) *Higher education and social justice*, Maidenhead: Open University Press.

[12] Johnstone, D.B. and Marcucci, P.N. (2007) *Worldwide trends in higher education finance: Cost-sharing, student loans, and the support of academic research*, UNESCO Forum on Higher Education (http://gse.buffalo.edu/org/inthigheredfinance/ files/Publications/foundation_papers/%282007%29_Worldwide_Trends_ in_Higher_Education_Finance_Cost-Sharing_%20Student%20Loans.pdf); Johnstone, D.B. and Marcucci, P.N. (2010) *Financing higher education worldwide: Who pays? Who should pay?*, Baltimore, MD: Johns Hopkins University Press.

[13] Callender and Jackson (2005) op cit.

[14] The most informative analysis is still provided by Esping-Andersen (1990) op cit, pp 23-6.

[15] Korpi, W. and Palme, J. (1998) 'The paradox of redistribution and strategies of equality: Welfare state institutions, inequality, and poverty in the Western countries', *American Sociological Review*, vol 63, no 5, pp 661-87. Although Marx et al (2013) have recently engaged in a critique of the paradox; see Marx, I., Salanauskaite, L. and Verbist, G. (2013) *The paradox of redistribution*

revisited: And that it may rest in peace?, Discussion Paper, Bonn: Institute for the Study of Labor (IZA).

[16] Barr, N. (2001) *The welfare state as piggy bank: Information, risk, uncertainty, and the role of the state*, Oxford: Oxford University Press.

[17] Johnstone, J. and Shroff-Mehta, P. (2001) 'Higher education finance and accessibility: An international comparative examination of tuition and financial assistance policies', in H. Eggins (ed) *Globalization and reform in higher education*, Maidenhead: McGraw Hill Education, pp 32-54.

[18] Jones, G., O'Sullivan, A. and Rouse, J. (2006) 'Young adults, partners and parents: Individual agency and the problems of support', *Journal of Youth Studies*, vol 9, no 4, pp 375-92.

[19] Eurostudent (2015) 'Composition of monthly income by type of housing and characteristics of students (Sweden)' (http://database.eurostudent. eu/76#countries%5B%5D=26).

[20] Eurostudent (2011) *Social and economic conditions of student life in Europe. Synopsis of indicators. Final report, Eurostudent IV 2008/09*, Blefield: Bertelsmann Verlag.

[21] Strömqvist, S. (2006) *Forms of student support in Sweden: Past, present and future*, International Institute for Educational Planning (IIEP), Paris: UNESCO.

[22] Eurostudent (2015) 'Form of housing by characteristics of students (Sweden)' (http://database.eurostudent.eu/56#countries%5B%5D=26).

[23] Eurostudent (2015) 'Recipients of family/partner contribution and importance of income source by characteristics of students (Italy)' (http:// database.eurostudent.eu/81#countries%5B%5D=13).

[24] Ibid.

[25] Ibid.

[26] Ibid.

[27] Eurostudent (2015) 'Form of housing by characteristics of students (II) (Italy)' (http://database.eurostudent.eu/56#countries%5B%5D=13).

[28] Ibid.

[29] Author's analysis of Eurostudent (2011) *Social and economic conditions of student life in Europe, National profile of England/Wales*, Eurostudent IV, Hannover: Eurostudent (https://eurostudent.his.de/eiv/report/data_overview.jsp?ssid =FA2AA479FEE88F3BEEAB88B08BAE72B3&sel_lang=&cnt_oid=23).

[30] BIS (Department for Business, Innovation & Skills) (2013) *Student Income and Expenditure Survey 2011/2012*, London: BIS (www.gov.uk/government/uploads/system/uploads/attachment_data/file/301467/bis-14-723-student-income-expenditure-survey-2011-12.pdf).

[31] The latest Student Income and Expenditure Survey 2014/15, which will provide an assessment of the impact of the 2012/13 changes to student finances, is due to come out in the next few months. In the meantime, all those interested in mapping the changes in student income can consult a less statistically rigorous, but a sociologically interesting project nonetheless, 'Save the Student', at www.savethestudent.org/money/student-money-survey-results.html

[32] BIS (2013) op cit.

[33] Eurostudent (2011) *Social and economic conditions of student life in Europe, National profile of England/Wales*, Eurostudent IV, Hannover: Eurostudent (https://eurostudent.his.de/eiv/report/data_overview.jsp?ssid=FA2AA479FEE88F3BEEAB88B08BAE72B3&sel_lang=&cnt_oid=23).

[34] Humphrey, R. (2006) 'Pulling structured inequality into higher education: the impact of part-time working on English university students', *Higher Education Quarterly*, vol 60, no 3, pp 270-86; Metcalf, H. (2003) 'Increasing inequality in higher education: The role of term-time working', *Oxford Review of Education*, vol 29, no 3, pp 315-29.

[35] Furlong and Cartmel (2009) op cit, p 113.

[36] Eurostat (2009) *Young people – education and employment patterns* (http://ec.europa.eu/eurostat/statistics-explained/index.php/Archive:Young_people_-_education_and_employment_patterns).

[37] Eurostudent (2011) *Social and economic conditions of student life in Europe, National profile of Italy*, Eurostudent IV, Hannover: Eurostudent (https://eurostudent.his.de/eiv/report/data_overview.jsp?ssid=B16C1E22101B327AE571272751BD0B81&sel_lang=&cnt_oid=10).

[38] Ibid.

[39] Eurostudent (2011) *Social and economic conditions of student life in Europe, National profile of England/Wales*, Eurostudent IV, Hannover: Eurostudent (https://eurostudent.his.de/eiv/report/data_overview.jsp?ssid=FA2AA479FEE88F3BEEAB88B08BAE72B3&sel_lang=&cnt_oid=23).

[40] Eurostudent (2015) 'Employment rate during the current semester by characteristics of students (Sweden)' (http://database.eurostudent.eu/89#countries%5B%5D=26).

[41] Eurostat (2009) op cit.

[42] Eurostudent (2015) 'Students' motivation to work by social background (Italy)' (http://database.eurostudent.eu/96#countries%5B%5D=13).

[43] Ibid.

[44] BIS (2013) op cit.

[45] Ibid, p 337.

Chapter 4

[1] Wright Mills, C. (2000) *The sociological imagination*, Oxford: Oxford University Press.

[2] Bynner, J. (2005) 'Rethinking the youth phase of the life course: The case for emerging adulthood?', *Journal of Youth Studies*, vol 8, no 4, pp 367-84.

Chapter 5

[1] Watts, S. and Stenner, P. (2012) *Doing Q methodological research: Theory, method and interpretation*, London: Sage.

[2] Ibid.

[3] Furlong, A. and Cartmel, F. (2006) *Young people and social change: Individualization and risk in late modernity*, Maidenhead: Open University Press, pp 3-8.

[4] Ibid.

Chapter 6

[1] The influence of HE stratification on young people's experiences of university in cultural terms has been best explained by Reay, D., Crozier, G. and Clayton, J. (2009) '"Strangers in paradise"? Working-class students in elite universities', *Sociology*, vol 43, no 6, pp 1103-21; Basit, T. and Tomlinson, S. (eds) (2012) *Social inclusion and higher education*, Bristol: Policy Press.

Part 3

[1] Coles, B. (1995) *Youth and social policy: Youth citizenship and young careers*, London: UCL Press.

[2] Standing, G. (2011) *The precariat: The new dangerous class*, New York: Bloomsbury.

Chapter 7

[1] Arnett, J.J. (2006a) *Emerging adulthood: The winding road from the late teens through the twenties*, Oxford: Oxford University Press.

[2] Dean, H. (2010) *Understanding human need*, Bristol: Policy Press.

[3] Arnett has defended his view against the previously mentioned criticisms by youth sociologists: see Arnett, J.J. (2006b) 'Emerging adulthood in Europe: A response to Bynner', *Journal of Youth Studies*, vol 9, no 1, pp 111-23.

[4] Many studies have stressed the presence of familism in southern European youth policies, for example, Micheli, G. and Rosina, A. (2010) 'The vulnerability of young adults on leaving the parental home', in C. Ranzi (ed) *Social vulnerability in Europe. The new configuration of social risks*, Basingstoke: Palgrave Macmillan, pp 189-218; van de Velde, C. (2008) *Devenir adulte: Sociologie comparée de la jeunesse en Europe*, Paris: Presses Universitaires de France; Moreno, A. (2012) 'The transition to adulthood in Spain in a comparative perspective: The incidence of structural factors', *Young*, vol 20, no 1, pp 19-48; Leccardi, C. and Ruspini, E. (2006) *A new youth? Young people, generations and family life*, London: Ashgate.

[5] Antonucci, L., Hamilton, M. and Roberts, S. (2014) *Young people and social policy in Europe: Dealing with risk, inequality and precarity in times of crisis*, Work and Welfare in Europe, Basingstoke: Palgrave Macmillan.

[6] Chevalier, T. and Palier, B. (2014) 'The dualisation of social policies towards young people in France: Between familism and activation', in L. Antonucci, M. Hamilton and S. Roberts (eds) *Young people and social policy in Europe: Dealing with risk, inequality and precarity in times of crisis*, Work and Welfare in Europe, Basingstoke: Palgrave.

[7] Gentile, A. (2014) 'The impacts of employment instability on transitions to adulthood: The mileuristas young adults in Spain', in L. Antonucci, M. Hamilton and S. Roberts (eds) *Young people and social policy in Europe: Dealing with risk, inequality and precarity in times of crisis*, Work and Welfare in Europe, Basingstoke: Palgrave Macmillan.

[8] See, for example, Brannen, J., Moss, P. and Mooney, A. (2004) *Working and caring over the twentieth century: Change and continuity in four-generation families*, Basingstoke: Palgrave Macmillan; Kohli, M. (1999) 'Private and public transfers between generations: Linking the family and the state', *European Societies*, vol 1, no 1, pp 81-104; Biggart, A., Bendit, R., Cairns, D., Hein, K. and Morch, S. (2010) *Families and transitions in Europe: State of the art report*, FATE, EU Research on Social Sciences and Humanities, Brussels: European Commission.

[9] This is reported by several works: Smith, D.J. and Rutter, M. (1995) 'Time trends in psychosocial disorders of youth', in M. Rutter and D.J. Smith (eds) *Psychosocial disorders in young people: Time trends and their causes*, Chichester: John Wiley & Sons, pp 763-81; Dey, I. and Morris, S. (1999) 'Parental support for young adults in Europe', *Children and Youth Services Review*, vol 21, no 11, pp 915-35; Jones, G., O'Sullivan, A. and Rouse, J. (2006) 'Young adults, partners and parents: Individual agency and the problems of support', *Journal of Youth Studies*, vol 9, no 4, pp 375-92.

[10] Walkerdine, V., Lucey, H. and Melody, J. (2001) *Growing up a girl: Psychosocial explorations of gender and class*, Basingstoke: Palgrave.

[11] I am referring in particular to the ideas presented in Beck, U. (1992) *Risk society: Towards a new modernity*, New Delhi: Sage; Beck, U. and Willms, J. (2004) *Conversations with Ulrich Beck*, Cambridge: Polity Press; Giddens, A. (1991) *Modernity and self-identity: Self and society in late modern age*, London: Polity Press in association with Basil Blackwell.

[12] Bourdieu, P. and Passeron, J.D. (1977) *Reproduction in education, society and culture*, London: Sage.

[13] Thomas Piketty has recently engaged in a conversation with the sociologist Mike Savage in the potential applications of his theories in social sciences: Piketty, T. and Savage, M. (2015) 'Thomas Piketty in conversation with Mike Savage', Theory, Culture & Society Blog, 29 September (www. theoryculturesociety.org/thomas-piketty-in-conversation-with-mike-savage-part-three/).

[14] This is a term coined in Miller, D. (1981) 'The "sandwich" generation: Adult children of the Aging', *Social Work*, vol 26, pp 419-23.

[15] See note 13 above.

[16] Brunton, A., Foster, L., Haux, T. and Deeming, C. (2015) *In defense of welfare 2*, Bristol: Policy Press.

Chapter 8

[1] Arnett, J.J. (2006) *Emerging adulthood: The winding road from the late teens through the twenties*, Oxford: Oxford University Press.

[2] These findings can be found in Eurostudent (2011) *Social and economic conditions of student life in Europe*, Hannover: Eurostudent, p 72 (www.eurostudent.eu/download_files/documents/EIV_Synopsis_of_Indicators.pdf).

[3] Eurostat (2009) *Young people – Education and employment patterns*, Brussels: Eurostat.

[4] ONS (Office for National Statistics) (2016) 'Contracts that do not guarantee a minimum number of hours: March 2016', Newport: ONS (www.ons.gov.uk/employmentandlabourmarket/peopleinwork/earningsandworkinghours/articles/contractsthatdonotguaranteeaminimumnumberofhours/march2016/pdf).

[5] Jones, G. (2016) 'Italy pushes labour flexibility to limit with job vouchers', *Daily Mail*, 11 March (www.dailymail.co.uk/wires/reuters/article-3487460/Italy-pushes-labour-flexibility-limit-job-vouchers.html).

[6] *La Repubblica* (2015) 'Boeri: "I voucher lavoro, la nuova frontiera del precariato"', 29 May (www.repubblica.it/economia/2015/05/29/news/boeri_i_voucher_lavoro_la_nuova_frontiera_del_precariato_-115554918/).

[7] INPS (2015) 'Voucher: il sistema dei buoni lavoro' (www.inps.it/docallegati/Mig/Doc/Informazione/UfficioStampa/Comefareper/Vademecum_voucher_04_2015.pdf).

[8] See Furlong, A. and Cartmel, F. (2005) *Graduates from disadvantaged families: Early labour market experiences*, Bristol: Policy Press; Kahn, L. (2010) 'The long-term labor market consequences of graduating from college in a bad economy', *Labour Economics*, vol 17, no 2, pp 303-16.

[9] Standing, G. (2011) *The precariat: The new dangerous class*, New York: Bloomsbury.

[10] della Porta, D., Silvasti, T., Hänninen, S. and M. Siisiäinen (2015) *The new social division: Making and unmaking precariousness*, Bristol: Policy Press.

[11] Standing (2011) op cit, p 59.

[12] Metcalf, H. (2003) 'Increasing inequality in higher education: The role of term-time working', *Oxford Review of Education*, vol 29, no 3, pp 315-29.

[13] Humphrey, R. (2006) 'Pulling structured inequality into higher education: the impact of part-time working on English university students', *Higher Education Quarterly*, vol 60, no 3, pp 270-86.

[14] This is stated by Furlong, A. and Cartmel, F. (2009) *Higher education and social justice*, Maidenhead: Open University Press, p 123.

[15] Bradley, H., Abrahams, J., Bathmaker, A.-M., Beedell, P., Hoare, T., Ingram, N., Mellor, J. and Waller, R. (2013) *The Paired Peers project year 3 report: A degree generation?* (www.bristol.ac.uk/media-library/sites/spais/migrated/documents/report.pdf

[16] Purcell, K. and Elias, P. (2010) *The impact of paid and unpaid work and of student debt on experience of higher education*, Futuretrack Working Paper 2, Warwick: Institute for Employment Research.

[17] Bradley et al (2013) op cit.

Chapter 9

[1] Eurostudent (2011) *Social and economic conditions of student life in Europe. Synopsis of indicators. Final report, Eurostudent IV 2008/2009*, Blefield: Bertelsmann Verlag (www.eurostudent.eu/download_files/documents/ EIV_Synopsis_of_Indicators.pdf)

[2] Rhodes, D. (1999) 'Students and housing', in J. Rugg (ed) *Young people, housing and social policy*, London: Taylor & Francis, pp 65-85.

[3] This has been described extensively in Chapters 2 and 3. See in particular Schwarz, S. and Rehburg, M. (2004) 'Study costs and direct public student support in 16 European countries – Towards a European higher education area?', *European Journal of Education*, vol 39, no 4, pp 521-32.

[4] Callender, C. and Kemp, M. (2000) *Changing student finances: Income, expenditure and the take-up of student loans among full- and part-time higher education students in 1998/99*, Research Brief no 213, London: Department for Education and Employment (http://webarchive.nationalarchives. gov.uk/20130401151715/http://www.education.gov.uk/publications/ eOrderingDownload/RB213.pdf).

[5] Cook, T.D. and Furstenberg, F.F. (2002) 'Explaining aspects of the transition to adulthood in Italy, Sweden, Germany, and the United States: A cross-disciplinary, case synthesis approach', *The Annals of the American Academy of Political and Social Science*, vol 580, no 1, pp 257-87.

[6] Laurison, D. and Friedman, S. (2015) *Introducing the class ceiling: Social mobility and Britain's elite occupation*, LSE Sociology Department Working Paper Series, London: London School of Economics and Political Science (www.lse.ac.uk/ sociology/pdf/Working-Paper_Introducing-the-Class-Ceiling.pdf).

[7] Callender, C. (2006) 'Access to higher education in Britain: The impact of tuition fees and financial assistance', in P.N. Teixeira, D.B. Johnstone, M.J. Rosa and H. Vossensteyn (eds) *Cost-sharing and accessibility in higher education: A fairer deal?*, New York: Springer, pp 105-32.

[8] Korpi, W. and Palme, J. (1998) 'The paradox of redistribution and strategies of equality: Welfare state institutions, inequality, and poverty in the Western countries', *American Sociological Review*, vol 63, no 5, pp 661-87. See the critical study by Marx, I., Salanauskaite, L. and Verbist, G. (2013) *The paradox*

of redistribution revisited: And that it may rest in peace?, Discussion Paper, Bonn: Institute for the Study of Labor (IZA).

[9] See also the critique by Barr, N. (2001) *The welfare state as piggy bank: Information, risk, uncertainty, and the role of the state*, Oxford: Oxford University Press.

[10] Johnstone, J. and Shroff-Mehta, P. (2001) 'Higher education finance and accessibility: An international comparative examination of tuition and financial assistance policies', in H. Eggins (ed) *Globalization and reform in higher education*, Maidenhead: McGraw Hill Education, pp 32-54.

[11] Van de Velde, C. (2008) *Devenir adulte: Sociologie comparée de la jeunesse en Europe*, Paris: Presses Universitaires de France.

[12] Leccardi, C. and Ruspini, E. (eds) (2006) *A new youth? Young people, generations and family life*, Aldershot: Ashgate.

[13] Arnett has offered a 'popular' coverage of his concept in Marantz Henig, R. (2010) (2010) 'What is it about 20-somethings?', *New York Times*, 18 August (www.nytimes.com/2010/08/22/magazine/22Adulthood-t.html).

[14] Silva, J. (2013) *Coming up short: Working-class adulthood in an age of uncertainty*, Oxford: Oxford University Press.

[15] Korpi and Palme (1998) op cit. This notion has been recently criticised by Marx et al (2013) op cit.

Conclusion

[1] Bell, D.N.F. and Blanchflower, D.G. (2011) *Youth unemployment in Europe and the United States*, Bonn: Institute for the Study of Labor (IZA).

[2] Furlong, A. and Cartmel, F. (2005) *Graduates from disadvantaged families: Early labour market experiences*, Bristol: Policy Press.

[3] IFS (Institute for Fiscal Studies) (2016) 'What and where you study matter for graduate earnings – but so does parents' income', Press release, 13 April (www.ifs.org.uk/uploads/publications/pr/graduate_earnings_130416.pdf).

[4] Hartley-Brewer, J. (2015) 'University was never meant to be for everybody. Young people have been sold a lie', *The Telegraph*, 19 August, (www.telegraph. co.uk/education/universityeducation/11811928/University-was-never-meant-to-be-for-everybody.-Young-people-have-been-sold-a-lie.html).

[5] As I have explained in the Introduction and in Chapter 1, the student body in Europe has become more socially diverse as a consequence of the mass expansion of HE that began in the 1990s and continued in the 2000s across Europe.

[6] Pintelon, O., Cantillon, B., van den Bosch, K. and Whelan, C.T. (2013) 'The social stratification of social risks: The relevance of class for social investment strategies', *Journal of European Social Policy*, vol 23, no 1, pp 52-67.

[7] Piketty, T. (2014) *Capital in the twenty-first century*, Cambridge, MA: Harvard University Press; Piketty, T. (2014) *The future of inequality: Making progressive politics work*, London: Policy Network.

[8] Morel, N., Palier, B. and Palme, J. (2011) *Towards a social investment welfare state? Ideas, policies and challenges*, Bristol: Policy Press.

[9] Hacker, J.S. (2011) *The institutional foundations of middle-class democracy*, London: Policy Network.

[10] Finch, J. (1984) *Education as social policy*, London: Longman.

[11] Torry, M. (2014) *Money for everyone: Why we need a Citizen's Income*, Bristol: Policy Press.

[12] Antonucci, L. (2016) *Basic income and social policy in Europe: What could shape a social-democratic proposal*, FEPS Brief, Brussels: Foundation for European Progressive Studies (FEPS) (www.feps-europe.eu/assets/b2851660-5349-415b-997b-4220dea1314d/abstract-lorenza-antoncipdf.pdf).

[13] Garben, S. (2012) *The future of higher education in Europe: The case for a stronger base in EU law*, LSE 'Europe in Question' Discussion Paper, London: London School of Economics and Political Science.

[14] European Commission (2014) *Do changes in cost-sharing have an impact on the behaviour of students and higher education institutions? Evidence from nine case studies, vol 1*, Luxembourg: Publications Office of the European Union (http://ec.europa.eu/education/library/study/2014/cost-sharing/comparative-report_en.pdf).

[15] *The Guardian* (2015) op cit, Introduction.

[16] Woodman and Wyn (2014) op cit, Introduction.

[17] Parker, S. (2013) *The squeezed middle: The pressure on ordinary workers in America and Britain*, Bristol: Policy Press.

[18] Atkinson, A.B. (2014) 'After Piketty?', *The British Journal of Sociology*, vol 65, no 4, pp 619-38.

[19] MacDonald, R. (2011) 'Youth transitions, unemployment and underemployment. Plus ça change, plus c'est la même chose?', *Journal of Sociology*, vol 47, no 4, pp 427-44.

[20] Mason, P. (ed) (2012) *Why it's kicking off everywhere: The new global revolutions*, London: Verso.

[21] BIS (Department for Business, Innovation & Skills) (2016) *Success as a knowledge economy. Teaching excellence, social mobility and student choice*, London: BIS (www.gov.uk/government/uploads/system/uploads/attachment_data/file/523396/bis-16-265-success-as-a-knowledge-economy.pdf).

Annex

This is a short summary of the methodology used to conduct the study. For the full methodology (including the full list of items and the statistical analyses) see https://policypress.co.uk/student-lives-in-crisis. The research explored the experiences of young people in university in England, Italy and Sweden by employing a mixed-methodological strategy and a cross-national research design. In addition to policy analysis, the research combined a Q-methodology survey completed by 84 students across the three countries with 33 follow-up in-depth and semi-structured interviews. The research was guided by two core research questions: how do young people's experiences in university vary across socioeconomic backgrounds? How are young people's experiences in university shaped by different welfare sources? The methodological strategy used is inductive, as the research aimed to capture new relationships between young people's experiences in university (with regard to finance, housing, wellbeing and education), welfare sources and socioeconomic backgrounds.

Combining Q-methodology and in-depth interviews

Q-methodology is an instrument that allows the exploration of subjective viewpoints and combines rigorous quantitative techniques with qualitative interpretation.[1] It is used in particular to explore 'personal experiences' as well as 'values' and 'beliefs'. In practice, in a Q-methodology study participants are asked to position predefined statements in a predefined grid (for example, as in this case, from +5, representing most agreement, to −5, representing least agreement). The usual grid used in Q-methodology consists of a prearranged frequency distribution with the shape of a normal distribution, which reflects the observation that extreme opinions tend to be concentrated on fewer items, while most items attract more moderate opinions.

What distinguishes Q-methodology from other approaches aimed at exploring individual views is the possibility of presenting a range of viewpoints in the form of items (defined as the Q-sort), which are sorted by participants (defined as the P-set) according to their subjective evaluation.[2] Crucially, these items are not sorted one by one, but altogether, as they are compared with each other by participants to provide the participants' global viewpoint on a certain matter.[3] The second method employed in this mixed-methodological design is the follow-up in-depth interviews. In-depth interviews have not only provided additional material in relation to Q-methodology, but have also permitted further exploration of the link between subjective and objective elements emerging from the Q-sort and from the analysis of the individual data. Table A.1 summarises how the quantitative and qualitative material has been used in the different stages of the methodological design to capture both individual and structural elements.

Table A.1: A summary of the different data collected in the study with an explanation of their different functions in the research design

Method	Data	Function
Q-method	Q-sorts	• Cluster experiences • Select the most representative participants for interviews • Explore the links between subjective experiences in relation to structures
Open questions (survey attached to Q-methodology)	Qualitative written material	• Explore reasons behind the Q-sort
Questionnaire (survey attached to Q-methodology)	Data on demography, objective socioeconomic background, housing and welfare sources	• Identify objective differences to help the interpretations of Q-sorts
Follow-up in-depth interviews	Qualitative audio material	• Help the interpretation • Clarify the links between subjective experiences and structural conditions • Find unexpected themes

Methodological procedure

The methodological procedure of this study is fully visualised in Figure A.1.

Preparation of items and the pilot

Q-methodology is based on different assumptions compared to the use of traditional factor analysis. Q-methodology is *not* driven by the aim of finding a statistically representative sample of participants; the aim is to conduct an in-depth study of variation of subjectivities by including a limited number of individuals. Therefore, the issue of

Figure A.1: An overview of research procedures adopted in this study

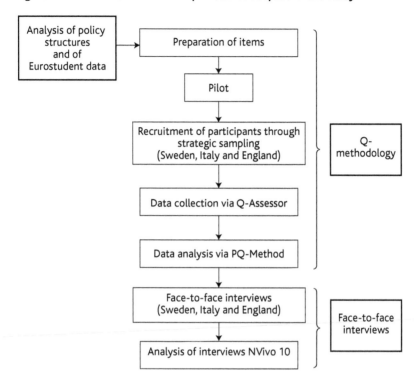

sampling concerns the Q-sorts (the list of statements) rather than the individuals involved in the study, who are considered 'the variables' of the study.[4]

An effective Q-set is characterised by its coverage and its balance. Coverage refers to the capacity of the Q-set to cover a wide range of opinions on a certain topic within the population (the *concourse*). In order to find the appropriate items, I focused on the different areas emerging from the literature: young people's experiences (including items on finances, housing, wellbeing and educational outcomes); welfare mixes, social origins and contextual factors (attitudes to welfare/youth transitions).

The other important characteristic of the Q-set is the balance of statements, which for this study consisted of the need to guarantee a representation of items valid for different contexts. I initially identified 100 items from the literature, which were reduced during the pilot. Student unions and young people from England, Sweden and Italy were asked to read and comment on the items that were least significant. The piloting had three objectives: elicitation of items (indicating the items that were least relevant, until reaching the final number of 52); checking the meaning/relevance of items in different national contexts; and refining the wording.

Capturing cross-national inequality

In order to obtain a 'theoretically variegated' sample, the two central goals were to have an equal number of young people from the three countries, and to have participants from different socioeconomic backgrounds. In respect to having participants from different socioeconomic backgrounds, I took into account:

• *Occupational background* refers to the parental occupational position, which follows the International Standard Classification of Occupations (ISCO-88),[5] aggregated into three categories: routine and manual; intermediate; managerial and professional.

• *Educational background* refers to the highest educational attainment of students' parents measured with the International Standard Classification of Education (ISCED),[6] aggregated into three categories: elementary (or primary) education (corresponding to ISCED 0-2); secondary education (corresponding to ISCED 2-4); and university level (tertiary education) (corresponding to ISCED 5-6).

The assessment of socioeconomic background was conducted by merging the information for both mothers and fathers of respondents according to Table A.2. In the event of a discrepancy between the mother and father's socioeconomic backgrounds, the nomenclature combined this discrepancy (for example, lower intermediate for young people with intermediate and low socioeconomic backgrounds).

Table A.2: Combining occupational position and educational background of mother/father in the study of youth transitions

		Occupational position of mother/father		
		Routine and manual	*Intermediate*	*Managerial and professional*
Educational background of mother/father	*Elementary*	Low socioeconomic	Low socioeconomic	Intermediate
	Secondary	Low socioeconomic	Intermediate	Upper
	University	Intermediate	Intermediate	Upper

As a consequence of institutional stratification, certain institutions might have a higher representation of students from a certain socioeconomic background. In order to recruit young people from different socioeconomic backgrounds I recruited participants in a variety of institutions:[7]

- England is characterised by a binary distinction between new (ex-polytechnics) and old universities. Students from low socioeconomic backgrounds tend to be substantially less represented in old universities, and in particular in universities from the Russell Group. Due to this pronounced dimension of 'horizontal stratification', recruiting young people from both old and new universities was used as an efficient strategy for ensuring representation of different socioeconomic backgrounds.

- Italy represents an example of a unitary system in which HE institutions are considered to be of the same quality and standard. The stratification arising from the North–South divide makes it crucial to cover both geographical areas in order to capture different groups of young people; for this reason, I recruited participants from universities in Milan and Naples.

- Sweden represents an example of 'diversified systems' where HE differs in quality, selectivity and prestige between ex-technical universities (*högskola*) and historical academic universities, which tend to attract different groups of young people. In this case, in order to capture both groups, I opted to recruit students from Lund University (a traditional historical university) and Malmö University, a *högskola* university college, both in Southern Sweden.

Table A.3 summarises the dimension of stratification of the different national contexts and illustrates the institutions and the types of key actors involved in the fieldwork.

Recruiting participants

One of the most challenging parts of the research was recruiting participants across three countries and six cities. Not only did this involve a significant amount of travel for a single researcher (across countries and within countries), but it also meant understanding the comparative differences in recruiting students in the three countries.

Table A.3: The national dimensions of stratification, institutions and key actors involved during fieldwork

	National dimension of stratification	Institutions involved during the fieldwork and city	Key actors involved during fieldwork
England	Old university	University of Bristol (Bristol)	Lecturers
	New university and location	University of Teesside (Middlesbrough), University of the West of England (Bristol)	
Sweden	Full university	Lund University (Lund)	Lecturers/student unions
	University college (*högskola*)	Malmö University (Malmö)	
Italy	Universities in the North	Università Statale di Milano, Università Cattolica, Università Bocconi (Milan)	Student unions
	Universities in the South (Mezzogiorno)	Università Federico II, Università Orientale (Naples)	

The first part of the fieldwork was conducted between April and October 2012, after constructing a database of 'key actors' to help recruit participants, and setting up a website with the goal of promoting the study.

I presented my research face-to-face with potential participants in Malmö, Lund, Milan, Naples and Bristol. In Sweden and England, where student unions have a strict confidentiality policy, I presented my research at the beginning or the end of lectures. In Italy, where unions have more informal contact with students, I was invited to present my research at events organised by the student unions.

This research recruited young people from undergraduate degrees. As there is no set-in-stone definition of 'youth' employed in the literature, I set 27 years as a cut-off age, in order to incorporate the less linear transitions of young people who entered university after a period of labour market participation. The sampling strategy of this research followed the following strategic sampling criteria: gender balance (a minimum of 10 female and 10 male participants for each country); having young people from at least two educational fields;[8] and having young people from different socioeconomic backgrounds (low, intermediate and upper) in each country. The sampling strategy was implemented in an adaptive way: during the Q-sorting and completion of surveys, I monitored the gender balance and variability of socioeconomic backgrounds and fields of study. When needed, I redirected my recruitment strategy to improve variability.

Collecting data

An information sheet was circulated to potential participants after the presentations or was shared by the key actors on my behalf. A link to the Q-study was sent through via email after the students had consented to participate.

The Q-Assessor first requires participants to put the statements into three broad categories: disagree, neutral and agree (see Figure A.2).

Second, participants were asked to review the items that they put in the three boxes and to express their agreement (from +1 agree to +5 agree), their neutrality, or their disagreement (from −1 disagree to −5 disagree). This is shown in Figure A.3.

In addition to the sorting, the participants were asked to fill in a questionnaire with compulsory and optional questions on their objective conditions: demographic data (for example, name, gender, field of study); assessment of socioeconomic background; objective use of welfare sources (state support, family sources and labour market participation); and housing condition.

Analysis of Q-sort

The data collected in Q-Assessor on Q-sorting were inserted into PQMethod, the specific software used for Q-method analysis. Principal component analysis (PCA) was used as the extraction method of choice. I performed two types of factor analysis in this research. First, I conducted a three-country analysis that included participants

Figure A.2: Snapshot of the first stage of Q-sorting

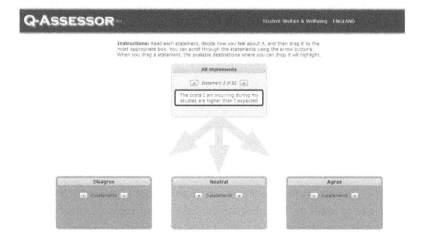

Figure A.3: Snapshot of the second stage of Q-sorting

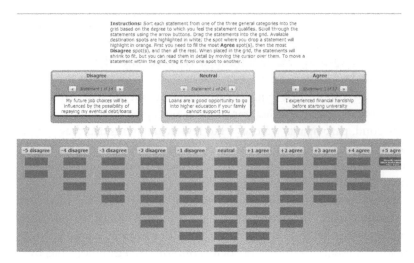

from England, Italy and Sweden to capture the variation of young people's experiences of university in relation to welfare structures. I performed a three-country analysis by selecting Q-sorting from 51 young people (17 per country) out of the total of 84 young people who completed the survey (the selection was necessary as the number of items needs to be equal or lower than the number of participants analysed). Second, I performed three within-country analyses (one for each country) involving all 84 students (approximately 30-40 per country). The rationale for this analysis was to clarify the function of each welfare mix within each country. The reader interested in the results of the performed analyses, and on the statistics behind the study, can consult the methodological annex in the book's website https://policypress.co.uk/student-lives-in-crisis.

Follow-up semi-structured interviews

The second part of the fieldwork consisted of face-to-face follow-up interviews with participants in six cities across the three countries: Bristol and Middlesbrough for England, Milan and Naples for Italy, and Lund and Malmö for Sweden. The interviews were conducted between November 2012 and January 2013. Given the limited resources available, I decided to select 33 participants (11 from each country) to interview. The selection of participants was informed by the Q-factor analysis, which identified the 'most representative cases' of the three-country analysis according to the criteria explained above, and also of the within-country analyses. The interviews were semi-structured, and a general list of themes to explore during the interviews emerged from the conceptual framework: the role of welfare sources, the different areas of young people's experiences (financial position, housing, wellbeing and education) and social origins (the exploration of the dynamic dimension of categorical socioeconomic background measured through the survey and a discussion of cultural capital).

Interpreting factors: from factors to profiles

The first step in the interpretation of factors (which led to the identification of the profiles) was to capture the entire item configuration. I used the systematic tool for comparing across factor arrays proposed by Stenner and Watts, namely, the 'crib sheet'.[9] This is constructed by comparing the score of each item across factors and preparing, for each factor, a sheet that includes the items ranked at +5 (most agreement), the items ranked higher in one factor than in other factors, the items ranked lower in one factor than in other factors and the items ranked at −5 (least agreement). The crib sheet provides a summary of the items that the profile offers as an instrument to compare profiles. Following the logic of abduction, after forming the crib sheets it was possible to formulate, for each factor, hypotheses regarding the whole viewpoint. I then used the other data, such as the *objective* ancillary information (welfare sources and socioeconomic background), to help in interpreting the viewpoint.

The 33 one-hour face-to-face semi-structured interviews were analysed by using audio coding in order to describe and organise codes, implemented with the audio coding instruments of the software NVivo 10, a widely used instrument in qualitative research. Two types of coding were employed. The first was a theoretical coding to validate/test the links between the subjective views and the objective conditions emerging from the analysis of the Q-sorts. The second was an inductive-orientated coding procedure to identify themes that were not specified a priori, but only emerged during the interviews. The final step consisted of integrating the findings from the interviews with the results of the Q-sort by putting together the different hypotheses formulated with the findings from the audio coding. A full discussion of the limits and strengths of this research are included in the methodological annex present in the book's website https://policypress.co.uk/student-lives-in-crisis.

Notes

[1] Baker, R., Thompson, C. and Mannion, R. (2006a) 'Q-methodology in health economics', *Journal of Health Services Research & Policy*, vol 11, no 1, pp 38-45.

[2] Watts, S. and Stenner, P. (2012) *Doing Q methodological research: Theory, method & interpretation*, London: Sage.

[3] Stenner, P.H., Cooper, D. and Skevington, S.M. (2003) 'Putting the Q into quality of life; the identification of subjective constructions of health-related quality of life using Q methodology', *Social Science & Medicine*, vol 57, no 11, pp 2161-72.

[4] Watts and Stenner (2012) op cit.

[5] ILO (International Labour Organization) (2004) 'International Standard Classification of Occupations, ISCO-88', Geneva: ILO (www.ilo.org/public/english/bureau/stat/isco/isco88/index.htm).

[6] UNESCO (2014) 'ISCED: International Standard Classification of Education' (www.uis.unesco.org/Education/Pages/international-standard-classification-of-education.aspx).

[7] Shavit, Y., Arum, R.T., Gamoran, A. and Menahem, G. (2007) *Stratification in higher education: A comparative study*, Stanford, CA: Stanford University Press.

[8] Considering that the five educational fields put in the survey were medicine and dentistry and allied to health (for example, nursing); other sciences, engineering, technology and IT; human and social sciences (including law, business, economics and psychology); creative arts, humanities and languages (for example, English literature, history); education; and others.

[9] Watts and Stenner (2012) op cit.

Index

Page references for notes are followed by n

Europe 2020 strategy 20
European social model 3–4
European Union (EU)
  higher education policy 1, 2, 20,
    21, 167
  youth policy 22, 167
Eurostudent 46, 55–8, 131, 185n
Eurydice 43, 45–6

F

family formation 25
family support 15, 23–4, 117–18,
  119–21, 122–4, 129, 155, 156–7
  England 27
  facing difficulties, but with hope for
    the future 109–10
  good in the present, worried about
    the future 96, 111–12
  having a great time 101, 113–14
  housing 29–30
  and inequality 55–9, 64, 65,
    115–16, 143, 162, 168
  Italy 27
  positive, but temporary, period 111
  and semi-dependence 124–9
  struggling and hopeless 80–1, 108
fees 4, 7, 11, 21, 34, 144–5
  England 33, 34, 35, 36, 37, 47–8,
    49, 53
  and inequality 64
  Italy 34, 36–7, 53–4
finance 11, 75, 104
  facing difficulties, but with hope for
    the future 77, 85, 87–8, 89
  good in the present, worried about
    the future 77, 95–6
  having a great time 77, 99
  positive, but temporary, period 77,
    90, 92
  semi-dependence 67, 72, 74
  state support 143
  struggling and hopeless 77, 78,
    80–1
Finland 131
France
  family support 23, 120
  labour market participation 131
  working-class students 10
fuori corso students 45

G

Gelmini, Mariastella 19, 44–5
Generation Y 3, 128, 167–8
Gentile, A. 120
Germany 131
Giddens, A. 9, 121
grants 4, 7, 34, 145
  England 36, 39, 41, 43, 46, 47,
    48–9, 53
  Italy 36, 38, 42, 50, 53–4
  Sweden 36, 37–8, 41, 44, 50
Guardian, The 167–8

H

Hacker, Jacob 165
Hartley-Brewer, Julia 163
higher education (HE) 6, 159–60,
  168–70
  access 22
  costs 1, 2, 3, 4, 11, 28–9, 32
  destinations 22
  European problems and national
    solutions 165–7
  for everybody 1–2, 163–4
  expansion 1, 2, 3, 12–13, 15,
    17–24, 32, 159
  and inequality 12–13, 18
  institutional stratification 8–9,
    18–19, 20, 107
  participation 22
  politics of living at university 28–32
  social and economic agendas 20–4
  social investment or addressing
    inequalities 164–5
  and socioeconomic background
    7–9
  and transitions 10–12
Hirsch, Fred 22–3
housing 11, 29–30, 32, 104
  European problems and national
    solutions 166
  facing difficulties, but with hope for
    the future 77, 85, 88, 89
  family support 55–6, 57–8, 59, 121
  good in the present, worried about
    the future 77, 96–7
  having a great time 77, 99, 101–2
  positive, but temporary, period 77,
    90
  and semi-dependence 70–1, 72,
    73, 74
  state support 143

Lightning Source UK Ltd.
Milton Keynes UK
UKHW021054260119
336179UK00012B/841/P